I0799915

IMAGES
of America

SCOTT COUNTY
ARKANSAS

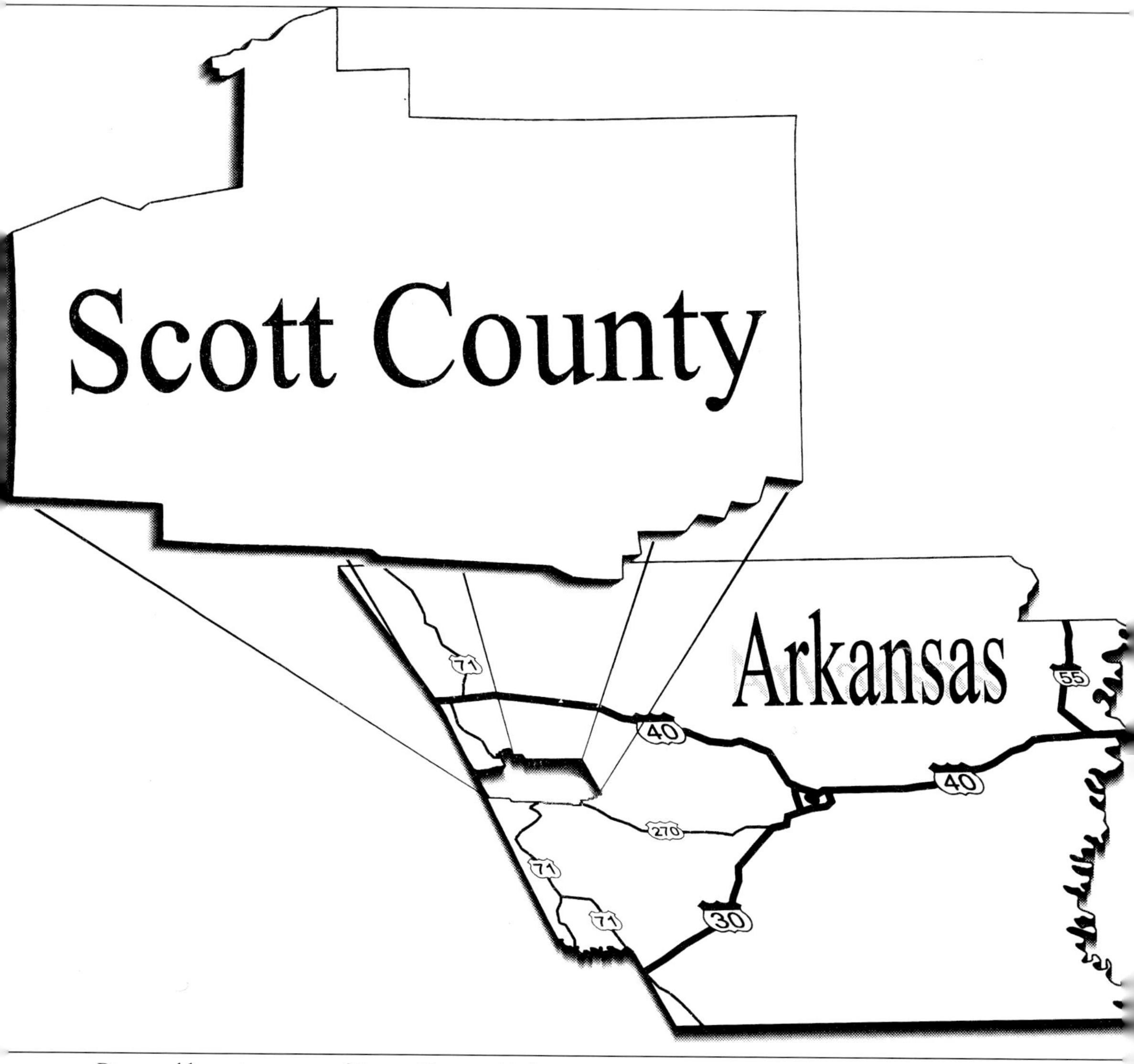

Pictured here is a map of Scott County/Arkansas.

IMAGES
of America

SCOTT COUNTY ARKANSAS

Wanda M. Gray

ARCADIA
PUBLISHING

ISBN 978-0-7385-0243-4

Published by Arcadia Publishing
Charleston SC, Chicago IL, Portsmouth NH, San Francisco CA

Printed in the United States of America

Library of Congress Catalog Card Number applied for.

For all general information contact Arcadia Publishing at:
Telephone 843-853-2070
Fax 843-853-0044
E-Mail sales@arcadiapublishing.com
For customer service and orders:
Toll-Free 1-888-313-2556

Visit us on the Internet at www.arcadiapublishing.com

Contents

ACKNOWLEDGMENTS

Without the help of many individuals this book would not have been possible. My sincere gratitude is publicly extended to each of you for the friendship we have shared for many years and the assistance you have rendered in making this photographic history of Scott County, Arkansas, a part of the *Images of America* series. Much of the material for this book was assembled by the author over a period of 25 years while writing newspaper articles and books about the history of Scott County and its people.

However, there are those who the author wishes to thank especially for the timely and generous manner in which they have contributed historical data and photographs, many of which have never been published. Mr. B.O. Roop of Fayetteville, Arkansas, contributed his personal image of the boundary line marker between the Choctaw Nation and the Scott County boundary, which was also the Territory of Arkansas boundary. Sincere appreciation is extended to Mrs. Edna Maxell of Waldron, Arkansas, for her generous sharing of photographs in the Swinney collection. A simple thank you is insufficient to express to Mr. Don Carpenter and members of the Waldron Masonic Lodge for their helpfulness in providing information and photographs concerning this organization. Mrs. O. Ann Oliver of Waldron has been extremely helpful in providing images that depict the life and times of the county and deserves special credit in this book as do Juanita and Kello Holland. The value of this book has been greatly enhanced by the untiring efforts of Mrs. Ila Rhodes of Fresno, California, in providing many images from her family collection. A very special thank you is extended to her. A very special thank you is also extended to Mrs. Lou Nell Davis of Lamar, Arkansas; Mr. Edgar Hon of McLean, Virginia; and Mrs. Reba Nell Bethel Bergman for their timely assistance in providing just the right images. To my dear friends of a lifetime, Mrs. Della Mae Langston Meredith, and Mrs. Sharon Langston Goodner, of Waldron, Arkansas, I wish to express deep gratitude for the use of family images. A very special thank you goes to Bryce Self who just "happened by" from Redwood City, California, and Mrs. Lou Nell McCraw Davis, who made a special effort to bring me images that contributed so much to the quality of this book. Finally, the author wishes to express appreciation to Dr. John L. Ferguson, Executive Director of the Arkansas History Commission, for granting permission for the use of archival photographs.

INTRODUCTION

The social, economical, and technological changes that have enhanced this area since it was acquired in 1803 in the Louisiana Purchase are many indeed. Yet, on the eve of the 21st century, the people of Scott County continue to cherish their rural heritage and small-town lifestyles.

The adventuresome early settlers pushed into the county from the north, east, and south by boat, on horseback, and on foot to live off of the land. Soon, American Indian trails became primitive roads and wagons pulled by stout horses and the trusty oxen carried families to the area. The images of the landscape then took on a new dimension. Plentiful timber was cut, and log cabin homes were built; logs were split to make tables, chairs, benches, beds, and rail fences to pen the cattle, and trees were cut to clear the land for the planting of small plots of corn and vegetables. By 1850, 3,000 people inhabited the county officially established in 1833, and as it grew, so did the state.

The stouthearted men and women, with Spartan doggedness, were not deterred by the hardships and isolation that faced them. The land gave way to larger row-crop farms, churches, schools, post offices, improved roads, sawmills, gristmills, cotton gins, and the railroad. Several businesses were established to accommodate the population that had increased to 13,183 at the turn of the 20th century; however, a decade later in 1910, the population reached its zenith.

Though progress continued with the coming of the automobile, hard surfaced roads, radios, tractors, large modern sawmills, brick and soda pop plants, a creamery to process milk products, new courthouses, and water and sewer systems in Waldron, the population was in a gradual decline. However, even with the drought and Depression in the early 1930s, it was not until after 1940, when the timber had been cut out and people left to work in World War II defense plants, that the population began plummeting down to its lowest point—7,283 by the year 1960. This major emigration has come to be known as the "brain-drain" from which the county has never fully recovered.

The most progressive era of the county occurred about a half century behind that of the nation. After the 1950s, energetic business leaders were successful in gaining major improvement in the infrastructure of the county seat, Waldron. Factories were built, which provided employment for people and brought economic stability to the county. This resulted in the building of not only homes and farms but the population as well.

As we look to the year 2000, the landscape of the county is dotted with attractive ranches where livestock contentedly grazes. The Tyson Food processing plant and feed mills operate two to three shifts each day; another factory produces dog bones and school furniture, employing a number of people. There are several wood product producers, both large and small, including the high-tech planing mill at Mansfield, and we can boast of one manufacturer of international renown that produces air emission monitoring systems. In the 20th century, modern schools replaced the ones made of logs; when those schools reached capacity, a new elementary and middle school were built. A new library was built in 1983, as well as a newer and larger hospital with satellite services from Fort Smith. Since the 1960s, businesses have relocated, and new ones have been built on the Highway 71 Bypass to the west of the old Featherston Donation. This resulted in a decline in the downtown area, but it is currently undergoing some restoration.

The political life of the county has changed little since it harshness generated the Waldron War of the 1870s, and perhaps this has hindered the county in not sharing in the growth and development comparable with surrounding counties. But, politics aside, the people of the area are of the finest in the world. They care about their neighbors, they help when others are in trouble, and they have intrinsic Christian values. The environment created by country living builds strong families. These families will carry their heritage into the 21st century with a sureness and calmness experienced by few others.

Selected Bibliography

BOOKS:

Ashmore, Harry S. *Arkansas, A History. 2d ed.* New York: W.W. Norton and Co., 1984.

Baker, T. Harri and Jane Browning. *An Arkansas History for Young People*. Fayetteville, Arkansas: University of Arkansas Press, 1991.

Brown, C. J. *The WPA Guide to the 1930s*. Lawrence, Kansas: University Press of Kansas, 1941.

Cates, Michael. *History of Scott County, Arkansas*. Dallas: Curtis Media, 1991.

Claunts, P.M. *From Memory's Scrapbook: A History of the Early Events and Happenings in Scott and Sebastian Counties, Arkansas*. Waldron, Arkansas: Advance Reporter, 1938.

Goodner, Charles E. *Scott County in Retrospect*. Mansfield, Arkansas: Frank Boyd, 1976.

Goodner, Norman. *Scott County Days Gone By*. Mansfield, Arkansas: Frank Boyd, 1983.

Goodner, Norman. *A Scott County Scrapbook*. Mansfield, Arkansas: Frank Boyd, 1982.

Goodner, Norman. *A History of Scott County, Arkansas*. Siloam Springs, Arkansas: Bar D Press, 1941.

Gray, Wanda M. *Selected Historical and Genealogical Records*. Waldron, Arkansas: W.M. Gray, Publisher, 1993.

Gray, Wanda M. *Cemeteries of Scott County, Arkansas*. Waldron, Arkansas: W.M. Gray, Publisher, 1993.

McCuen, W. J. "Bill". *Historical Report of the Secretary of State*. Little Rock: State of Arkansas, 1986.

McCutchen, Henry Grady. *History of Scott County, Arkansas*. Printed in Arkansas: Henry Grady McCutchen, 1922.

Parman, Donald L., ed. *Window to A Changed World: The Personal Memoirs of William Graham*. Indianapolis: Indiana Historical Society, Publishers, 1998.

Poe, McDonald, Sr. *Forty-Nine Years of Law Practice*. Waldron, Arkansas: McDonald Poe Sr., Publisher, 1976.

Smith, Kenneth L. *Sawmill*. Fayetteville, Arkansas: The University of Arkansas Press, 1986.

Thompson, Seth. *The Muscadine Vine*. Waldron, Arkansas: Waldron News, 1983.

________. *A History of the Mansfield School District Area*. Mansfield, Arkansas: Mansfield High School, 1994.

COLLECTIONS:

Center Special Collection, 5634 Collins Lane, Fort Smith, Arkansas

Black, McCraw, Frizzell Collection, Lou Nell Davis, Lamar, Arkansas

Historian's Scott County Collection, Wanda M. Gray, Fort Smith, Arkansas

Holland Collection, Ila Rhodes, Fresno, California

Nunn Collection, Kello Holland, Waldron, Arkansas

Oliver Collection, Ann Oliver, Waldron, Arkansas

S. K. Leming Collection, 5634 Collins Lane, Fort Smith, Arkansas

Swinney Collection, Edna L. Maxell, Waldron, Arkansas

One

SETTLEMENT ERA 1820–1920

It was a stouthearted, venturesome breed of people who walked with rifles over their shoulders, or came by boat, horseback, or covered conveyance pulled by oxen and horses to the western frontier inhabited by Native Americans. As you will see from these images, the people who settled the area were plainly dressed and wore heavy cotton pants or overalls (except for Sunday). They had few personal belongings and had to live off the land. Like Judge Scott, early settlers were remarkable for their strong constitutions, simplicity of manners, and honesty of purpose. They were religiously devout and kept their promises sacred. The population increased for the next 67 years, though settlements were widely scattered. The coming of mail service helped to advance civilization, as did the coming of the gristmills, sawmills, cotton gins, and the railroad. As you reflect upon these images, it is hoped that you will catch a glimpse of the self-reliant, rugged individualism of the pioneers who had to make do with what they had.

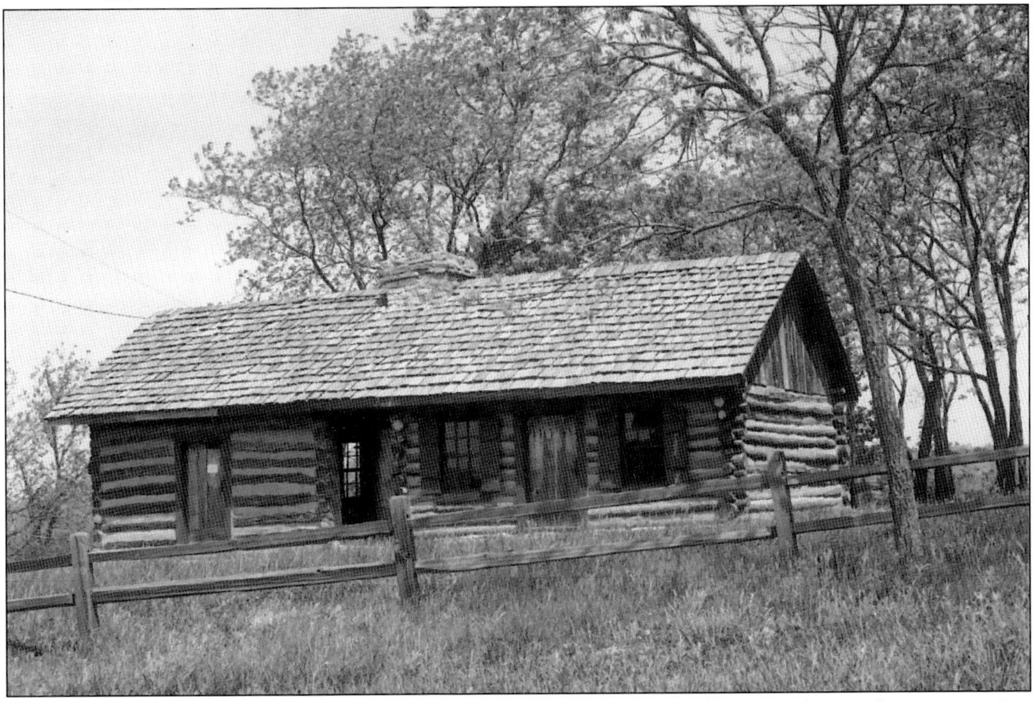

The second courthouse was a log building measuring 12 by 20 feet, similar to the one in this image, and was used by early settlers for the first permanent seat of justice at Winfield, Scott County, Arkansas, which was located on the York farm northeast of Waldron in 1843. This settlement was spearheaded by Edward Hardesty Featherston, brother of W.G. It was off the Red River Road and lasted less than three years before it was moved back to Poton Valley, later to be named Waldron. (Historian's Collection.)

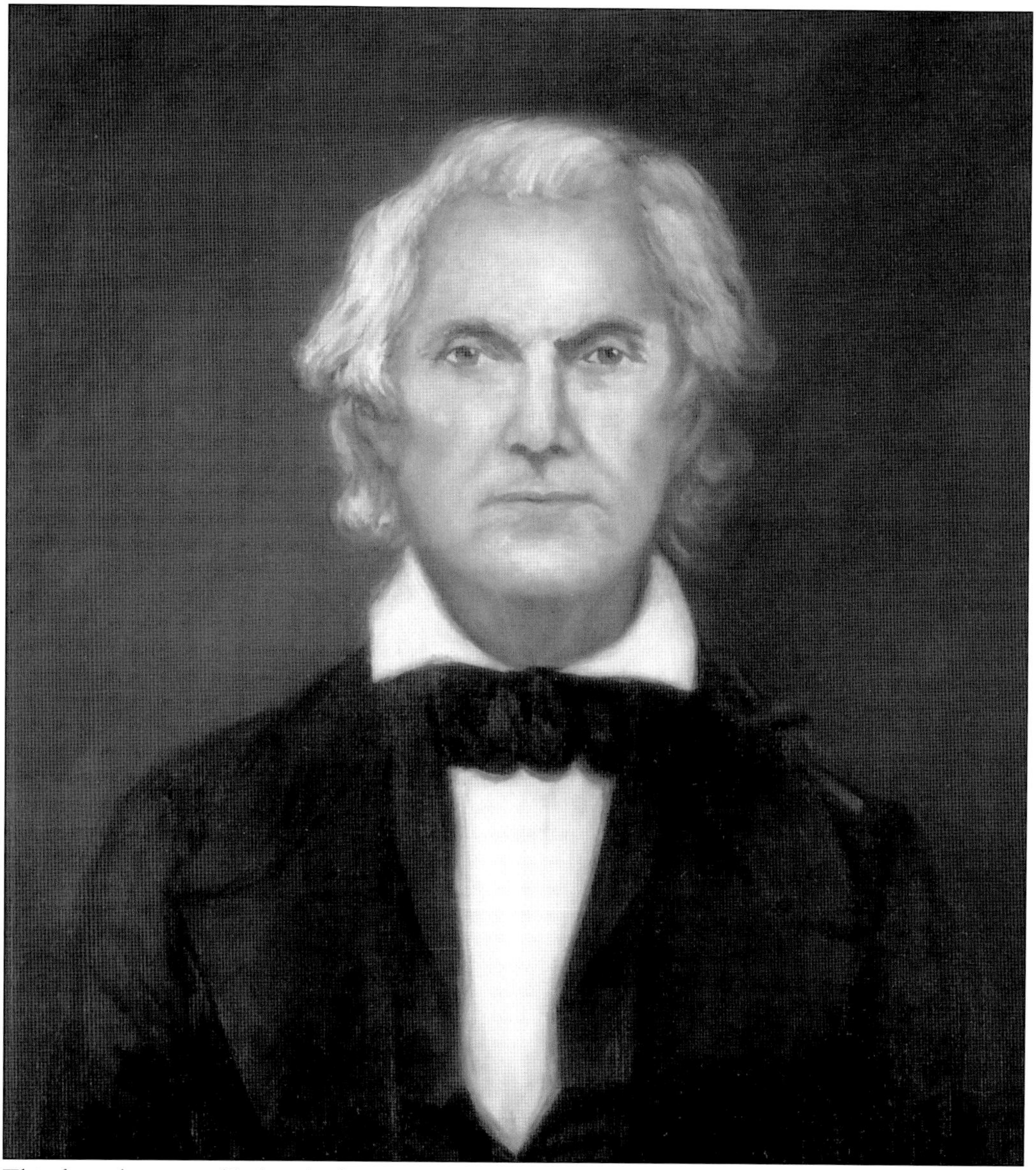

This formal image of Judge Andrew Horatio Scott was taken a few years after his appointment as a Superior Court judge in Arkansas Territory in 1819. He had followed the westward political expansion of this country to St. Genevieve and Potosi, Missouri, when he received President James Monroe's appointment. At Arkansas Post, he put into operation the organic law and first government of the territorial capital. He became a charter member of the first masonic lodge in the state and moved to Little Rock with the capital in 1821, where he became judge of the Circuit Court in 1827. With the removal of the Cherokees, he acquired Native American lands on a farm he named "Scotia" in Pope County in 1828, located on the military road, and he became the first county judge. True to his pioneer spirit and high sense of honor, he survived a duel that fatally wounded Superior Court Judge Seldon and defended his honor again when another fatally wounded challenger stepped forth. It is highly fitting that a county on the rugged frontier immortalized his name on November 5, 1833, when Scott County became the 25th county formed in the state. (Courtesy of Arkansas History Commission.)

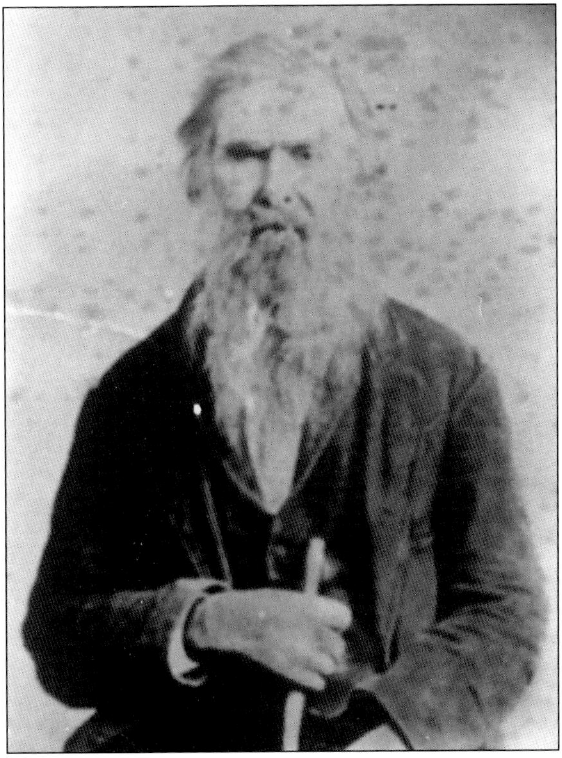

This image shows a bearded, matured Walter Cauthron (1797–1877). He was born in Georgia but headed west in 1820, when life west of the mighty Mississippi was a wild wilderness. He settled in the Petit Jean Valley, about 30 miles south of present day Fort Smith, by 1827. He successfully worked for the establishment of Scott County on November 5, 1833, and his log home and mercantile store on the southeast side of Booneville were used as the first temporary seat of justice for a few years. He served as Scott County Treasurer from 1836 to 1840 and was a very influential and highly respected citizen. When Sarber (now Logan) County was established in 1871, his land holdings were within that jurisdiction. (Courtesy of Kenneth N. Oliver, Tulsa, Oklahoma.)

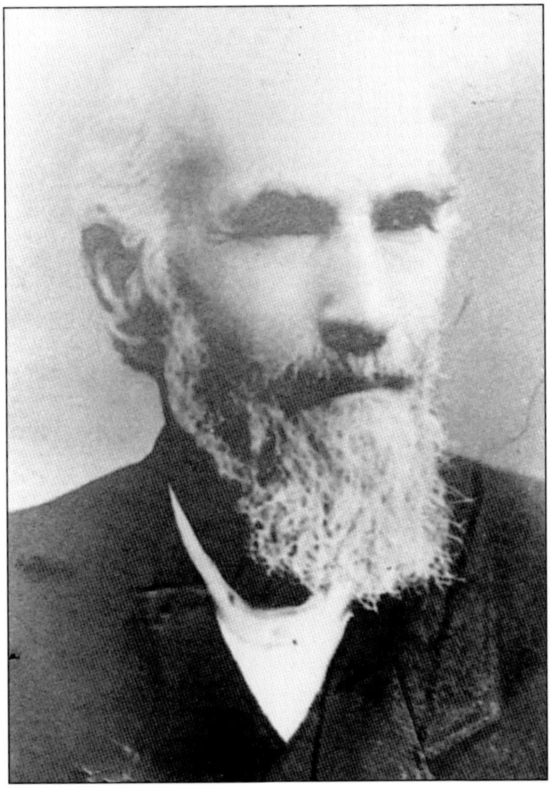

Serious-looking Rev. William Graham (1821–1894) was a circuit-riding Methodist Episcopal preacher in the county, visiting the areas of Bates, Hon, Waldron, Boles, Parks, Black Jack Ridge, and Abbott in 1844. After the Revolutionary War and by 1850, the Methodists emerged as the largest church denomination in the United States. It was their primary goal to spread the gospel to inhabitants of rural communities in frontier areas. Camp meetings became the best known form of worship of primitive Methodism, and they introduced "brush-arbor" meetings to the Baptists. (Courtesy of Professor Donald L. Parman, Purdue University, and graduate student, Jason Tetzloff.)

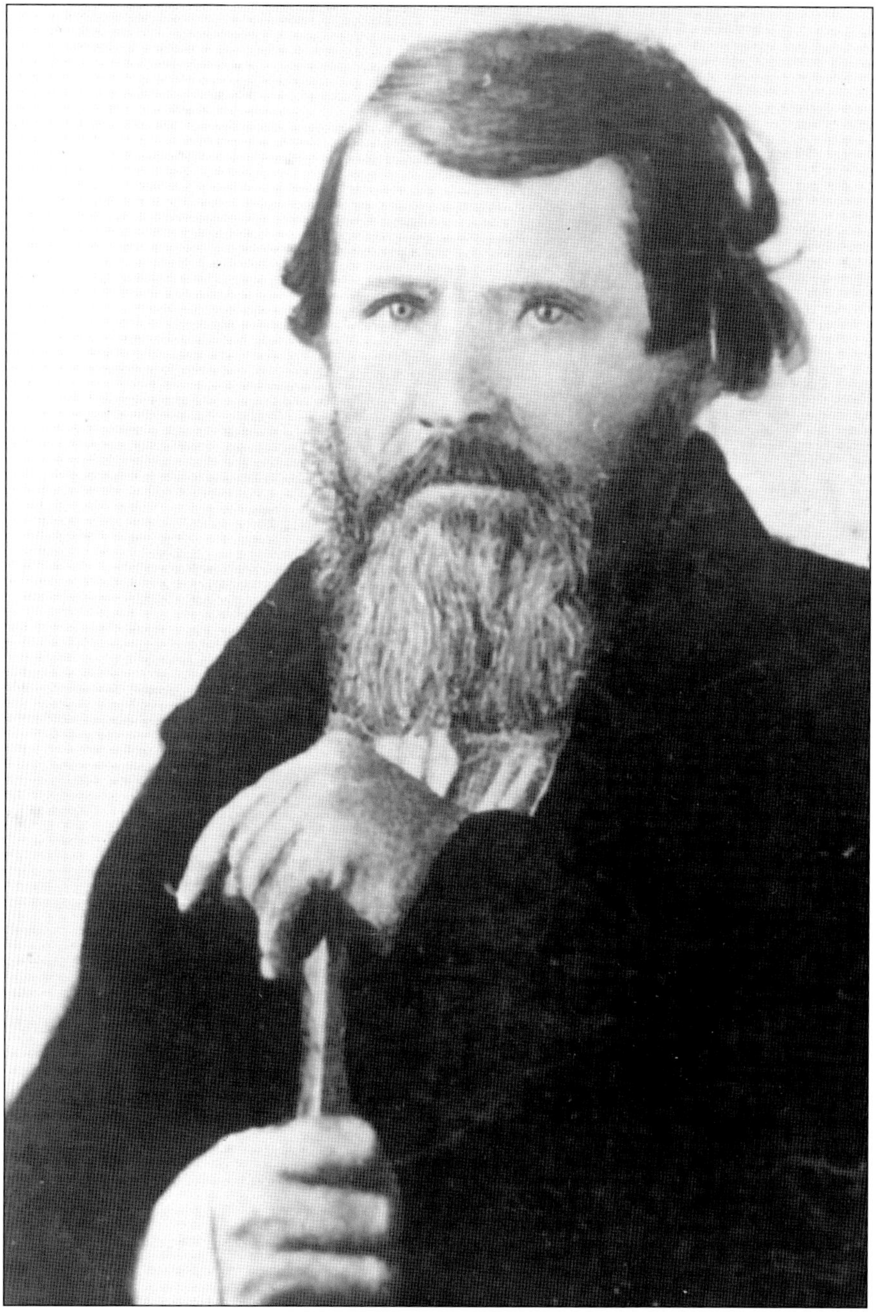

This is the last image taken of William Grandison (W.G.) Featherston (1807–1873), the son of Henry Featherston Jr. He came to Scott County via Smith and Lincoln Counties, Tennessee, and Franklin County, Arkansas. He settled on land in Scott County in 1835 on which the Poton Valley postal service was established in 1838. He gave 10 acres of his land for a town and county seat in 1846, and the town of Waldron was laid out. His home was on the now famous Texas or Red River Road, the traces of which are still visible behind the Dairy Kreme where the heavy-ladened wagons pulled up the high bank of the South Fork of the Poteau River. The old road has since become a paved street and honors his name. (Courtesy of Mrs. Bruce Raymond.)

A portrait of Jackson Hon (1810–1872), who was born in Kentucky and migrated with his young family from Illinois in the 1830s, depicts the formal attire of the early 1800s. Beady dark eyes, straight thin lips, and a firm, set jaw illustrate his serious and business-like manner. By the1860s, his land acquisitions, mainly around the Poteau (Hon) and the Poteau River, totaled 1,455 acres, making him one of the principal landowners in Scott County. He cultivated 400 acres, raised hogs, cattle, sheep, horses, and mules, and ran a distillery and blacksmith shop, without the help of slaves. The Stewart and Boultinghouse families from Illinois intermarried into the Hon family. (Courtesy of Ed Hon, McLean, VA.)

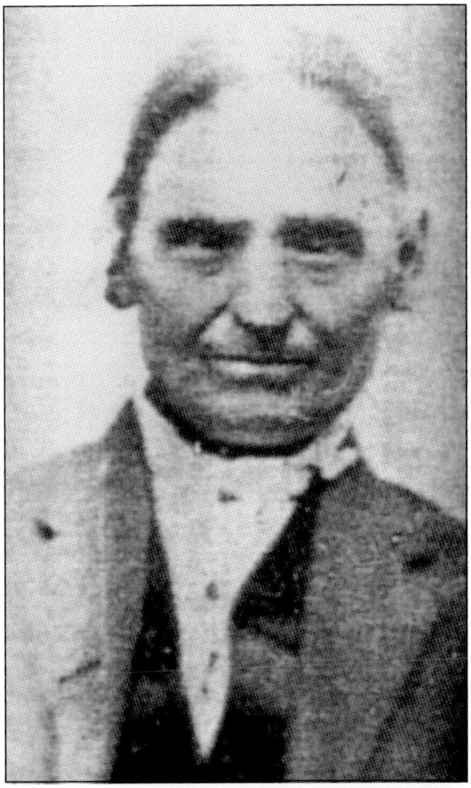

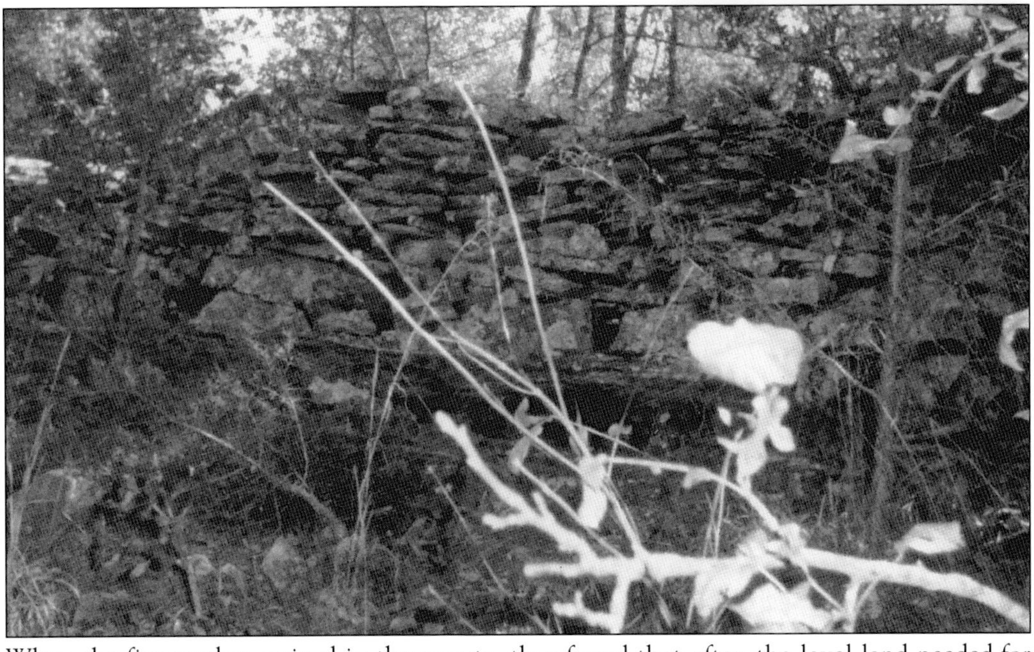

When the first settlers arrived in the county, they found that often the level land needed for pasture and cultivation was filled with native stones. According to local tradition, this rock fence, 6 feet high and over a mile long, was built by slaves as the land was cleared on a farm north of Waldron in the 1850s. (Historian's Collection.)

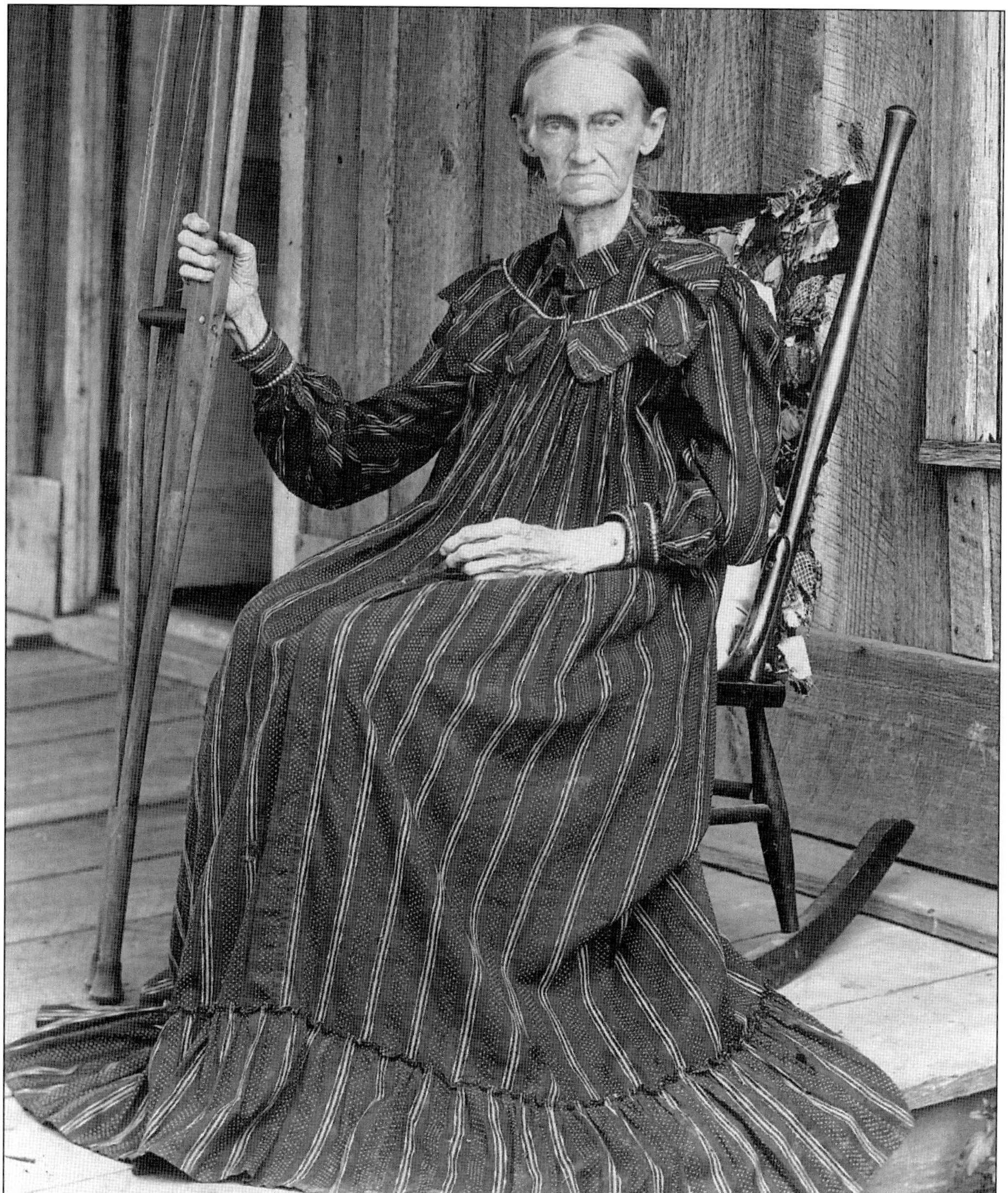

In an image taken shortly before her death, Sarah William Tomlinson Swinney rocks on the front porch of her home on Swinney Hill. She was born in the Tomlinson Township in 1834, on the slave plantation of her parents, Joseph Johnson Tomlinson and Olive Ann. It is likely that she played in the tavern and post office on the Texas Road near the toll bridge, at what later became known as Boothe. Around 1844, she and her husband, Matthew Swinney, acquired land about four blocks west of town that became known as Swinney Hill, and they built their home of rough sawed lumber. It is on this land that the Waldron Public School System was built. After Mr. Swinney, one of the first merchants of Waldron, was shot on his way to the store, she married James Null and had a daughter, Mattie F. Null. (Courtesy of Edna Maxell's Swinney Collection.)

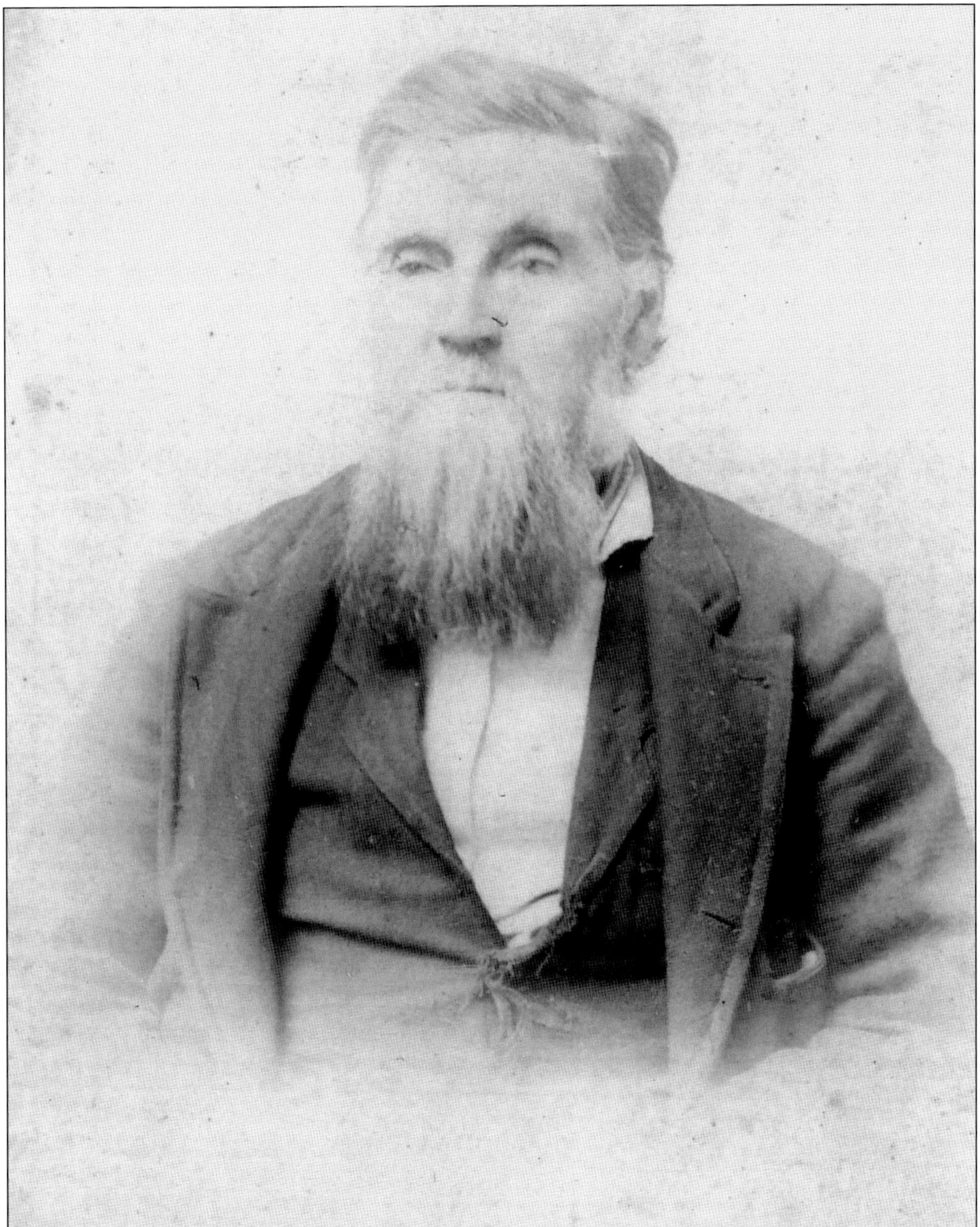

This image, of a bearded, rather stocky, Alfred C. Craig Sr. (c. 1840–1902), reveals a man who did not like to wear neckties. He was a very prosperous farmer in at least four states: Illinois, Texas, Mississippi, and Arkansas. He married three times and had a host of children. We get a glimpse of his personality, thoughtfulness, and education in a letter to his first wife, Mary Albinia Henderson. He wrote while serving in the Civil War on January 16th, 1865, telling her to "Remember Love who gave you this when other days shall come when He who has thine Earliest Love Lies in the Silent Toom [sic]. Presented to Mrs. Mary A. Craig by Alfred C. Craig her Husband in the army." (Courtesy Ila Rhodes, Fresno, CA.)

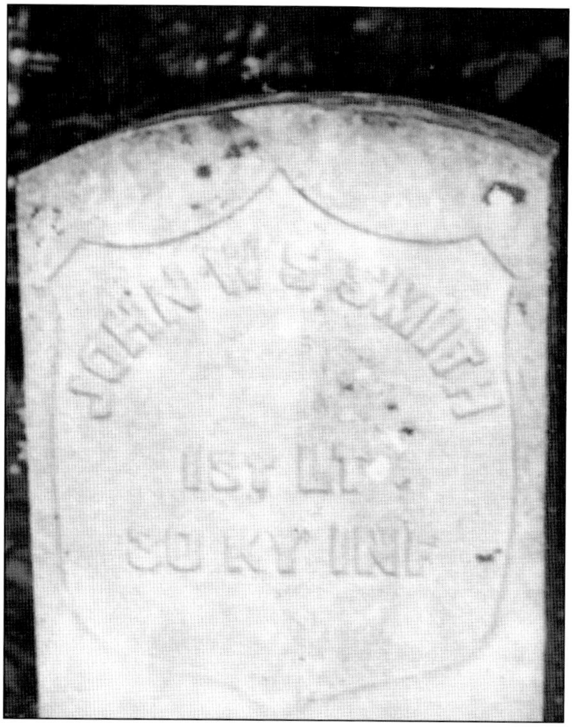

The white marble monument, embossed with a shield emblem, marks the grave of 1st Lt. John Wm. Seth Smith (1830–1898) in a grove of trees on the north slope of Round Mountain. He was born in Virginia and followed the western migration to the state of Kentucky, where he enlisted as a 2nd Lt. in Co. D, 27th Regiment, KY Volunteers on April 15, 1862. He was promoted to the rank of 1st Lt. of Company F in the 30th KY Mounted Infantry and mustered out on April 18, 1865. After the war, he went to Hill County, Texas, for a while before settling in the Tate community in northern Scott County, Arkansas, in 1883. Only his grave and that of his mother, Biddy Ann Fitzsimmons Smith, are in this burial site. (Historian's Collection contributed by Howard La Roche, Houston, TX.)

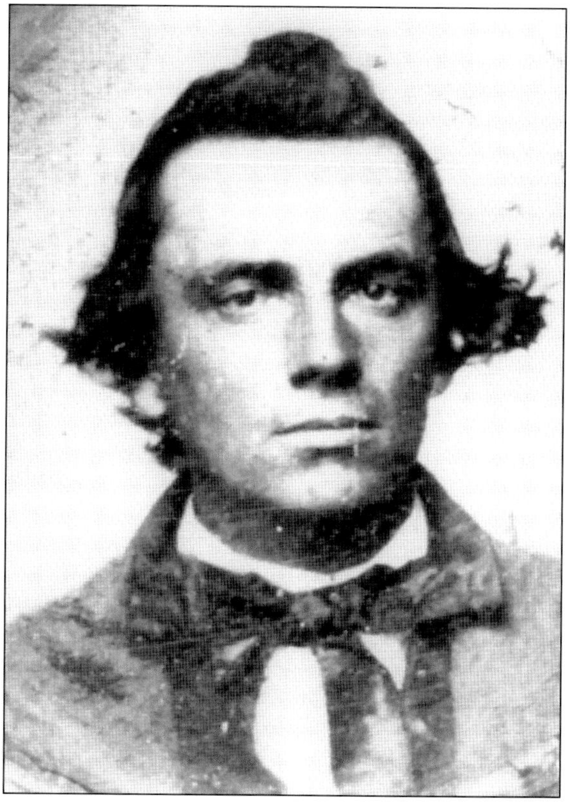

Peter Hon (1837–1862), son of Jackson B. Hon, had little success keeping his naturally curly hair straight enough for formal military duty. He enlisted in the 17th Arkansas Infantry, Confederate Army, and the dark trim on his coat is believed to represent the color worn by his company. He married Susan Boultinghouse prior to the Civil War, and they had one son, Isaac Monroe Hon, born in the spring of 1861. Peter died in the CSA hospital at Bentonville. (Courtesy of Edgar R. Hon, McLean, VA.)

The head dress and attire of Susan Boultinghouse Hon (1843–unknown), wife of Peter Hon, reminds us of Scarlett in the movie *Gone With the Wind*, which had a Civil War setting. The heavy, open-weave hair net with ribboned head band of the 1860s also became popular during World War II in the 1940s. The Hon, Boultinghouse, and Stewart families hailed from Illinois, with roots in Kentucky and Virginia, and intermarried several times. (Courtesy of Edgar R. Hon, McLean, VA.)

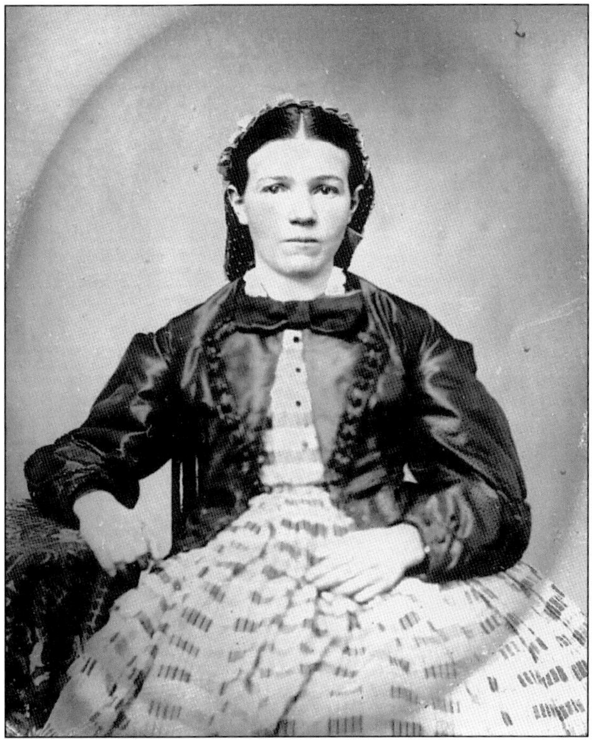

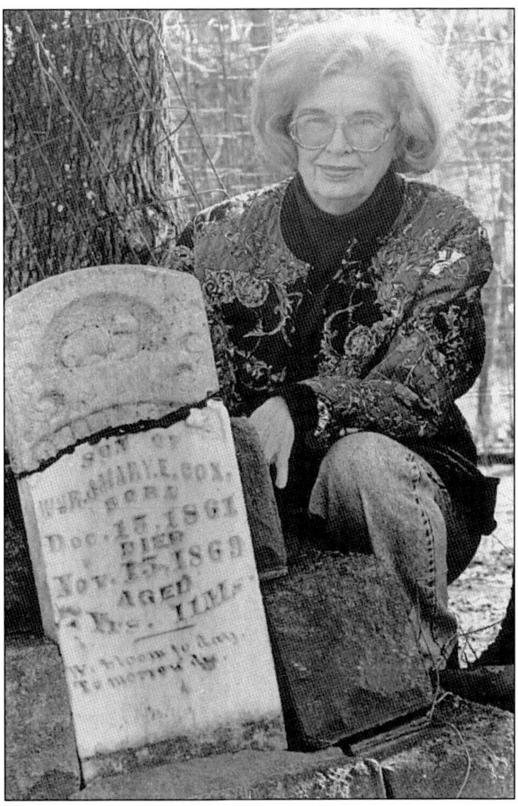

Directly behind the headstone, a large oak trees grows out of the ground atop the sacred burial ground of the son of William and Mary E. Cox. The author discovered the monument in the 1980s. The Cox's son was born in the middle of December 1861 and died in the middle of November in 1869, when he was seven years and eleven months old. He is buried in the oldest burial ground in Waldron, near the grave of W.G. Featherston across from the Methodist Church, in the backyard on private property. At the time of the burial, it would have been to the south of the church which faced Church Street. (Historian's Collection.)

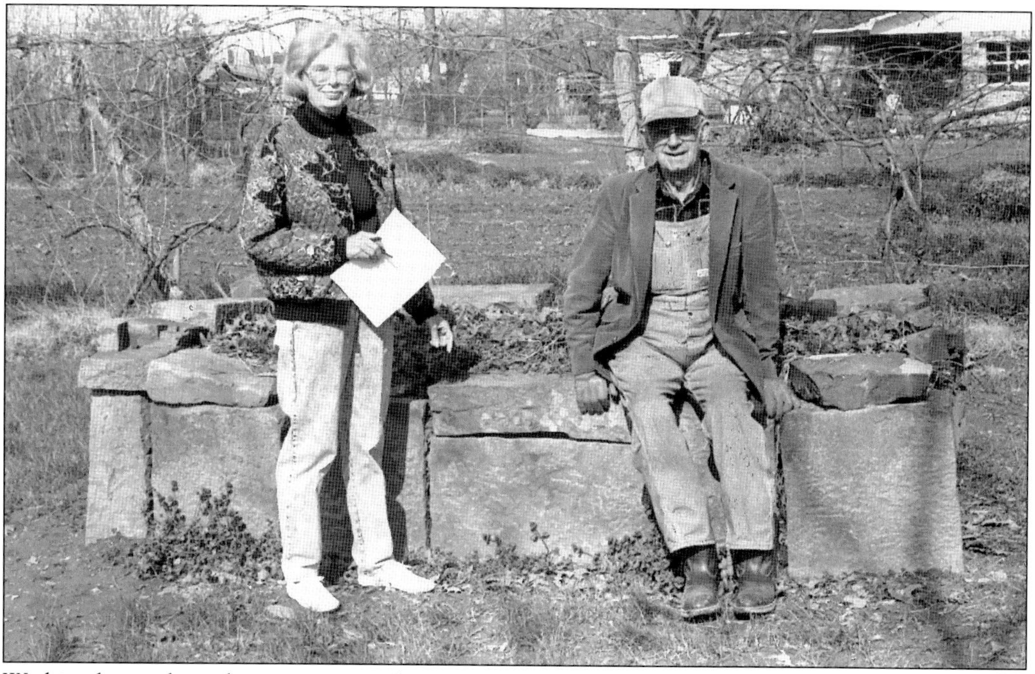

Within this rock enclosure, next to the turnip patch in the backyard of 425 Featherston Street, lies the body of the founder of Waldron, William G. Featherston, who died in 1873. This grave is 8 feet 6 inches long, 5 feet wide, and 30 inches high. The large thick stones were quarried with a few field stones lying on top. Shown here are Wanda M. Gray and Oscar Holland. (Historian's Collection, photographer Ronnie Mullenax.)

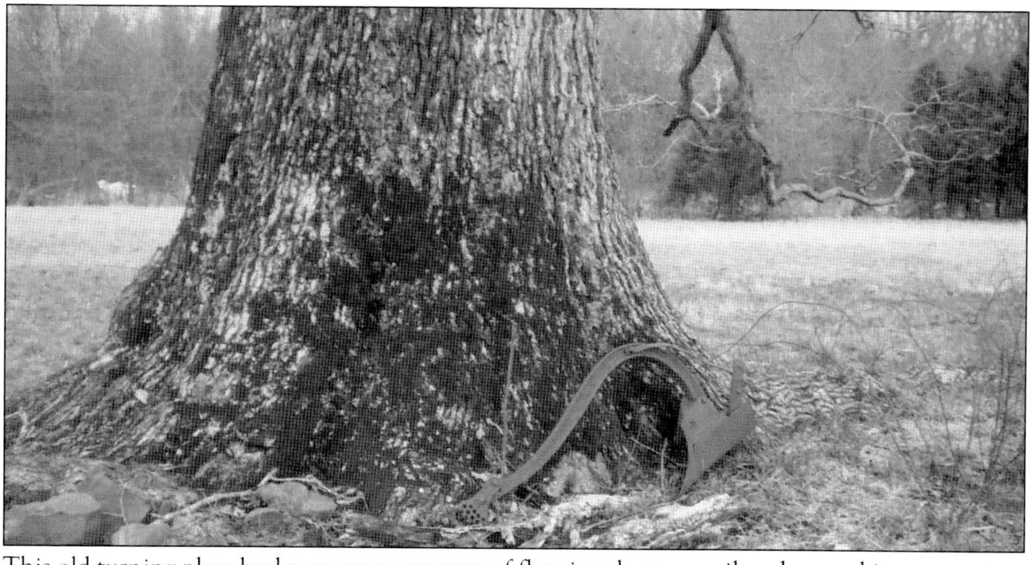

This old turning plow broke up many an acre of flat river bottom soil and earned its rest against the base of the Arkansas Champion White Oak Tree. In the 20th century, the single horse-drawn plow gave way to the gasoline-powered tractor. The rocks on the left of the tree cover a water well, indicating there was once a house nearby. The land belonged to Ed Thompson and now belongs to his son, Dale. It is located west of Waldron on the north side of the Poteau River. (Historian's Collection.)

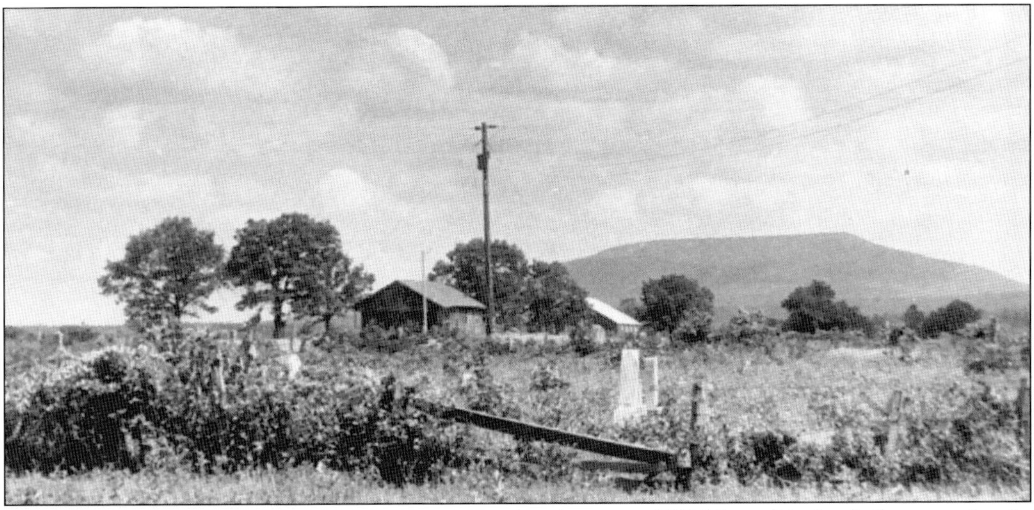

Pictured here is the Pleasant Grove Cemetery, 6 miles east of Waldron. Under billowing clouds, with Pilot Mountain looming in the background, many hardworking settlers of the community were laid to rest. The home of John Belter and Mamie Feeser, of German descent, is located directly behind the graveyard and was established in the 1850s. This historic burial ground has been restored and enlarged and is maintained regularly by a cemetery committee. (Historian's Collection.)

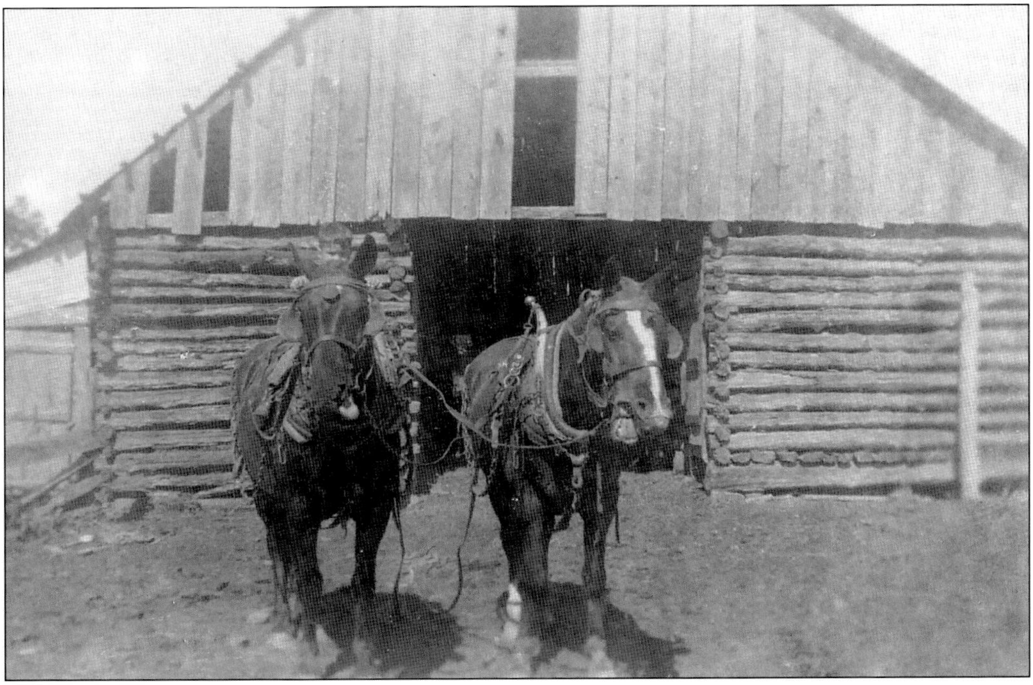

This log barn was built in the 1870s by Obadiah Neal, who came to Arkansas from Georgia with two brothers and settled east of Waldron off of the present Highway 248. He worked as a successful farmer. A church, cemetery, and school were established within a short distance of this barn known as Liberty, but all that remains today is the cemetery, known as the Neal Cemetery. The well-fed team of harnessed horses are patiently waiting either the plow or the wagon and belonged to Tommy Langston. (Courtesy of Della Meredith.)

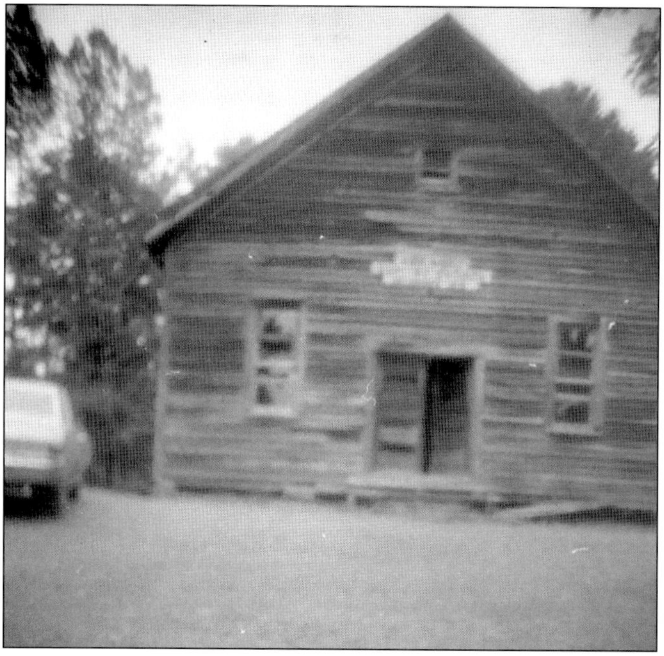

The New Home Church at Cross Creek in the western part of the county was a "box-style" building with the high-pitched roof and clapboard siding that came into fashion after the turn of the 20th century. It had sash windows and was built upon field stones for a foundation. Arley Browning owned this property in 1983. (Historian's Collection.)

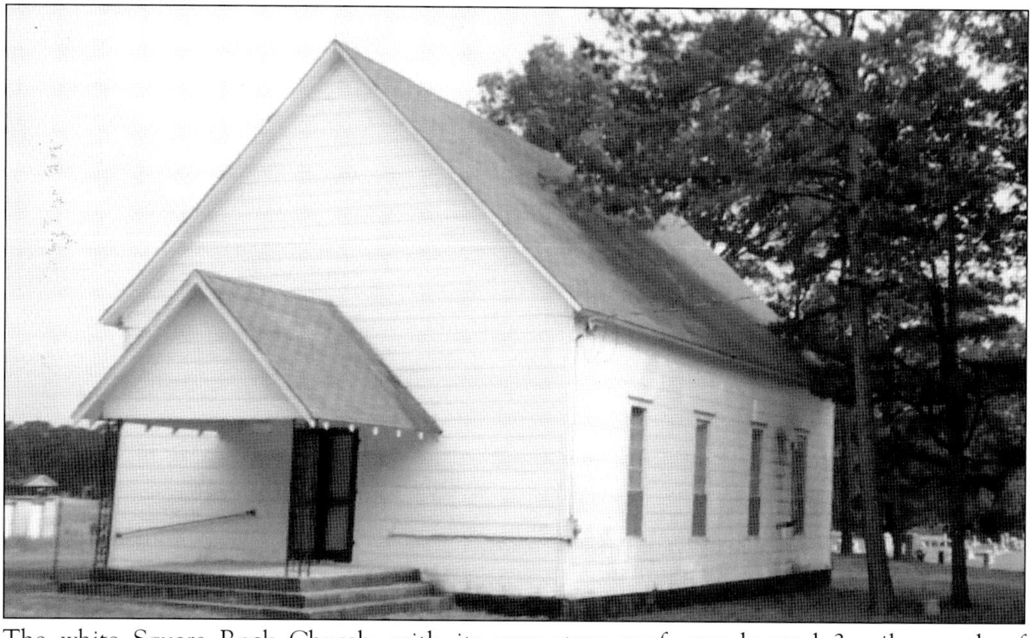

The white Square Rock Church, with its very steep roof, was located 3 miles north of Waldron. It was organized as early as 1842, according to circuit riding Methodist preacher, William Graham, who recorded in his diary, "there were in all twenty-one appointments . . . and when I came to see the work, my idle conceptions was nigh blown away . . . I held meetings in homes and not much used log school houses . . ." Graham was assigned in 1844 but mentioned that no one had been on the circuit for two years; he specifically stated that Square Rock was on his circuit. The recorded burials in the cemetery date back to the 1870s. It continues to be an active church and very active burial ground as it readies for the 21st century. (Historian's Collection.)

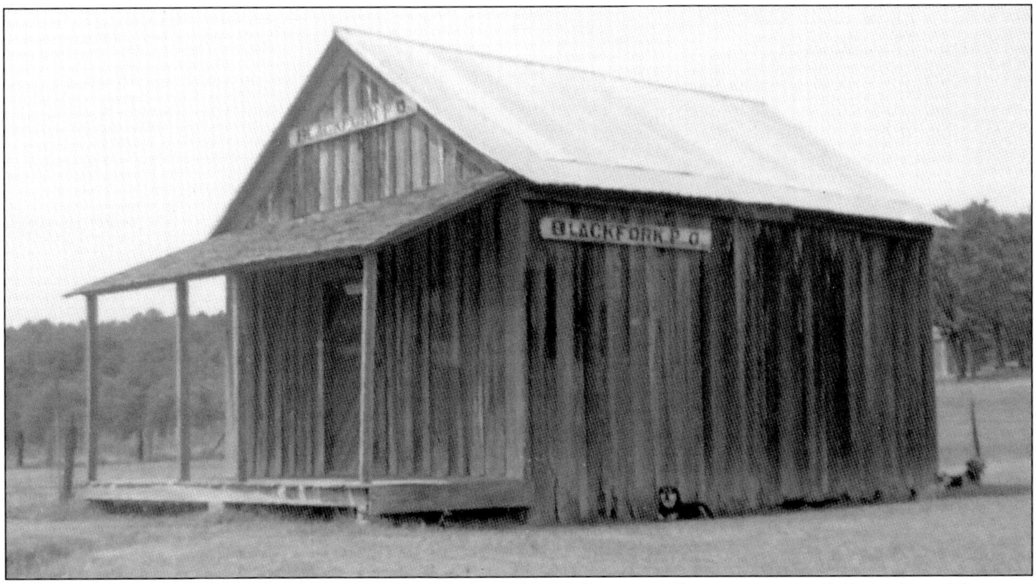

Within a short distance of the Choctaw Indian Nation, this unpainted board-and-batten rough-sawed lumber building, perched on native stones, housed the Black Fork Post Office. This building, preceded by a log structure, stood out as it was the only combination store and mail service in the forest-covered floor of the Black Fork Valley in the extreme southwest part of the county. Mail service began operation in 1877 and was not discontinued until a 104 years later. (Historian's Collection.)

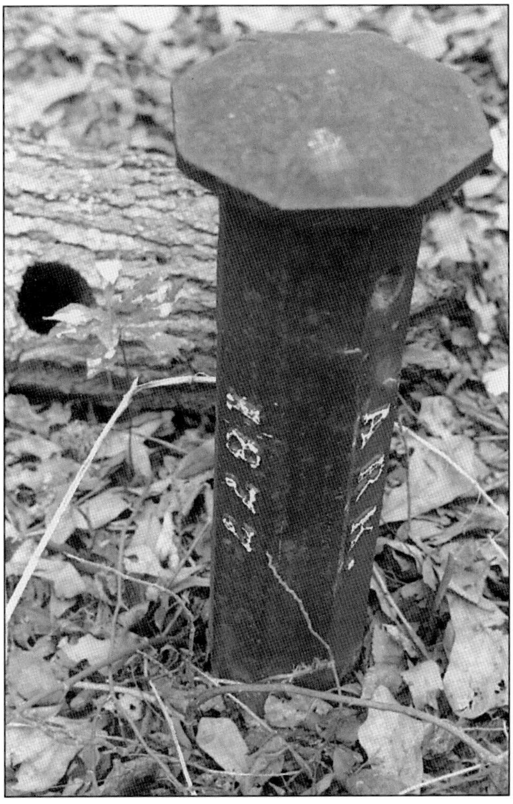

This 1877 survey marker separated Scott County and the Choctaw Indian Nation. Years of border disputes initiated the placement of these octagonal iron spikes at each mile on the western Arkansas boundary line. On every other flat surface they are inscribed "ARK., 1877, CHOC., 35 M." or the appropriate number. The 1820 Choctaw Treaty was the first major treaty to remove eastern Native Americans to the far west. Often times, neither the Native Americans nor the white man knew where the survey line was on the ground, which led to encroachments and continual conflicts. Another survey was authorized by the federal government in 1868 but halted after going only 8 miles. In 1875, Congress enacted 18 Statutes at Large 476 authorizing the 1877 resurveying and re-marking of the entire west boundary of the state of Arkansas. One hundred and twenty-four years later, some of these markers are evidenced. (Courtesy B. O. Roop, Fayetteville AR.)

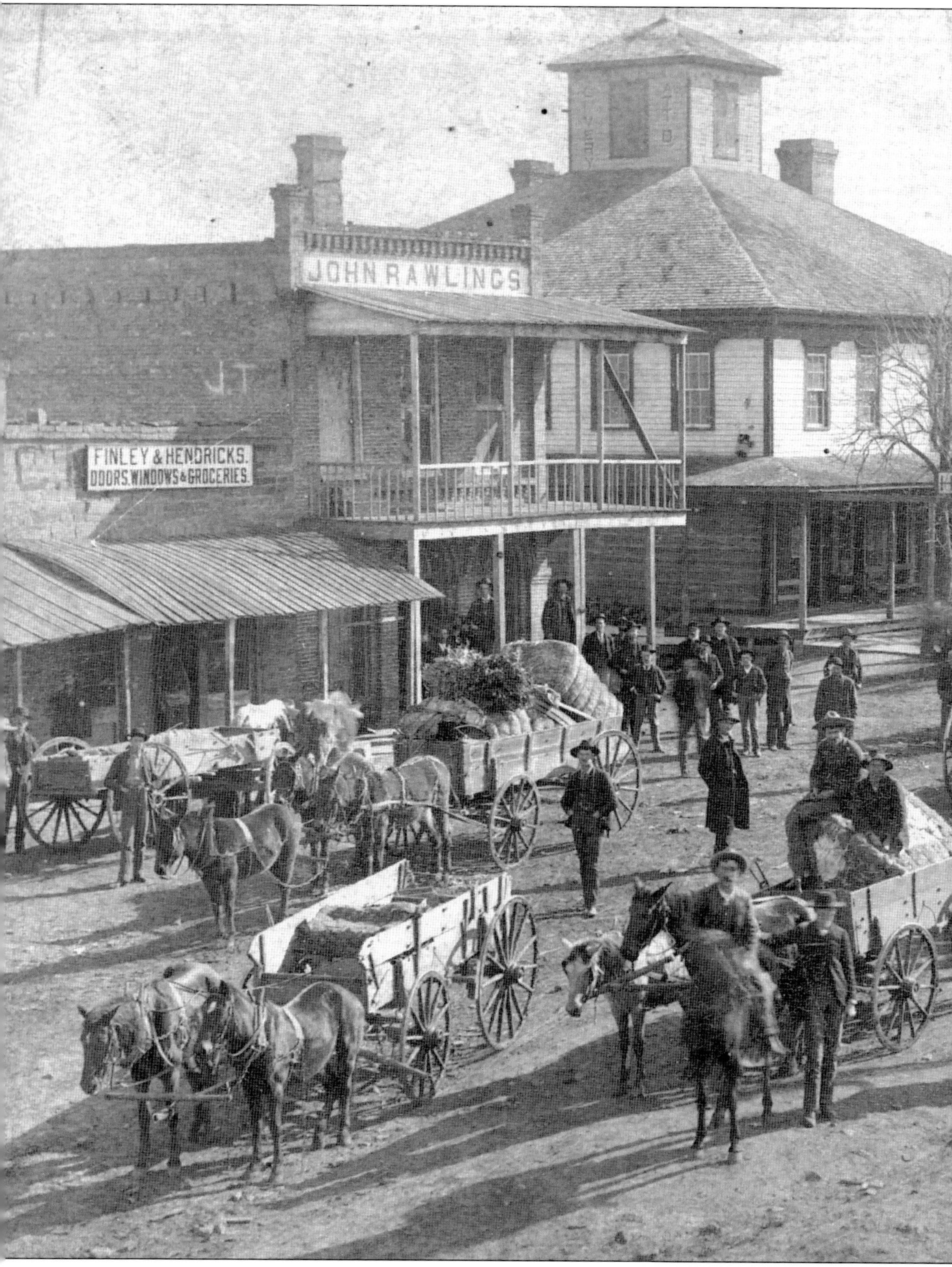
JOHN RAWLINGS
FINLEY & HENDRICKS.
DOORS, WINDOWS & GROCERIES.

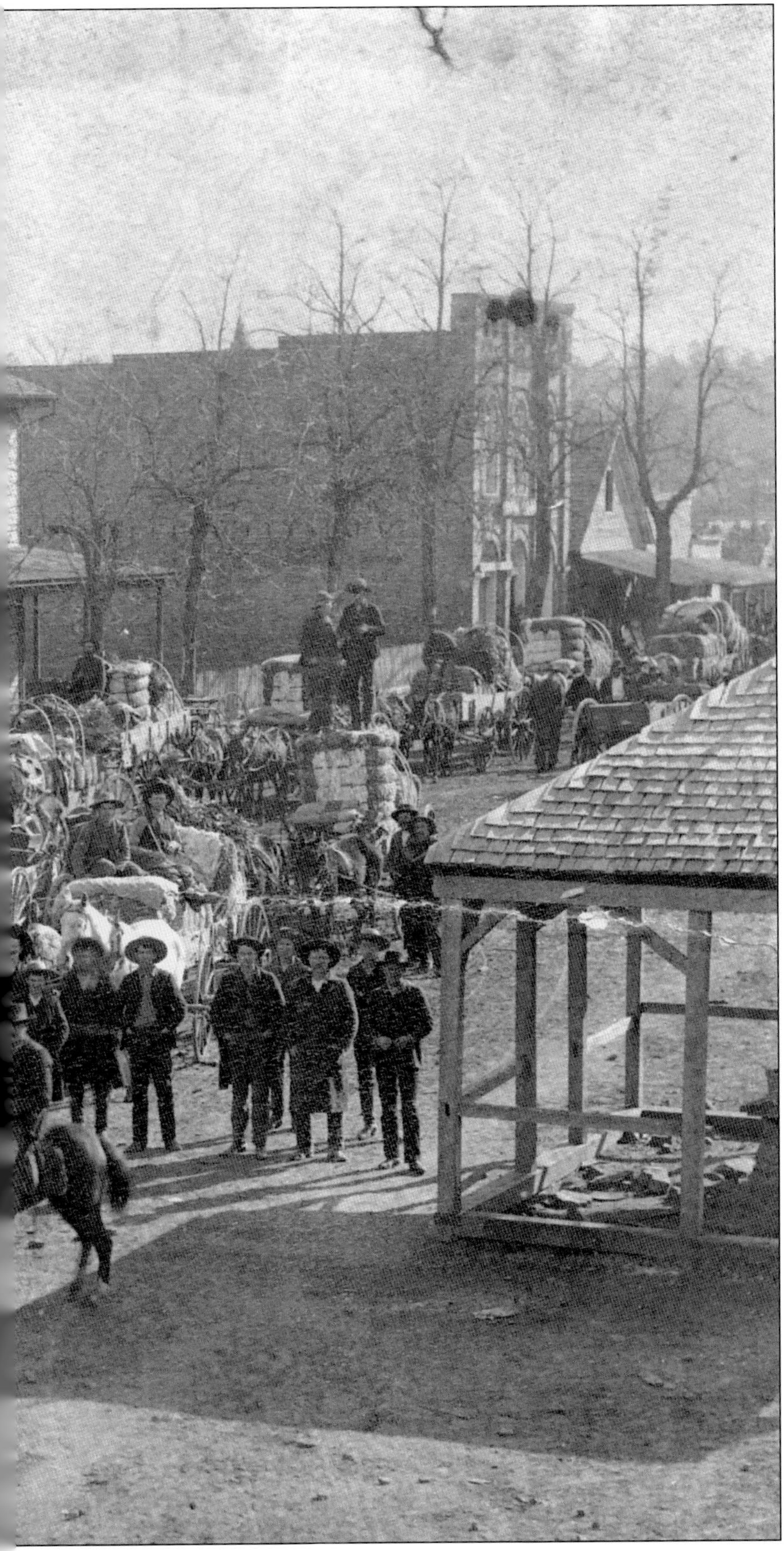

One could hear phonograph music on Main Street in the county seat of Waldron, which was dusty or muddy in the fall when the cotton wagons rolled into town. This view is looking south from Second Street. The people could quench their thirst at the town well, buy their coffee at Finley & Hendricks, or pick up cloth for a new dress from John Rawling's mercantile. Most farmers spent the night in the wagon yard rather than the commodious, 20-room Continental Hotel built in 1878. (Historian's Collection.)

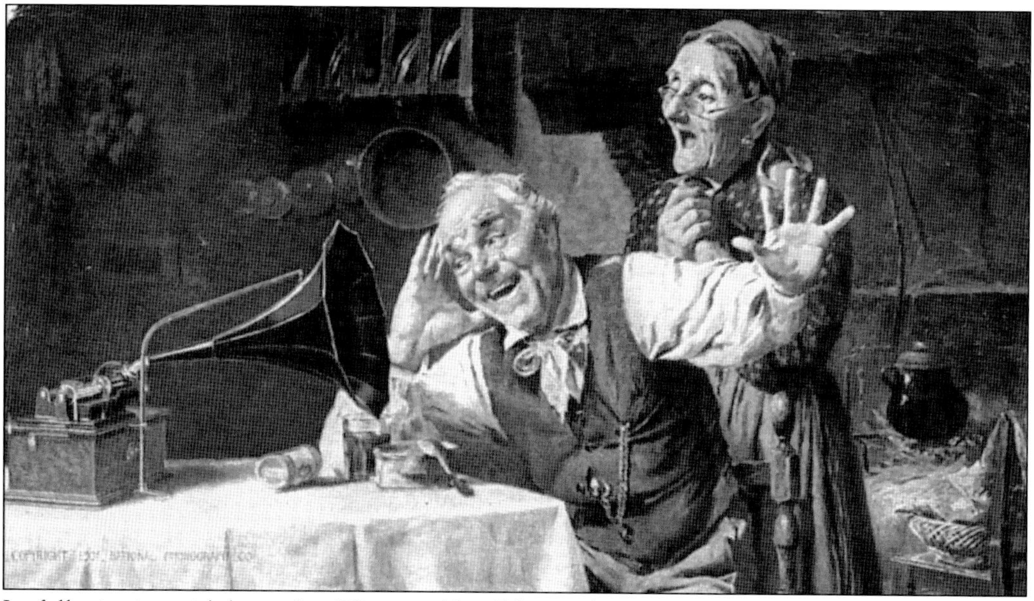

Joyfully singing with his wife is Thomas Alva Edison, the inventor of the phonograph, in 1877. The large shaped horn seems to overpower the little wooden box, which houses tinfoil and wax cylinders that record and reproduce sounds. The phonograph was developed into a wonderful musical instrument enjoyed in homes for generations. It was the forerunner of radio, stereos, and television. Edison was one of the most prolific inventors of the late 19th century who, at his death in 1931, had patented over 1,000 inventions. (Historian's Collection.)

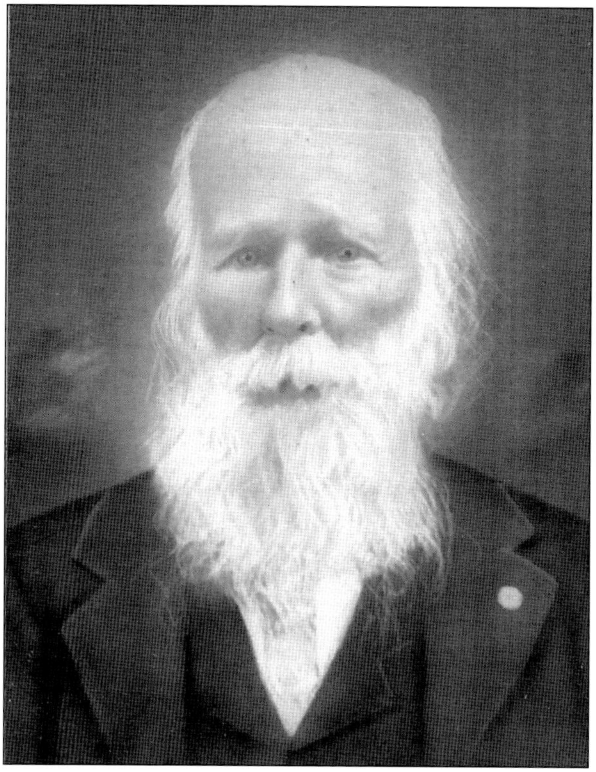

Dr. Elijah Leming (1819–1903), a compassionate pioneer, was one of the first professionally trained doctors in the county. He traveled on horseback, tending the sick in the rain, sleet, and snow. He first settled in the Birdsview community in 1858 but later built a log home on the old Springfield Military Road between Fort Smith and Fort Towson on the Red River. Today, it would be in north Waldron, on the west side of Highway 71B across from the Blythe Museum. He was active in politics, a leader in the community, a Republican, a Baptist, and a Mason. He was the Worshipful Master of Waldron Lodge in 1871, 1873, 1875, 1876, and 1879. (Courtesy of Waldron Masonic Lodge No. 132.)

The sharp, twinkling eyes of Thomas Chauncey Humphrey depict a man with a keen wit, a high degree of intelligence, and a youthful spirit. The square set of his jaws portrays a man of rugged individualism, which enabled him to conquer the wilderness. In 1935, this 89-year-old man was honored as the Senior Past Grand Master of the Masonic Grand Lodge for the state of Arkansas. During his long life, he distinguished himself as a doctor, an attorney, and a Mason, and he served two terms in the state House of Representatives (1875–1893). His father, Charles Humphrey, was the first sheriff of Scott County at the time of statehood (1836), serving three terms. (Courtesy Masonic Lodge, Waldron.)

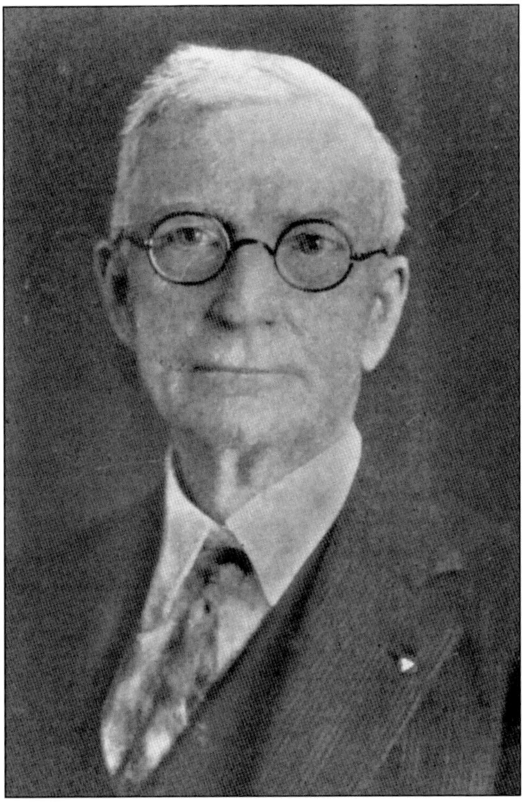

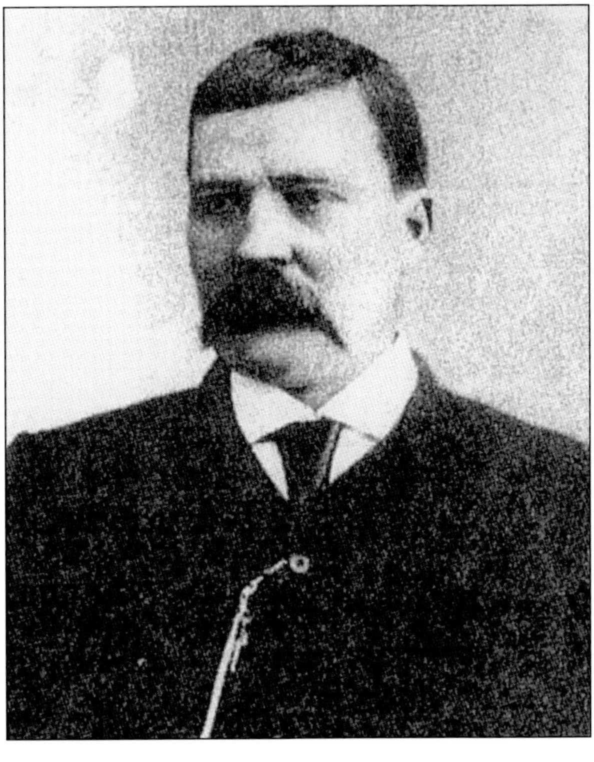

Richly dressed James William Harper operated a wholesale grocery in Mansfield. He also owned land the railroad was surveying in the 1880s that could have resulted in the naming of the town. At the end of a day, the surveyor was asked where he ended the survey and the surveyor replied, "in some man's field." Reportedly, from that comment, Mansfield got its name. However, the town of Mansfield was, most likely, named in honor of the Arkansas jurist, W.W. Mansfield.

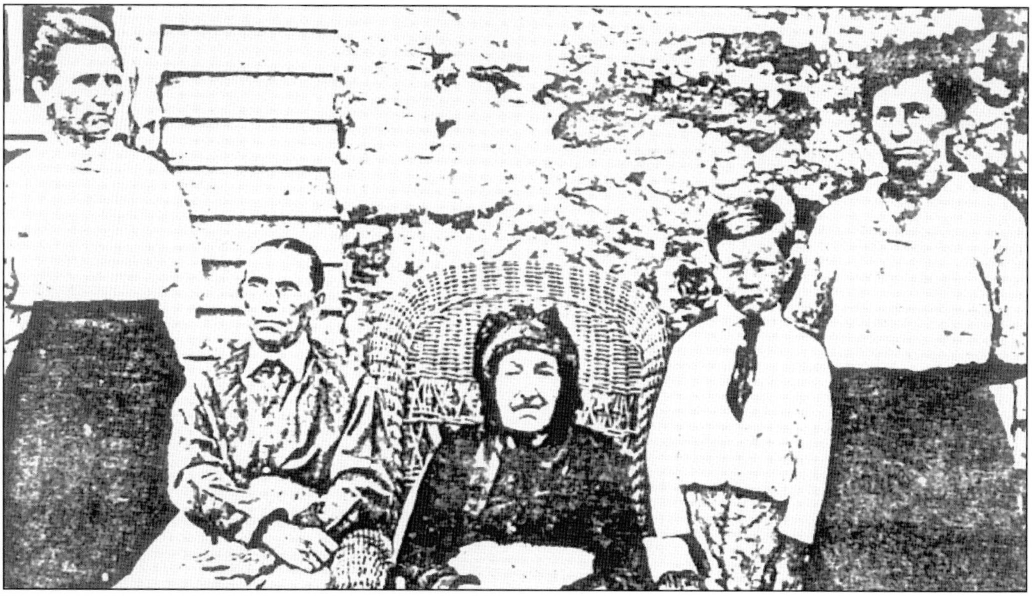

This widow brought her family to the county before 1880, where they spent the rest of their lives.They came to Arkansas from Lauderdale County, Tennessee. From left to right are as follows: Elmyra H. Hipp Farnsworth; Henrietta Hipp Hutchison Potts Shaw Payne; the matriarch, Kathryn Sawyer Hipp, widow of Holdrich; Milburn Williams; and Virginia Kathryn Hipp Williams. (Historian's Collection.)

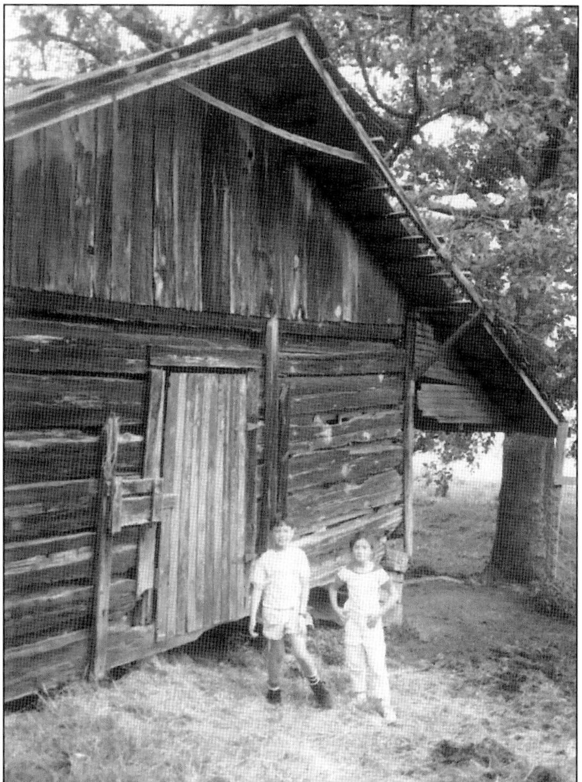

Former County Judge Rowland Chiles (1827–1899) patented 120 acres in Pleasant Valley east of Waldron in 1883 and built this hand hewn log barn, which is still standing over 100 years later. The heavy wooden latch holds the vertical plank door shut near where his great-great-great-grandchildren, Paul and Susan Holland, pose standing in loose hay on the ground. (Courtesy of Ila Rhodes, Fresno, CA.)

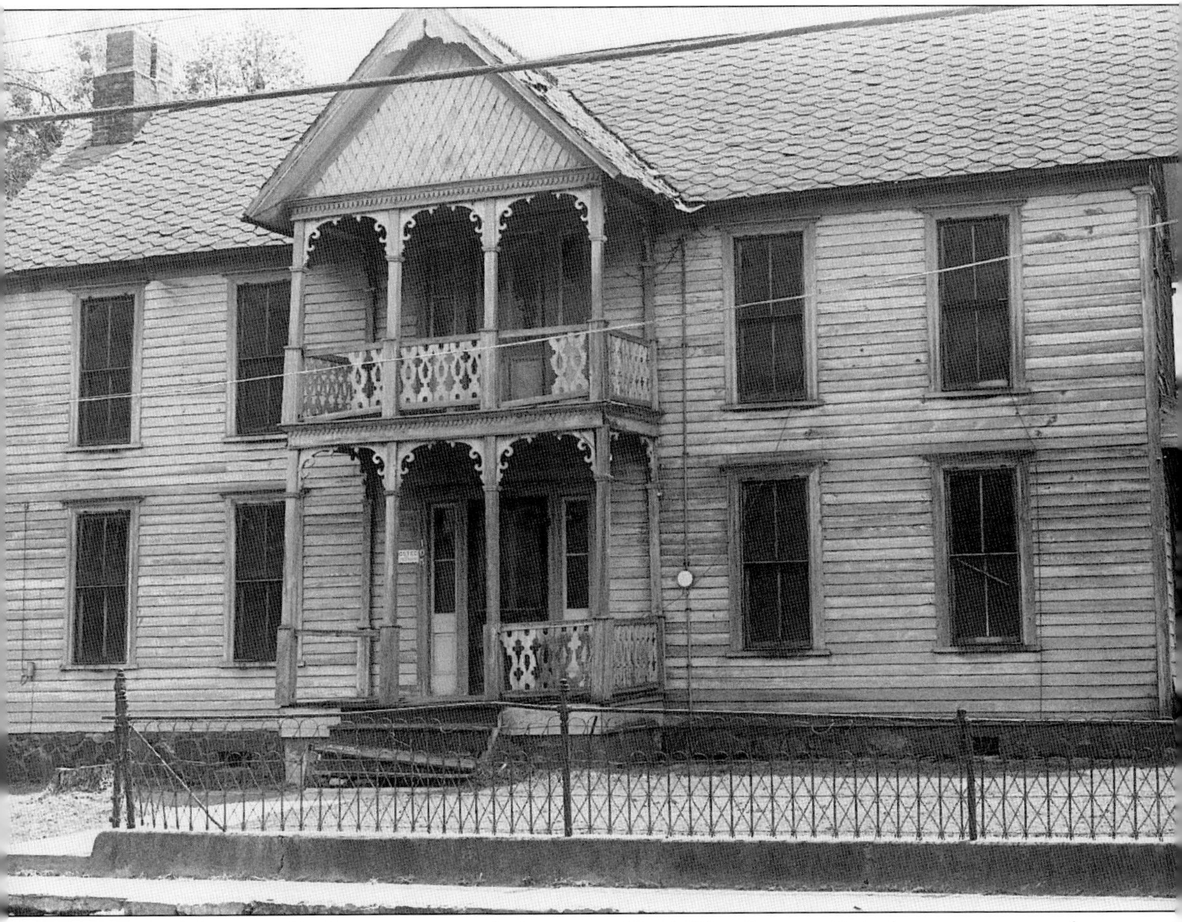

Carl H. and Juanita R. Supon acquired this post–Civil War home of timber magnate and businessman, John T. Forrester, at 115 Danville Street in Waldron. It began as a three-bedroom, one-story home built at the end of the Civil War. In 1886, it received a gable-roofed, two-story addition inspired by the decorative Eastlake style. The entire building was faced with horizontal weatherboard, with corner boards and cornice molding with iron cresting appearing along the ridges of the gabled roofs. A full porch adorned the west side of the building and gently mediated between the one-story south end of the house and its two-story addition. The floors were hand-planed pine boards, and ceiling boards and cedar wall boards, when exposed, proved to be in excellent condition. Square-headed nails were used in original construction, and the house had four working fireplaces, three downstairs and one upstairs. There were no closets built into the original structure or the later addition, but corner clothes closets were added in 1900. Attempts at restoration of this historic home failed, and necessity dictated that it be torn down in the 1980s, at which point the community suffered the loss of one of its oldest homes. (Historian's Collection, contributed by Juanita R. Supon.)

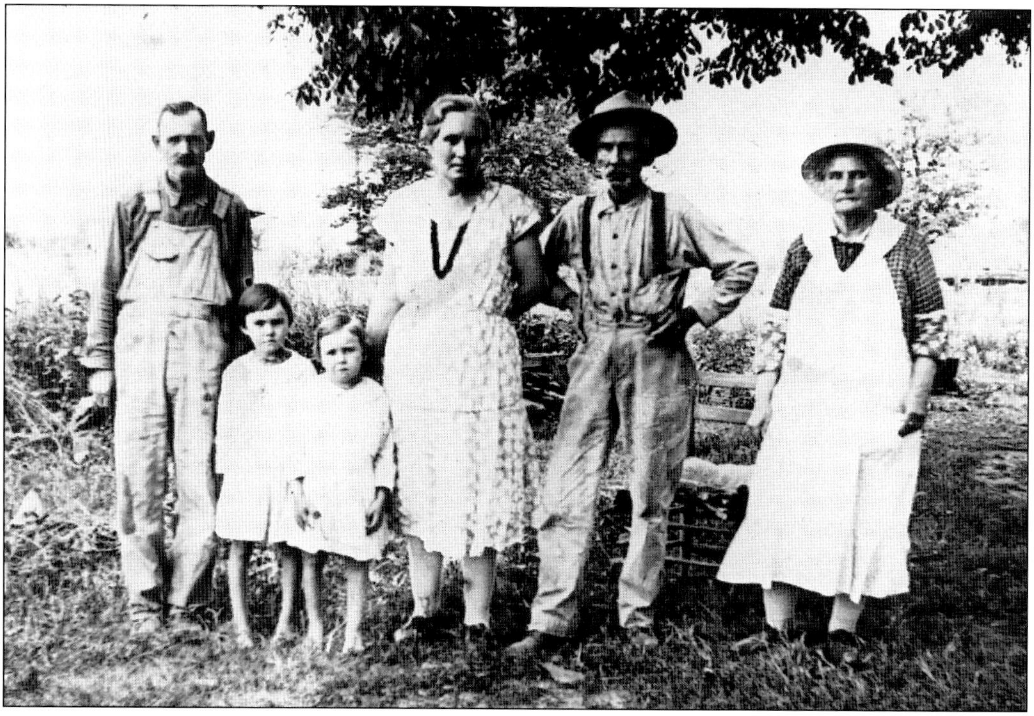

Taking a short break from the daily chores of farm life in this rural scene is a typical farm family: Jacob Craig (1887–1961), Edna, Ila, Fannie May Speaks Craig (1884–1959), Lewis Newton Speaks (1847–1943), and Josephine Fisher Speaks (1858–1944). The senior Speaks came to the county in the 1880s and lived the remainder of their lives there. Many of their descendants have continued to make the county their home. (Courtesy of Ila Rhodes, Fresno, CA.)

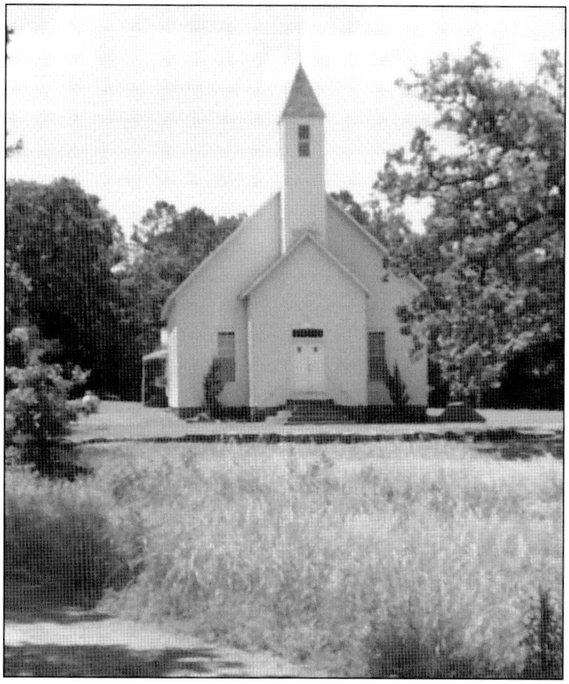

One of the best preserved historic church structures in the county is the Mt. Pleasant Methodist Church in the Greenridge community, about 10 miles east of Waldron on Highway 248. The land for this church was donated in 1884 by Alvin and Joseph Self, descendants of the religiously devout pioneer settlers arriving from Georgia in the 1860s. (Historian's Collection.)

This portrait of Mary Elizabeth Oldham (1860–1903), in a black formal dress, illustrates the appearance of ladies in 1882. The long dangling earrings have continued to be fashionable for the last 100 years, and the same holds true for neck scarves. The daughter of Joseph C. Oldham of West Fork, she married John Edwin Center and lived in Greenwood briefly, where her husband split rails for 10¢ each for her Uncle Joel Kinsley Oldham, her father's twin brother. About 1882, Mr. Center relocated his family to a farm near Waldron. (Historian's Collection.)

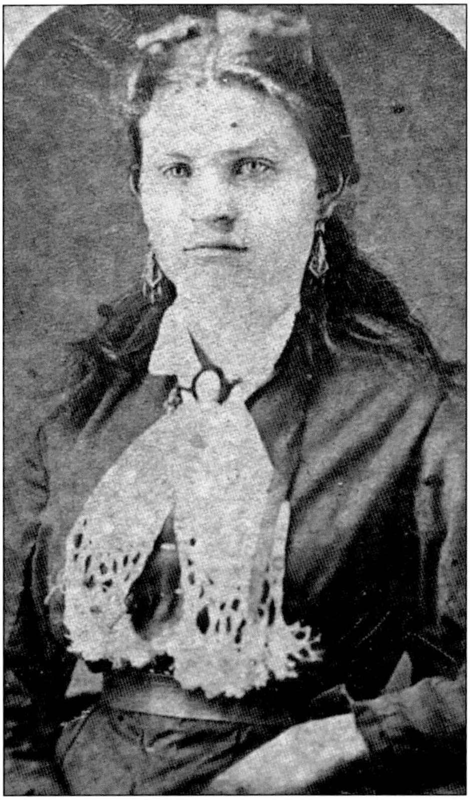

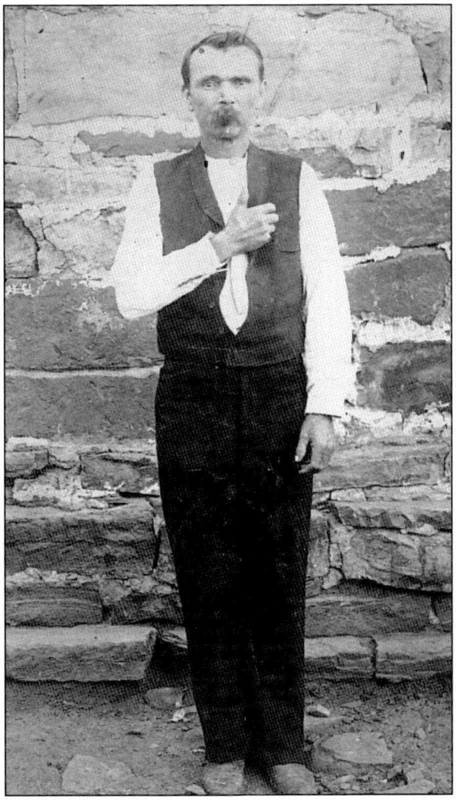

Pictured standing outside on the dirt against a crudely constructed native stone building is Walter T.L. Gipson. His black pants and vest indicate that he was a merchant, not a farmer. All that remains of the historic Gipson settlement on the north banks of the South Fork of the Poteau River, south of Bates, is the sprawling Gipson Cemetery. The old wagon road to Indian Territory meandered past the Gipson store and post office in 1887. (Historian's Collection.)

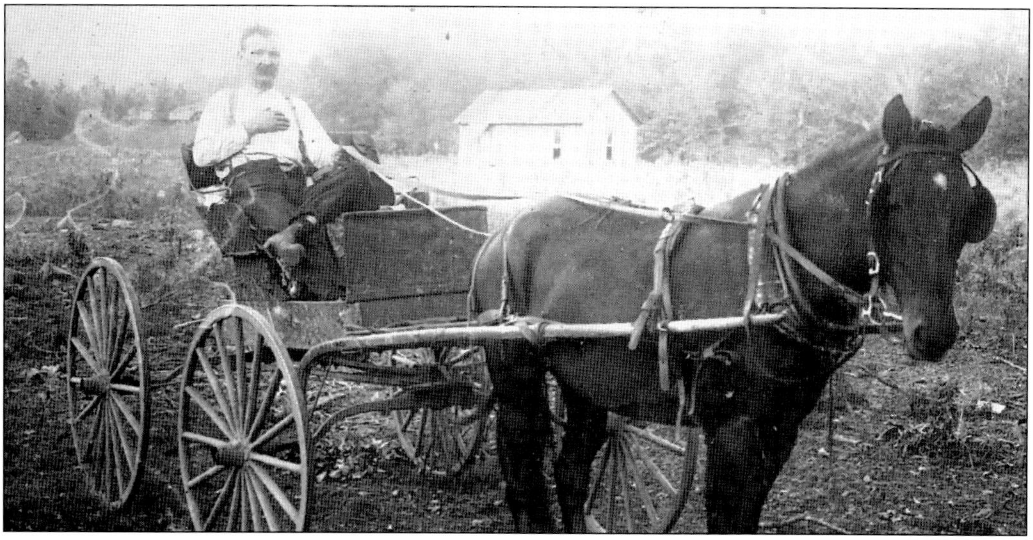

The horse-drawn buggy became a popular method of conveyance and a familiar sight in the county after the timber was cut and roads improved. It was much lighter and less cumbersome than the heavy wagons and could move along at about 10 miles an hour. This peaceful and serene 1890s image of Walter T.L. Gipson brings to mind the comment made by the literary genius, Washington Irving, "I pray that the revolutions that distract other parts of the . . . planet reach not here . . . that the inhabitants may long retain their happy ignorance . . . and respect for the fiddle." (Historian's Collection.)

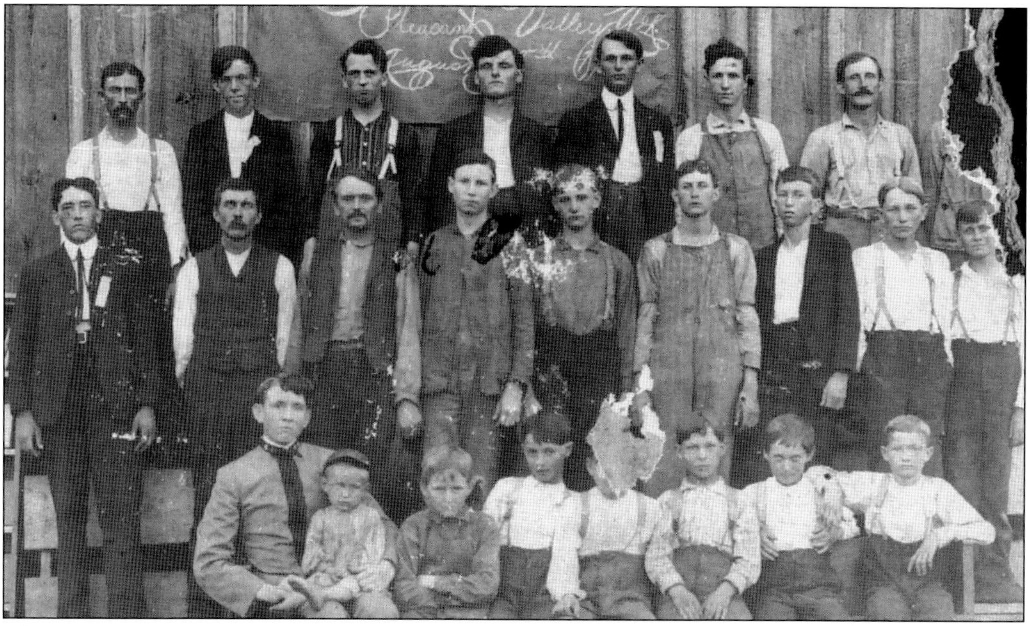

This "men only" gathering at the old Pleasant Valley schoolhouse, just before the turn of the 20th century, must have been a special occasion. Three men had special ribbons pinned on their lapels, winning prizes won perhaps in geography, judging from the globe on the bookcase that had been carried outside for the August event. Few today know of this school, which was located about 5 miles east of Waldron on the northeast corner of where County Road 87 intersects with Highway 80 East. (Courtesy of Ila Rhodes, Fresno, CA.)

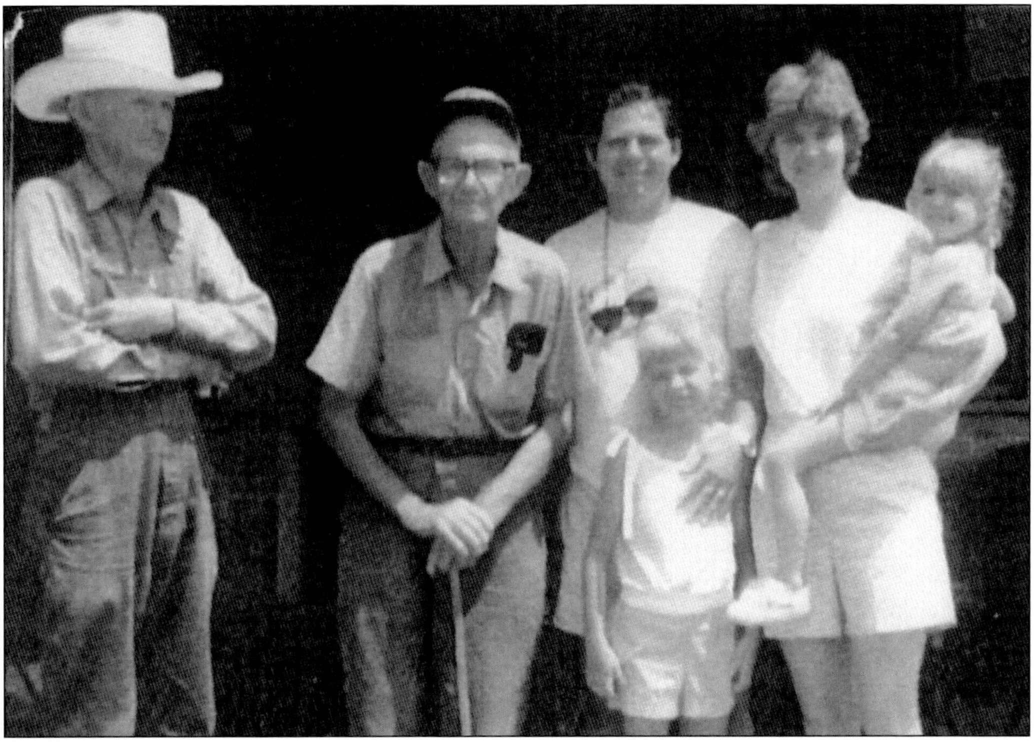

Pictured here is Emmet Miller (1903–1988), the time-honored reverend, former rancher, postmaster, and owner of the combination gas station, grocery store, and post office at Cauthron. He was well known for his love of singing gospel music at the popular Sunday afternoon "singings." Pictured from left to right are the following: Billy Rowe, Emmet's only child; Emmet; Tony Phillips; Theresa, age seven; and Theresa Ruth Ann Bergman Phillips holding Amanda, age three. (Courtesy of Reba Nell Bethel Bergman, Waldron.)

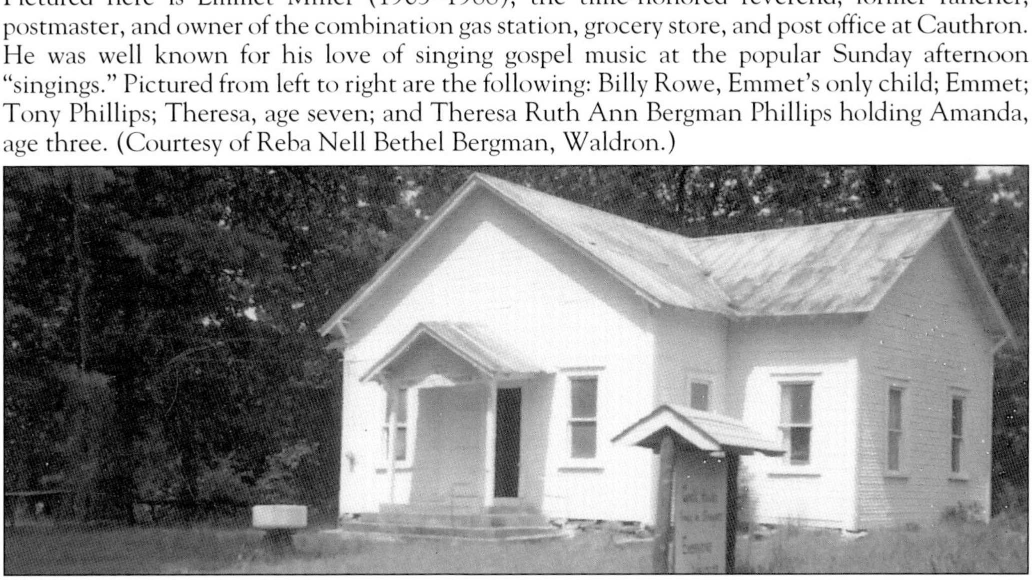

Seen here is the rusty metal roof of the two-room Shiloh Baptist Church near the Nella and Blansett communities. Located in the rugged but beautiful southwest part of the county, the church is still active. Many of the early settlers are buried in the cemetery behind the church. The spiritual life of settlers was very important, and a church has been in this area since settlers herded their trusty oxen over almost nonexistent roads over the mountains before 1840. At first, sermons were preached in log homes, then log churches, and then in improved church buildings. (Historian's Collection.)

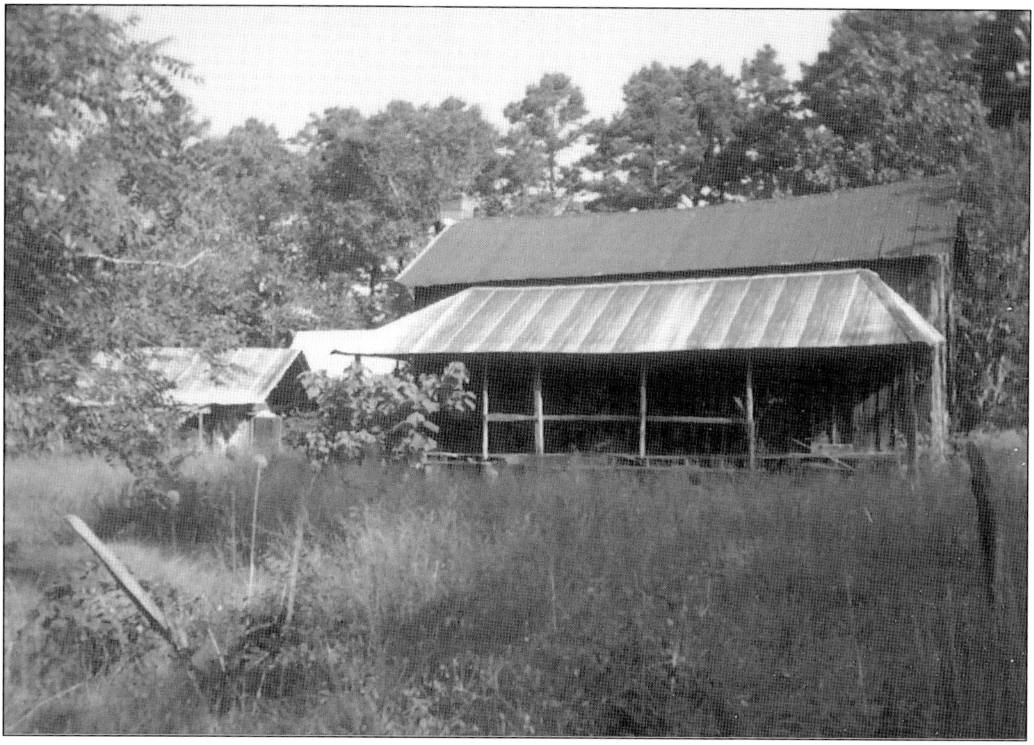

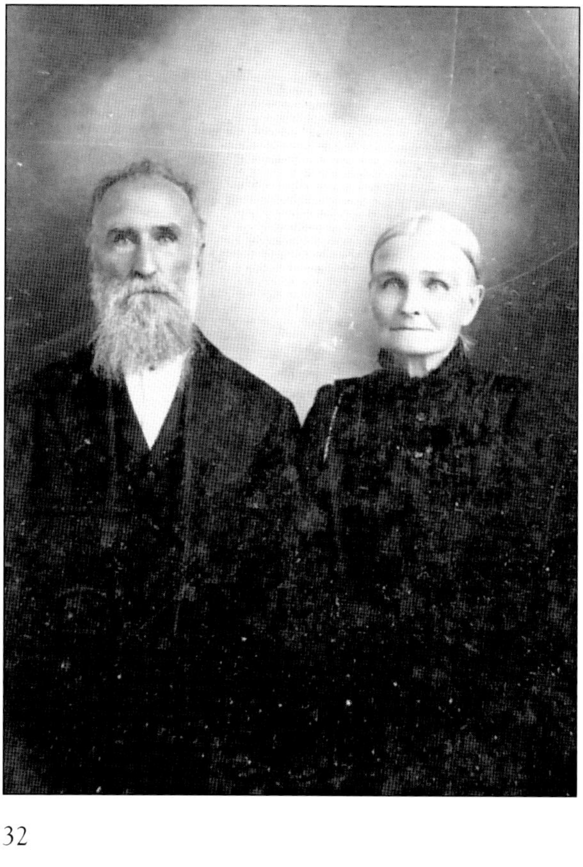

The corrugated roof covers the former home of Joseph A. Gist and his wife, Laura Taylor, a descendant of former President Zachary Taylor. It was built in 1894 of rough sewed lumber. The tall grass attests to the fertile soil in the Blansett community in the rugged and remote southwest part of the county. (Historian's Collection, photo by Leroy Livesay.)

In the 1800s and early 1900s, black attire was worn almost exclusively for formal occasions such as church services, weddings, funerals, and photography. It was also customary that men wear long beards, especially if they were businessmen or doctors. Samuel Graves Lafayette Chandler (1830–1906) and his wife, Elizabeth E. Stewart (1834–1908), left Georgia after the "scorched earth" military practice of General Sherman at the end of the Civil War and settled about 2 miles east of Cauthron. (Historian's Collection.)

A formal portrait of 20-year-old Nathaniel Lee Holland (1875–1942) shows the moustache and dark suit common in this era. Usually, a person had only one dress suit, which was used to wear to church, funerals, weddings, and to have pictures taken. In addition to farming the land, Mr. Holland was the owner and operator of the Holland Gin Company, a very large cotton gin in Waldron. (Courtesy of Ila Rhodes, Fresno, CA.)

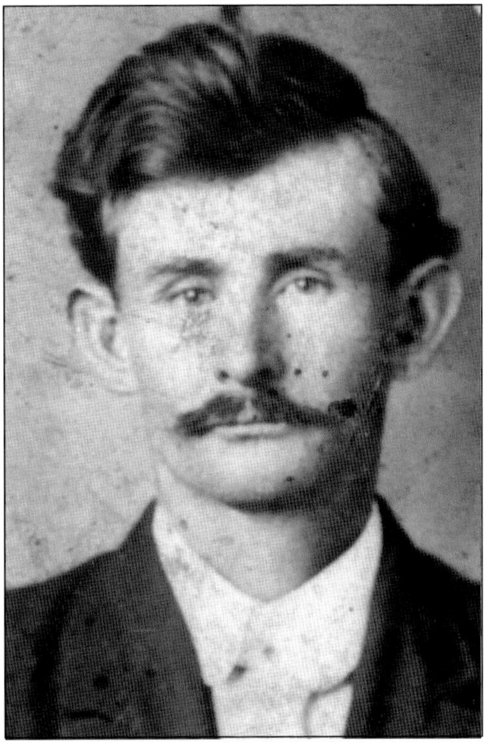

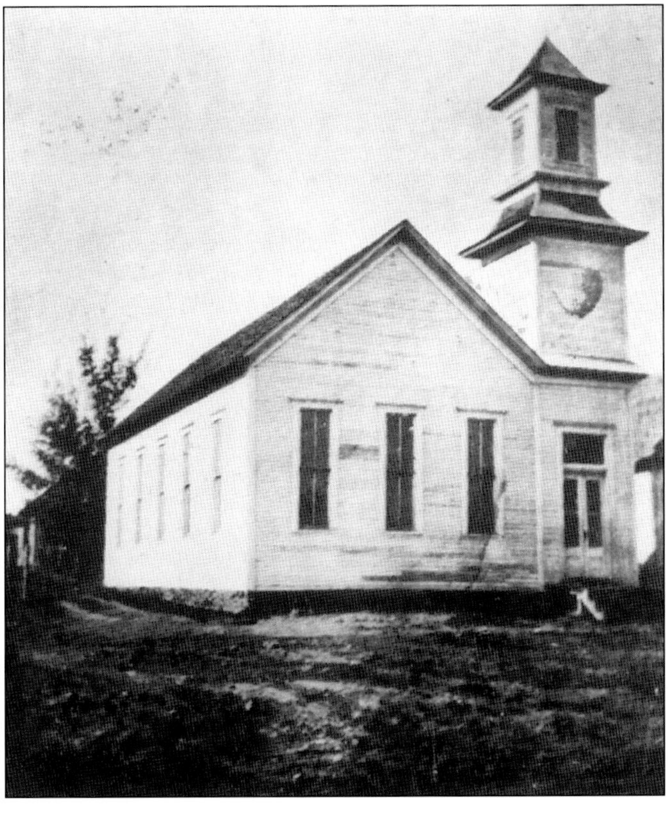

The lovely two-story frame North Methodist Episcopal Church, with a bell tower, stands tall ready to ring out the 19th century in a town that began as a Choctaw trading post. It has been active for over half a century in the settlement of Mansfield, formerly Chocoville, which was located a short distance to the west of the present town. The circuit riding Methodist preachers held meetings in the county as early as 1841 and were most likely the earliest organized church on this part of the frontier. They came when the buffalo, antelope, and bear were plentiful and roamed at will. (Courtesy of Harry Blackman.)

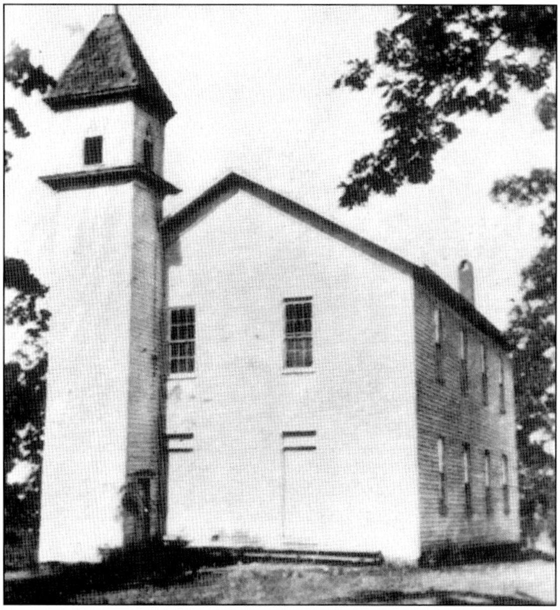

A post–Civil War wood-frame Presbyterian Church, with a bell tower, was located on the west end of Howard Street in Mansfield. It was one of many different denominations in the area that saw to the spiritual welfare of the people. (Courtesy of Harry Blackman.)

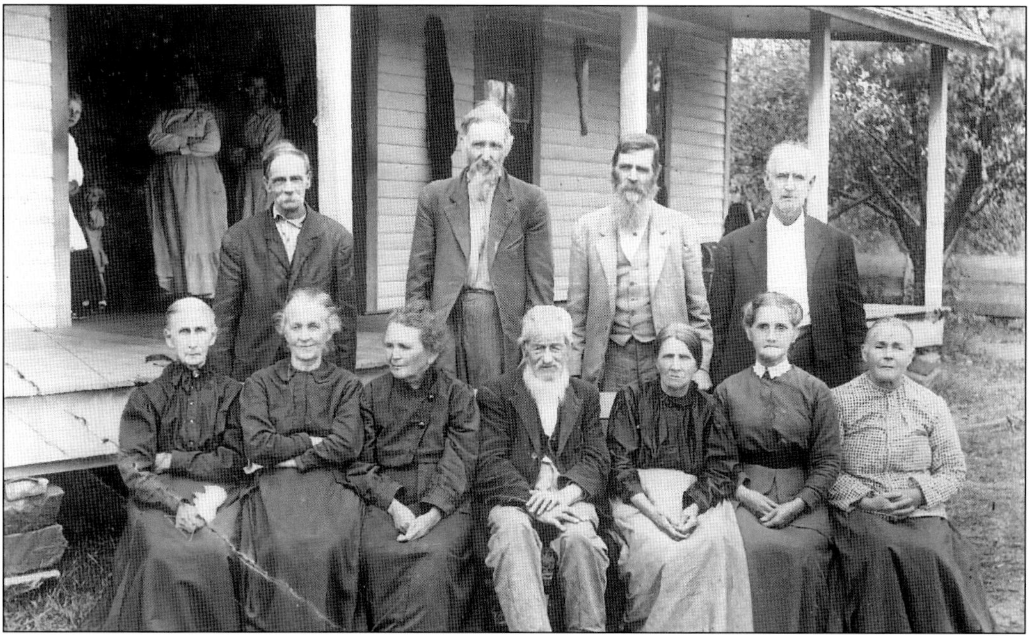

Found in a typical country setting is this log house with a "dog-trot" (open wide hallway) in the center that has been updated with clapboard siding. Note the items hanging on nails on the outside walls: a garment in the center, a handsaw on the right, and another aproned item on the left. Nails were put to use to hold clothing inside the house, as there were no closets built in the early home. It has the usual native stone piers used for a foundation. These "salt-of-the-earth" families living east of Waldron are exemplary of those settling in the county. Pictured from left to right are as follows: (front row seated) Emma Ashmore, Senora McCord, Mary Frizzell, Moses Killion, Sarah Johnson, Mrs. Davis, and Mrs. Murphy; (middle row standing) J.J. Ashmore, James A. McCord, E.F. Fair, and Rev. Davis; (third row standing) Thelma Lynch, Hershel Lynch, Fannie Holland, and Ella Lynch. (Courtesy of Ila Rhodes, Fresno, CA.)

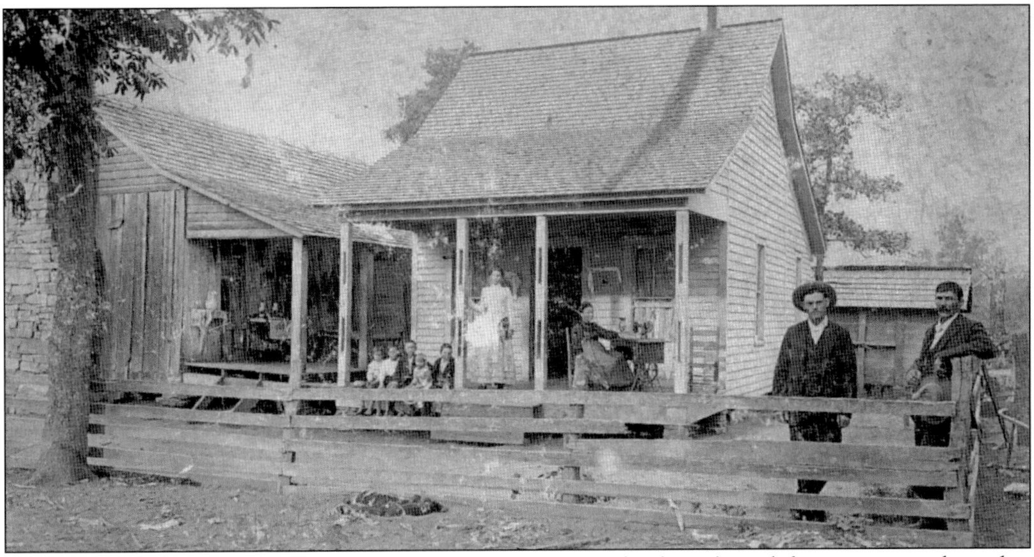

A hound dog, with a litter of nursing pups, rests near the board yard fence surrounding this typical country homeplace. Visiting in the yard at the fence corner are, from left to right, Jacob Wesley "Jake" Craig and Lewis Newton Speaks (1847–1943). The five boys neatly seated on the front porch, with dangling bare feet, belong to Josephine and Lewis N. Speaks. Pictured from left to right are Jess, Lewis, Fred, Tone, and Herb. May Craig (standing), wife of Jake, and Josephine Speaks, have moved the treadle sewing machine out on the front porch where it is cooler to sew. The porch of the old box house (left) with the natural rock chimney is still in use storing needed items. (Courtesy of Ila Rhodes, Fresno, CA.)

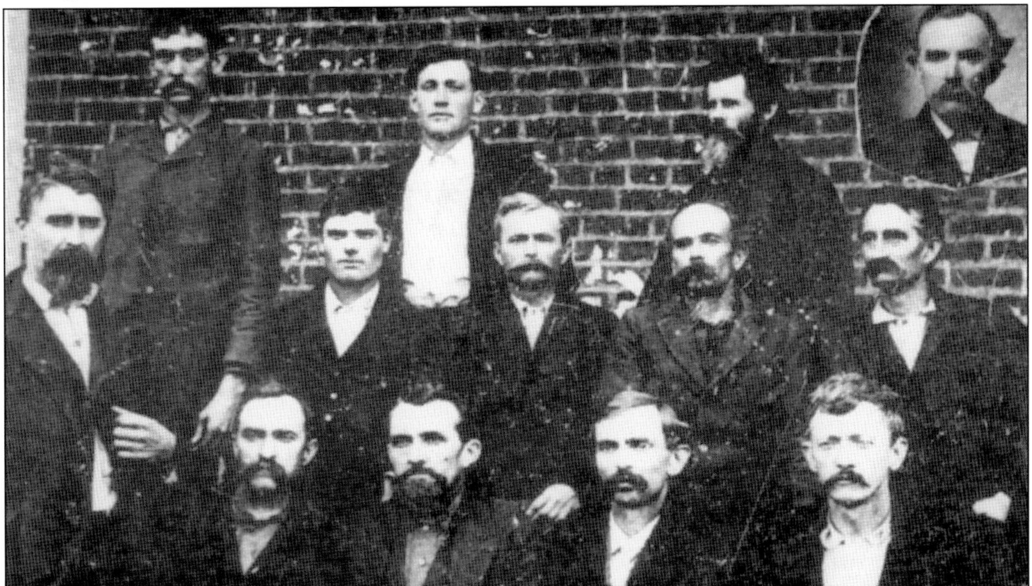

The images of these 13 serious-looking men represent the grand jury for Scott County called in 1901. Pictured from left to right are as follows: (front row) B.J. Claybrook, N.W. Eddy, Looper and J.L. Norris; (second row) Gus Pitts, Luther Johnson, E.R. Watson, H.C. Black, and G.W. Gatlin; (back row) Sid Edwards, J.M. Hale (Audie Hale's father), R.N. Millard, and T.J. Parker. (Courtesy of Arkansas History Commission.)

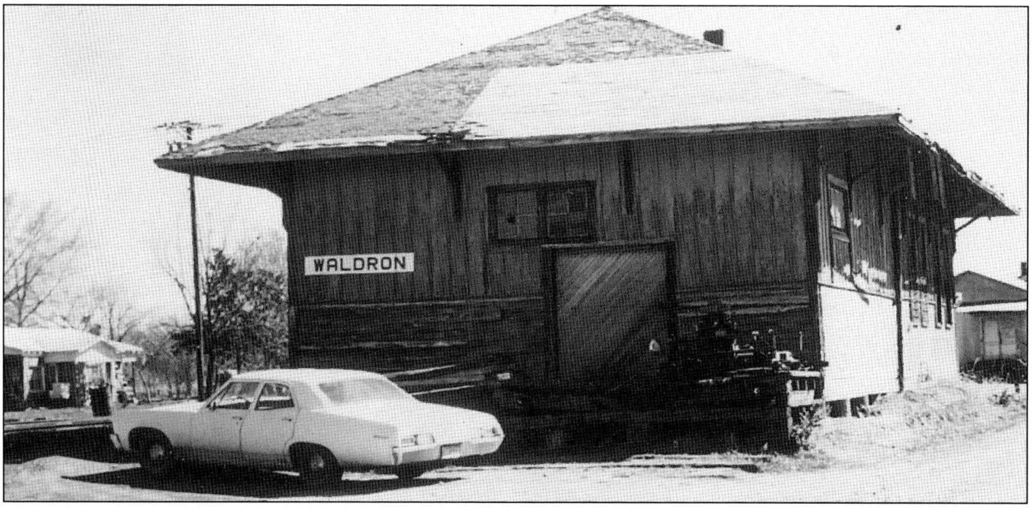

Showing signs of deterioration, in the past the depot was a festive, busy place when the train arrived with people gathering to visit, welcome and say goodbye to friends, receive goods and ship products, or just to see what was going on. The Arkansas Western Railway Company completed 32 miles of railroad to Waldron, Arkansas, in 1901, from Heavener, Oklahoma, where it connected with the Kansas City Southern north/south lines. Within a few years, this line was extended to the lumber-mill town at Forrester. The first train arrived in 1902, with scheduled stops at Godman, Bates, Cauthron, Harris, Bryan Spur, and Hon. Other stops were made on flag to pick up passengers. The train also carried farm produce, livestock, lumber, and milk cans. (Historian's Collection.)

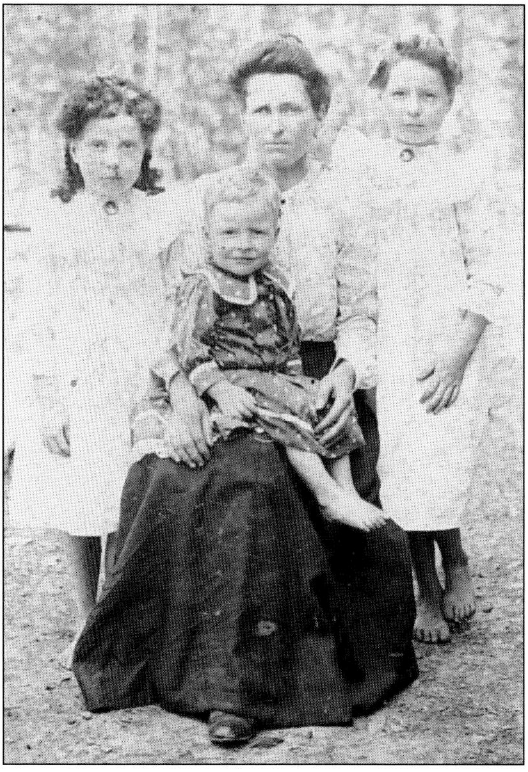

These children are finely dressed, except for their lack of shoes, in this 1902 photo of Kate Smith Pottridge (1873–1957) with daughters Emma (left) and Bessie (right), and Roy (on her lap). She was born at Whitney, Texas, in Hill County but came to the Tate community in the rugged mountainous area between Pilot and Round Mountain in Scott County with her family in 1883. She married H. Alvin Pottridge, and they had six children. It was not at all uncommon for children to go barefoot in the summer. (Historian's Collection, contributed by Howard La Roche, Houston, TX.)

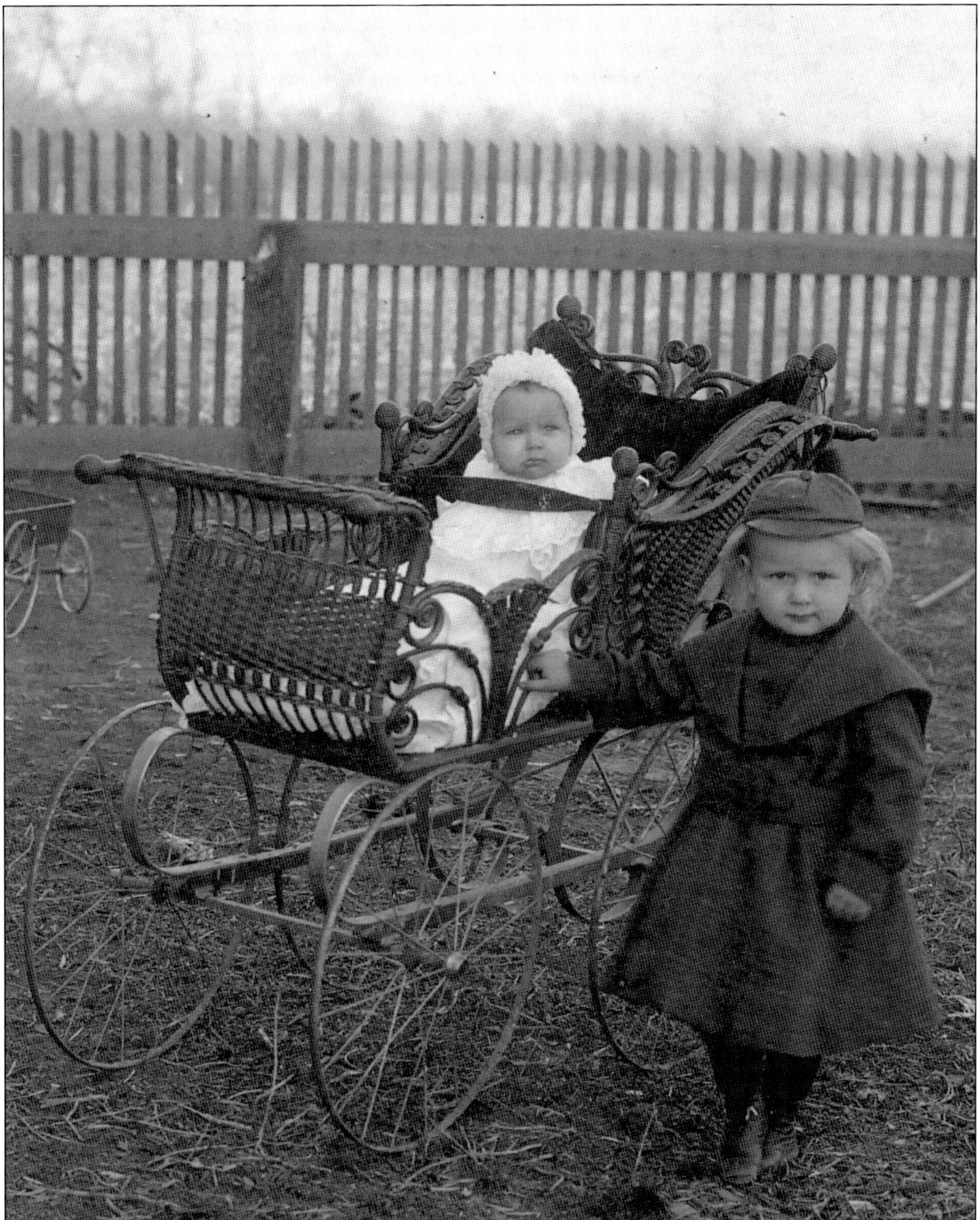

Inside the unpainted picket fence is a child's wagon with metal frame and spoked wheels and a rather large baby carriage on an iron foundation with wheels topped with woven wicker, stylish at the turn of the 20th century. The handsome and chubby child, two-year-old Ivis Leon Ballard (1901–1991), poses beside the carriage in his coatdress, dark stockings, black leather shoes (closed with a narrow strap), and a small, slightly billed cap. The baby in the carriage is unknown. Ivis Leon is the son of Thomas Jefferson Ballard and Molly Ellen Johnson and is the father of Wesley Leon "Wes" Ballard who married Betty Jo Judy. (Courtesy of Ila Rhodes, Fresno, CA.)

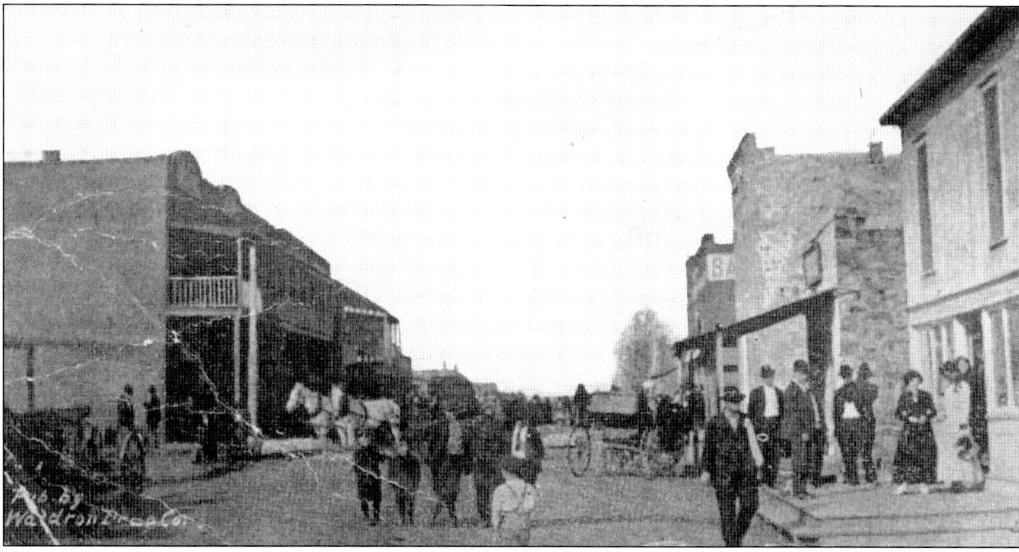

Ladies with long dresses, hats, and hightop buttoned shoes graced Main Street (looking north from Danville Street) on a Saturday in Waldron as men and boys leisurely went about their business. Within a few years, the prized team of greys pulling wagons would give way to the combustion engine-powered vehicles. The population had almost reached its zenith at over 13,000, business was brisk, and the community was growing with buildings rebuilt after the Civil War. (Postcard published by Waldron Drug Company, courtesy of Harry N. Blackman.)

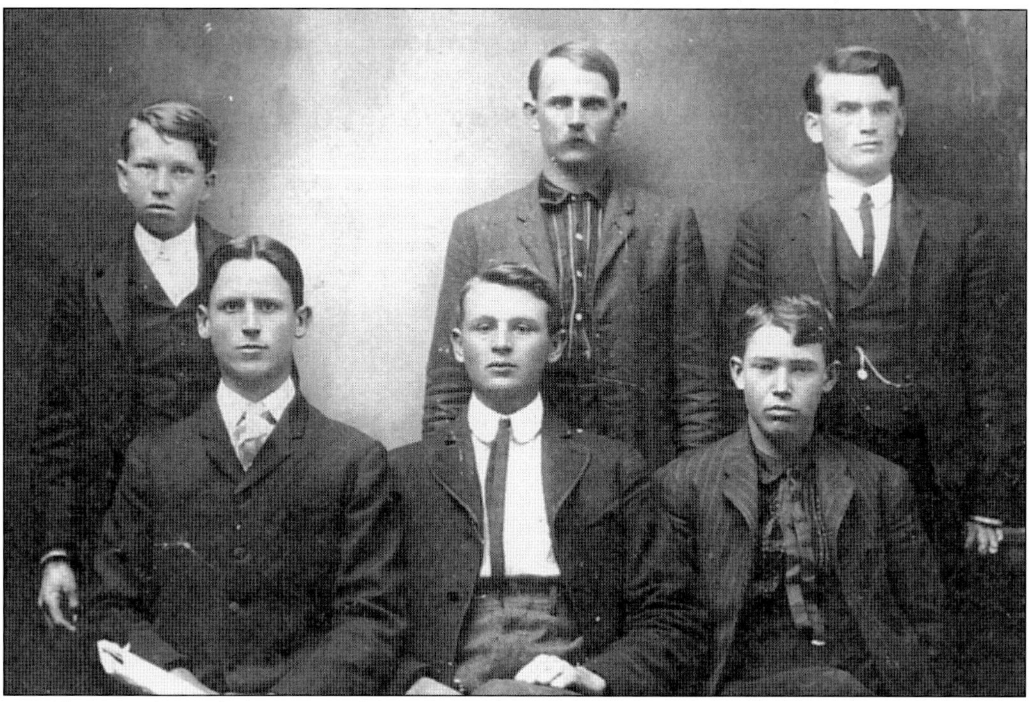

In addition to being first cousins, these six young men were strong leaders, teachers, businessmen, public servants, and politicians in the county. Pictured from left to right are as follows: (front row) John Wesley Black, Newt Black, and Talmadge Gant; (back row) Dan Frizzell, John Black, and Luna Black. (Courtesy of Ila Rhodes, Fresno, CA.)

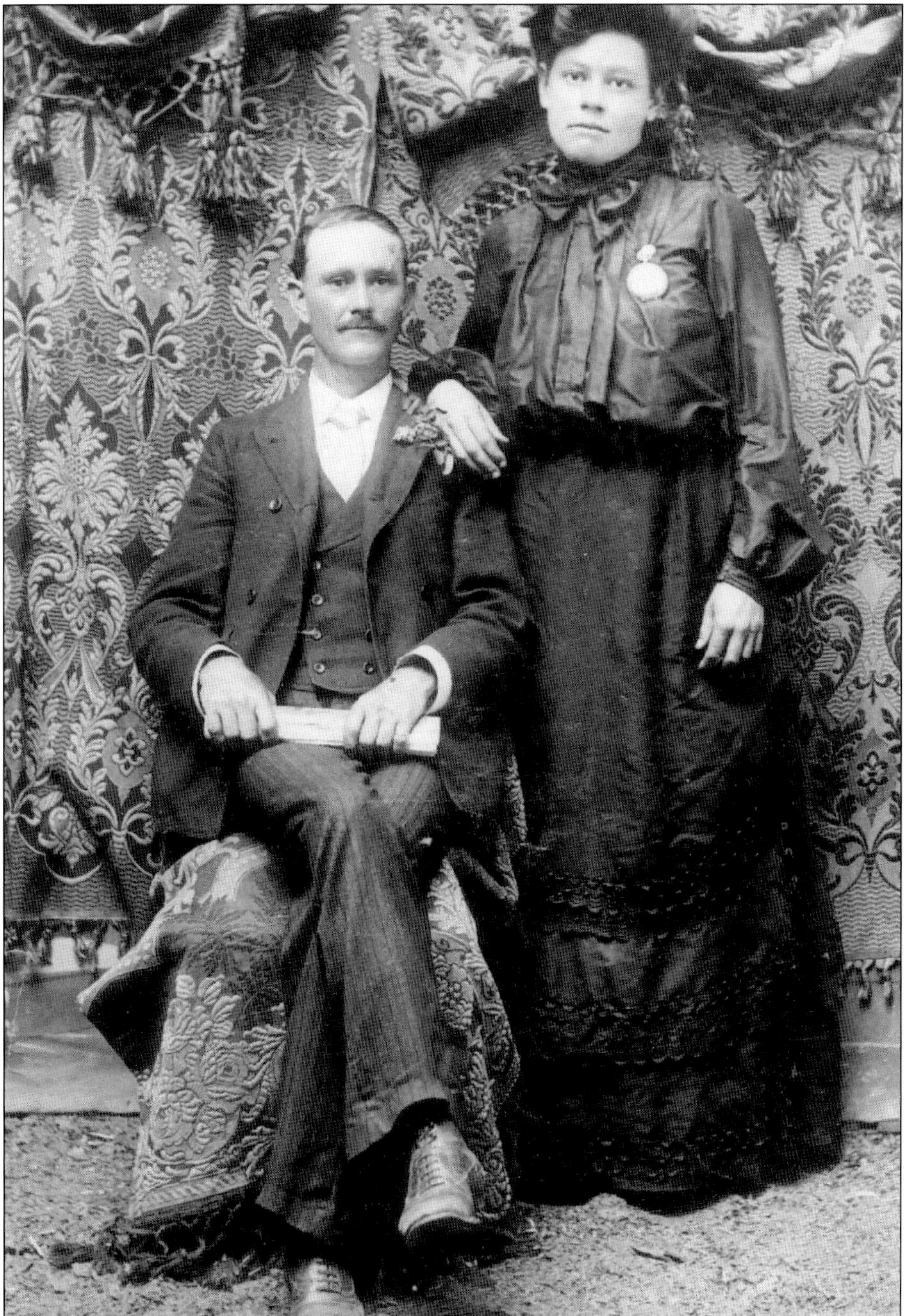

This dashing young man in flared striped pants and vest, Henry W. Roe (1875–1954), is seated in front of rather flamboyant drapes with his wife, Mary Bell McCormick, standing by his side. Holding his rolled up paper, he has a business-like appearance. Though he did some subsistence farming, his dainty hands were not made for farming, and he found an easier way to make a living—making and selling whiskey. Later, as the county was "dry," he purchased whiskey and resold it at twice the original price. He was murdered by those who thought that he had money buried on his farm. He is buried in the Pilot Cemetery. (Courtesy of Ila Rhodes, Fresno, CA.)

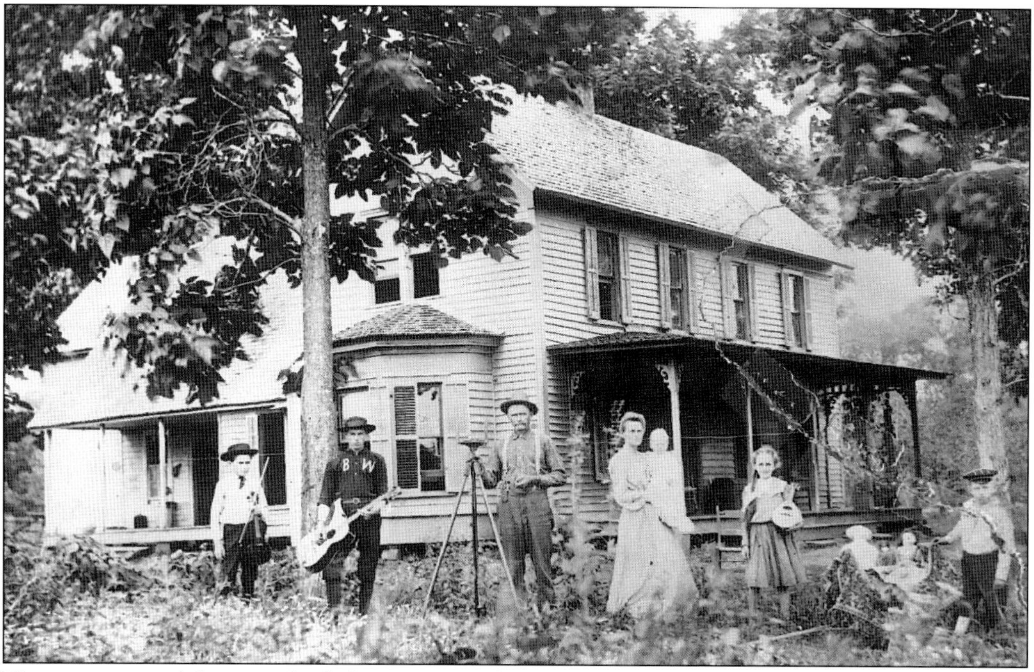

The east view of the tree-shaded, two-story plantation home of Henry Clay Bethel at Morgan Springs (near Bates) provides a vivid impression of a good life near Indian Territory on the western edge of the county. Pictured from left to right are the following: Claude (1891–1936) with violin; Carmen (1889–1983) with guitar; Henry Clay (1855–1917) with surveyors instruments; Ida Mae Bales Bethel (1869–1954) holding Justin (1905–1986); Bertha (1895–1949) with mandolin; and young Virgil (1898–1977) with doll carriage. The chair seen to the left of Bertha is beautifully displayed in the "memories room" of a descendant in Waldron, and was made by an ancestor. (Courtesy of Reba Nell Bethel Bergman.)

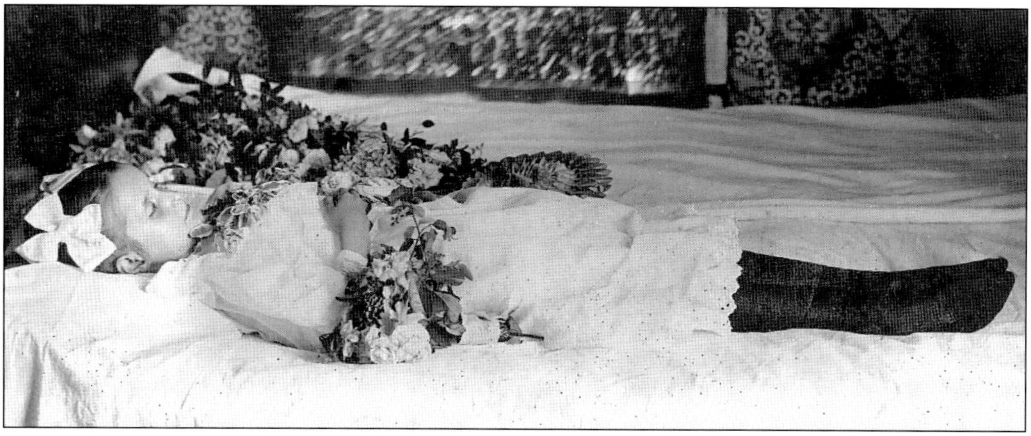

Peaceful in death, little Pansy Kling had a foot in both the 19th and 20th centuries. She was born in 1897 and died in 1905. This precious child is "laid out" according to customs of the time, on the bed in the family home where family and friends would sit up around the clock until burial. The white dress trimmed with eyelet embroidery is adorned by delicate fresh flowers. She was the step-sister of Houston McRae, daughter of Mattie H. Swinney McRae Kling, and granddaughter of Sarah William Tomlinson Swinney. (Courtesy of Swinney Collection.)

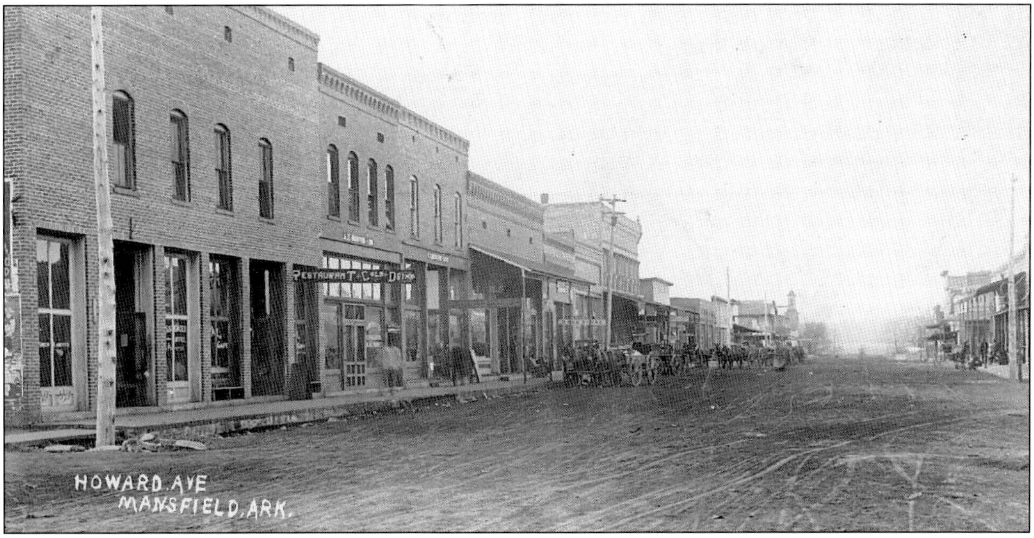

The wagons pulled by horses on the main street (Howard Street) of Mansfield in the northern part of the county have come to town for supplies. The poles had been put in the ground for electricity and telephone service but were not yet hooked up along the unpaved street with wooden sidewalks. The second brick building on the left belonged to pioneer Addision T. Boothe, while the first building advertised a restaurant with cold drinks. (Courtesy of Harry Blackman.)

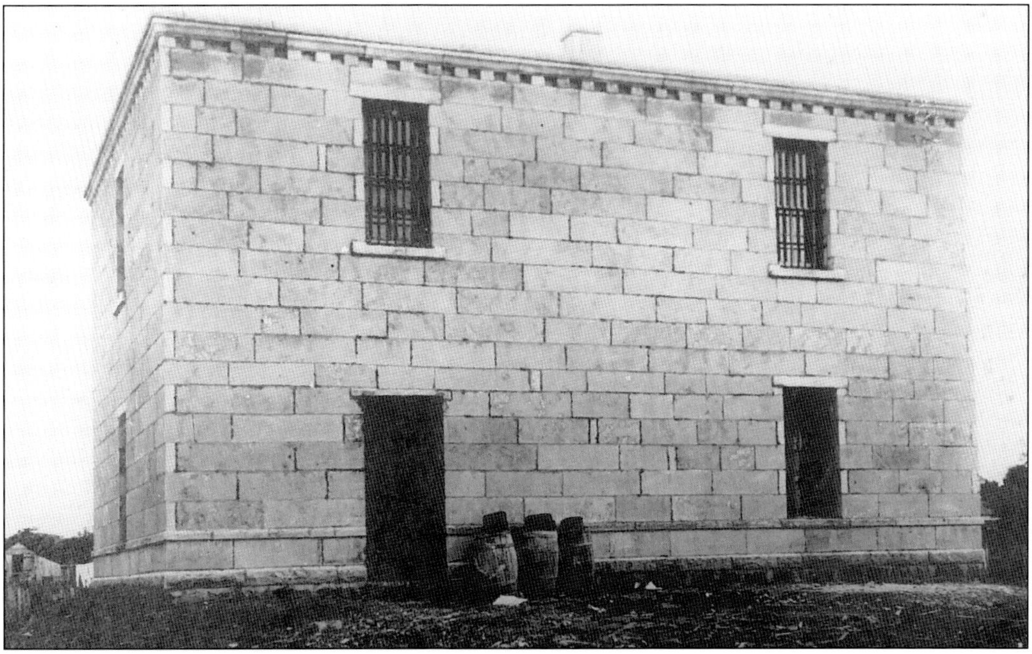

Judge W.A. Bates and Sheriff Thomas J. Center built one of the best stone jails in the state. A rather severe-looking, two-story building, it had outside walls constructed of large quarried stones two feet thick. It was built on an elevated area west of the courthouse in Waldron, replacing the dilapidated wooden jail from which escape was easy. This jail was used until 1935, when the new courthouse, replete with a jail on the third floor, was occupied. (Historian's Collection.)

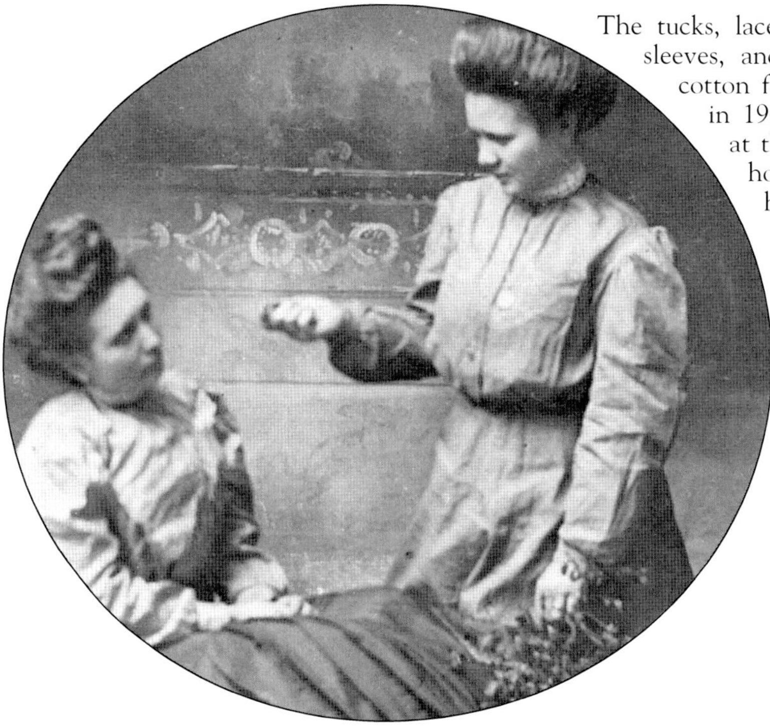

The tucks, lace, pleats, gathers, long sleeves, and long skirts made of cotton fabric for ladies apparel in 1907 dictated long hours at the ironing board. Seen holding mistletoe in one hand while gesturing to her sister, Georgia Anna, is Mary Elizabeth "Mollie" Center. The Center sisters were two of Waldron's most refined and lovely ladies (Historian's Collection.)

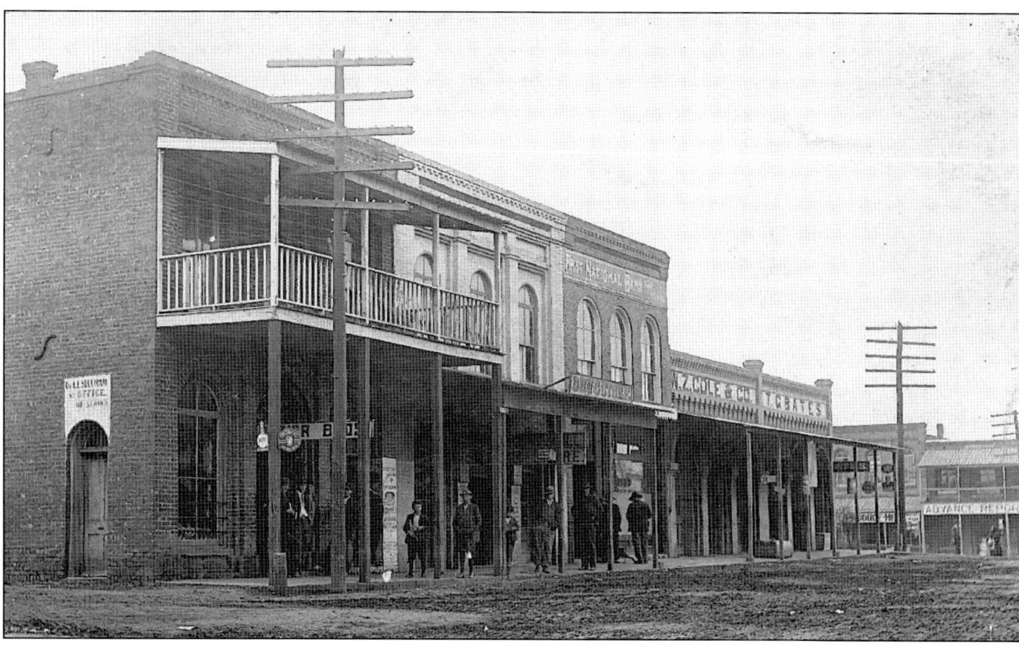

Looking north on the dirt-surfaced Main Street in Waldron from the corner of Fourth Street are seven brick buildings on the west side, denoting growth and progress. The coming of the railroad in 1903 instilled new life into the local economy, and by 1908, electricity and telephones had come to town, and the sidewalks were concrete and not made of boards. (Historian's Collection.)

The spacious two-story home of Postmaster George Abraham Chandler, located in the mountainous Brawley settlement in the southwest part of the county, was also used as the post office. This image was taken in October of 1909, and pictured from left to right are Charley L., Emma, Martha, George, George Elmer and his bride, Effie, and Ora Ethel Chandler. (Courtesy of Barbara Chandler Hansen.)

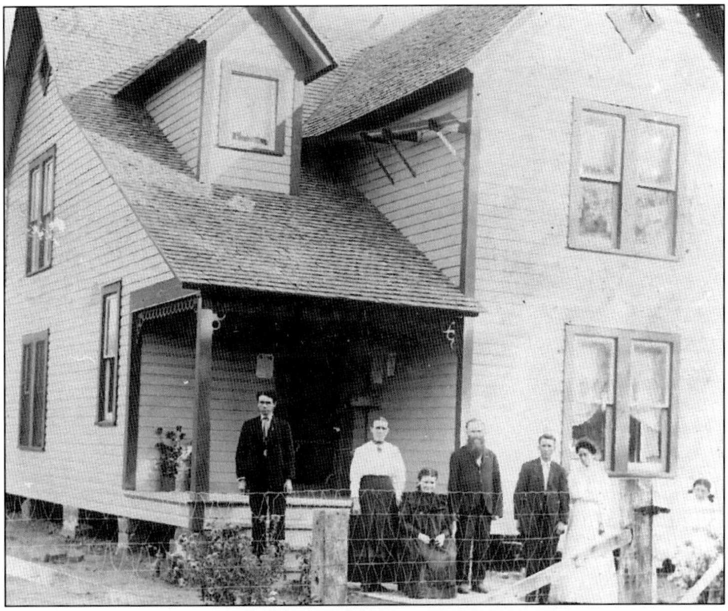

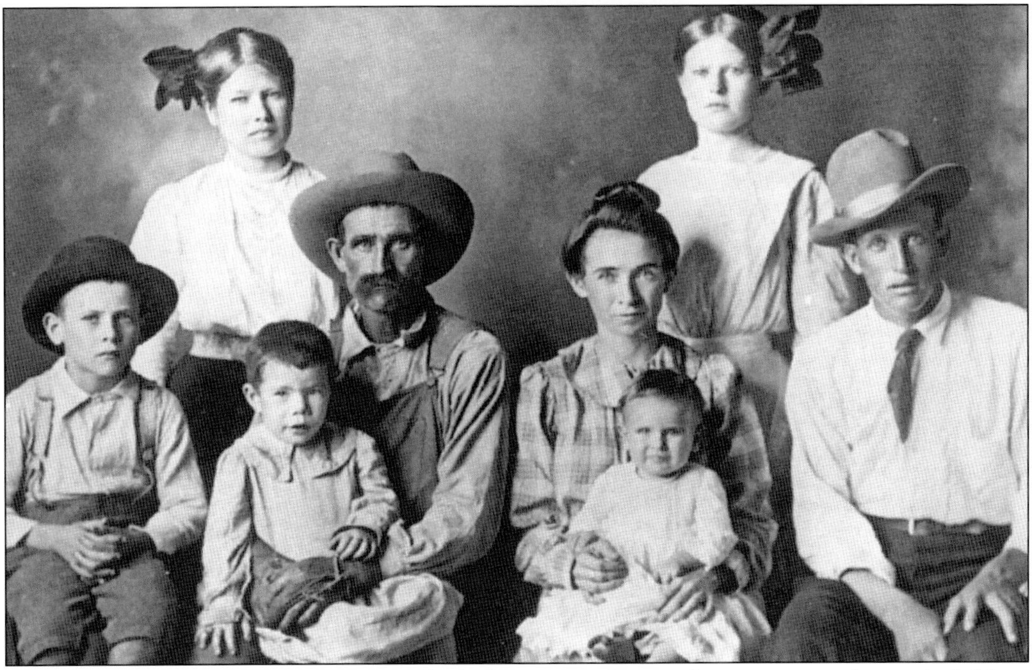

In 1909, older boys wore knee pants, little boys wore dresses for many months, and children were often barefoot, as this photo depicts. We might surmise from this image that unexpected company came to visit the work-wearied couple, Eli Hoyle Rhyne Jr. (1861–1917) and his wife, Minnie Eugenie Center. He arrived in Scott County in the 1880s, with two Native Americans and his dog from Indian Territory. Mr. Rhyne acquired 400 acres of land on which he worked from daylight until dark with his Winchester within easy reach. His farm was almost totally self-sufficient. Pictured in this photo from left to right areas follows: son Hoyle Lee Rhyne; Eli Hoyle Rhyne Jr. holding son Merl Rhyne; Minnie Eugenie Rhyne holding daughter Gertrude Rhyne; a Rhyne nephew; and standing, two Rhyne nieces. (Historian's Collection.)

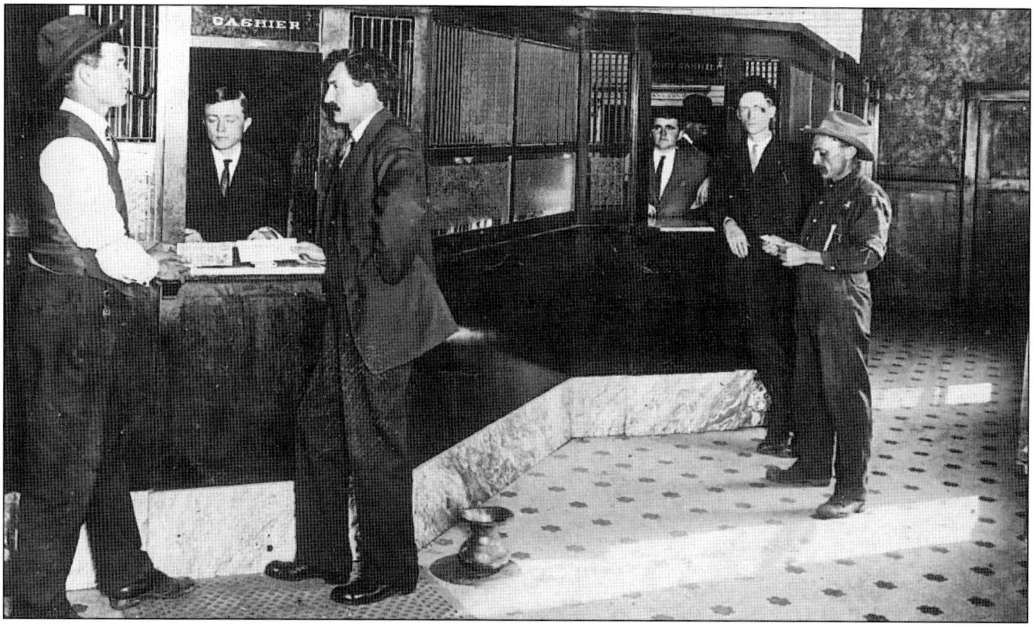

The new marbled floor and baseboard complimented the wooden cashier cage in the new Bank of Waldron. In order to heat the workers behind the teller windows, they had to run the stove pipe across the room to a flu on the outside wall. The cashier on the left is James L. Center. In 1901, when the bank was formed, it was in a frame building, on the corner of Main and Danville Streets. It remained on this site until the 1960s, when it moved two blocks on West Fourth Street. (Historian's Collection.)

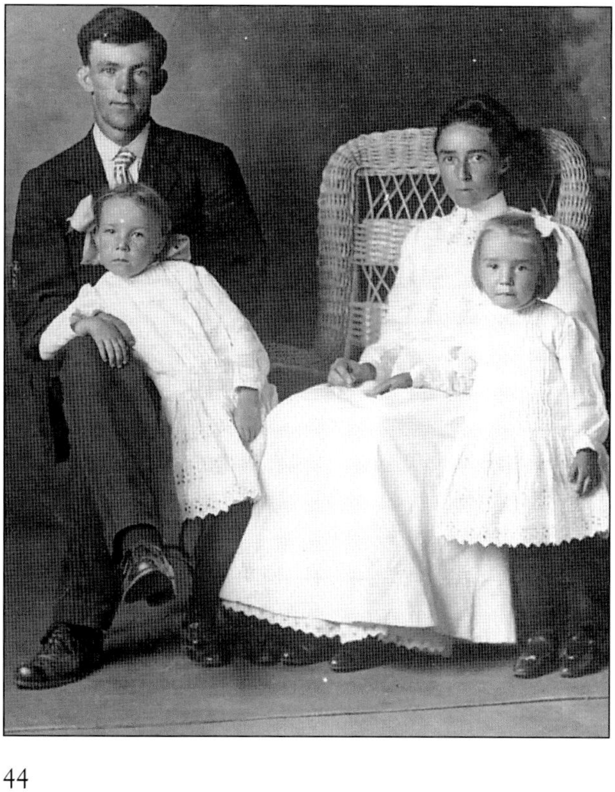

This formal family image of Thomas Jefferson Holland (1884–1966), sporting a new striped tie and highly shined shoes for the occasion, and wife Annie M. Norwood (1885–1938) with two of their five children, Ora and Lola, was probably taken by the outstanding photographer C.O. Pike at the Pike Studios in Waldron. The heavy white wicker furniture was popular during this time, as was eyelet embroidered material, used for the skirts of the girl's dresses and for Annie's dainty petticoat, a hint of which is showing. (Courtesy of Ila Rhodes, Fresno, CA.).

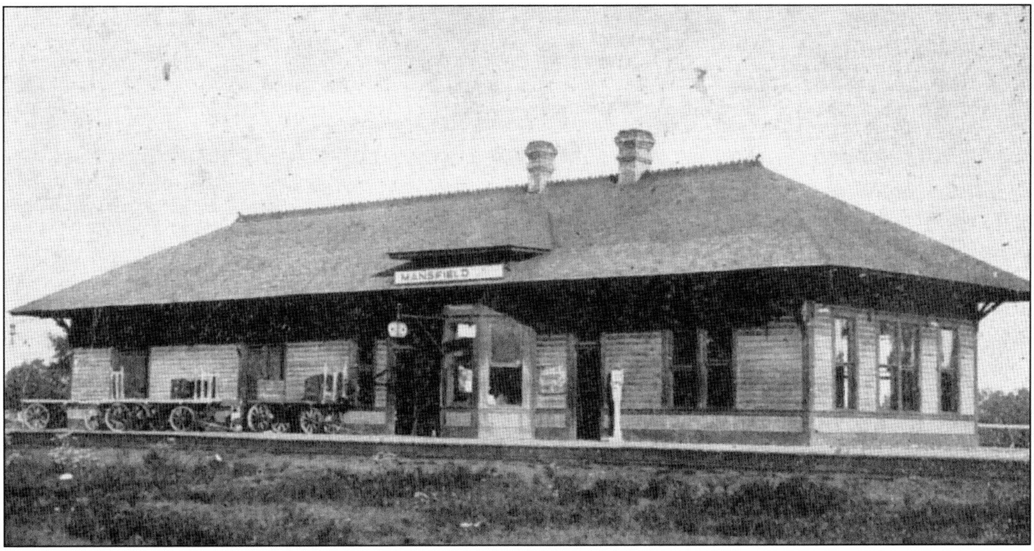

The Mansfield Railroad Depot invited travelers to parts unknown. Mansfield is just another town born of the Frisco and the Little Rock & Texas Railway in the 1880s, but this town has endured the test of time. Earlier depot buildings were destroyed, and this one, built in 1911, was torn down in 1972. (Courtesy of Harry Blackman.)

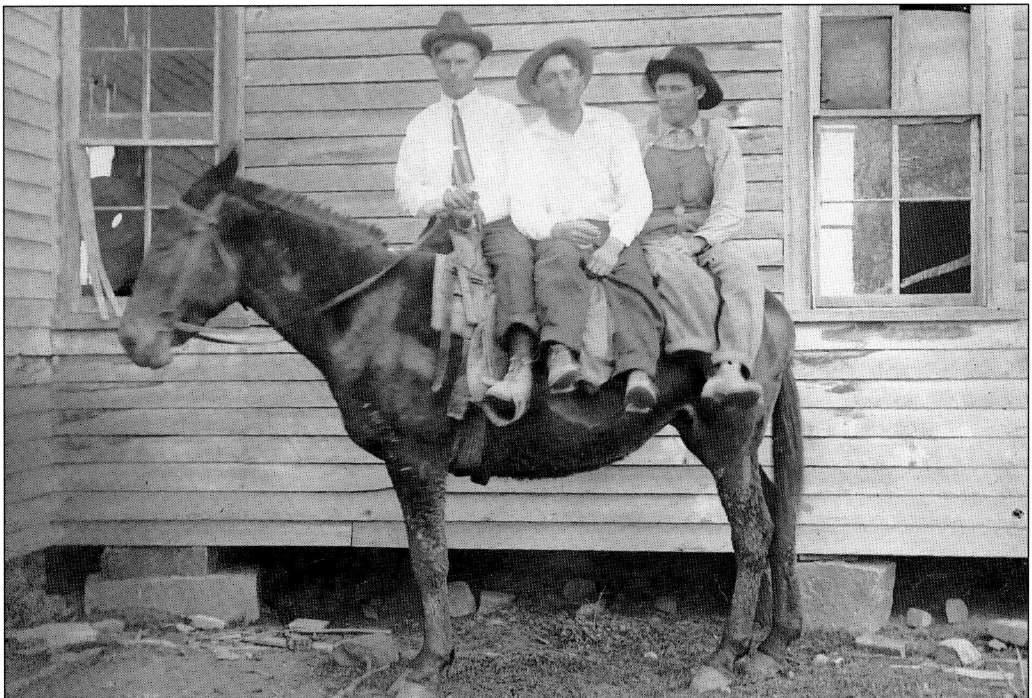

After church, which was not likely to be held in this old building, these three men are seen just "kickin'" around. The man with a white shirt and tie, the owner of the horse, shares a ride behind his saddle with Mirt Wilson (center) and another friend. One might say that a "horse's work" is never done, as this plow animal is used for riding on Sunday (Courtesy of Ila Rhodes, Fresno, CA.)

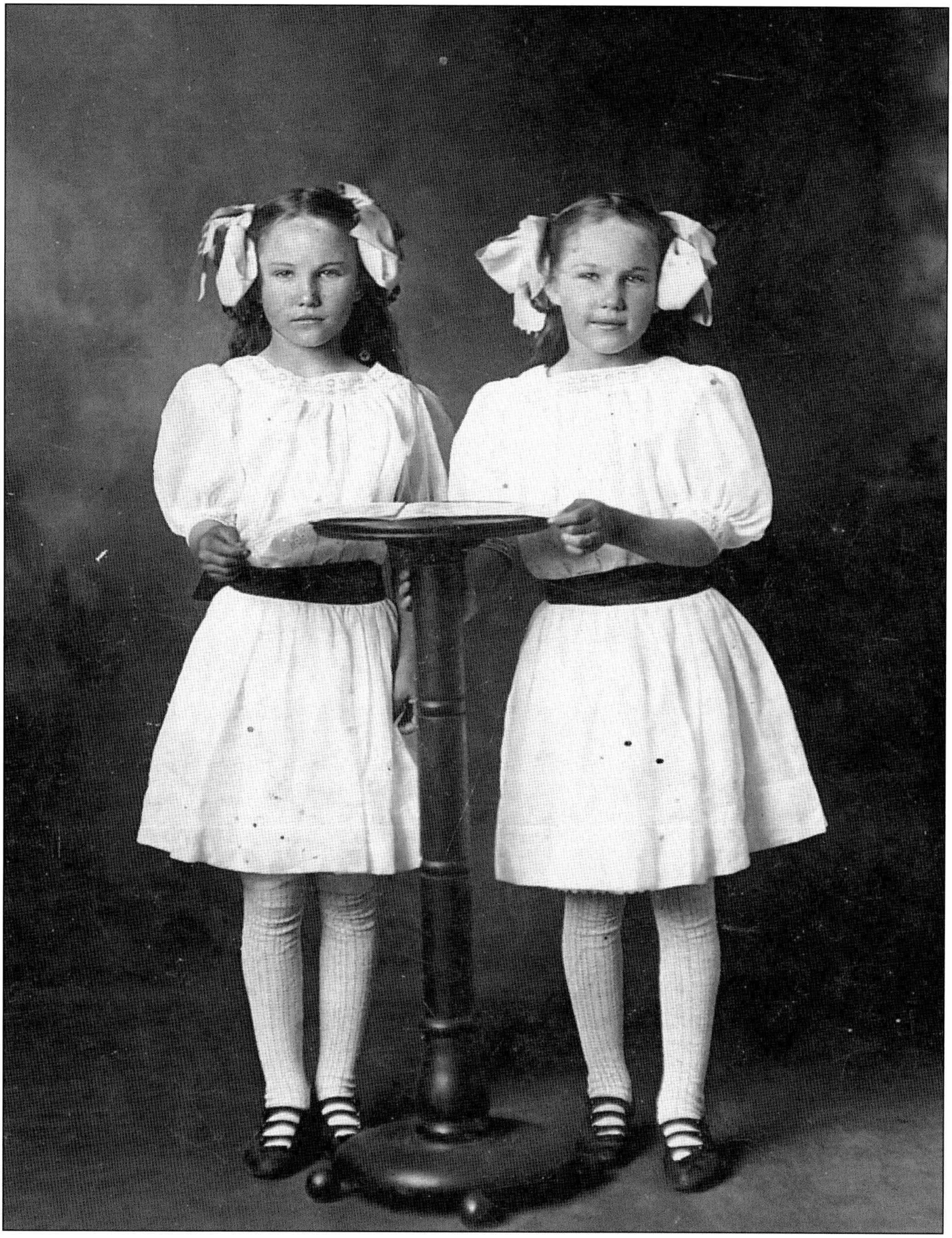

These two lovely ladies with buttons and bows are standing at the pedestal in the photography studio of C.O. Pike, located in the Pike block on Main Street just north of East Second Street. The twins, Hattie Day Craig (left) and Allie May Craig, look lovely with their white stockings matching their gathered white dresses with dark sashes. They are third generation descendants of Alfred C. Craig Sr. and his second wife, Elydia Fuller, and the daughters of Jacob Wesley "Jake" Craig (1877–1961) and his wife, Fannie May Speaks. (Courtesy of Ila Rhodes, Fresno, CA.)

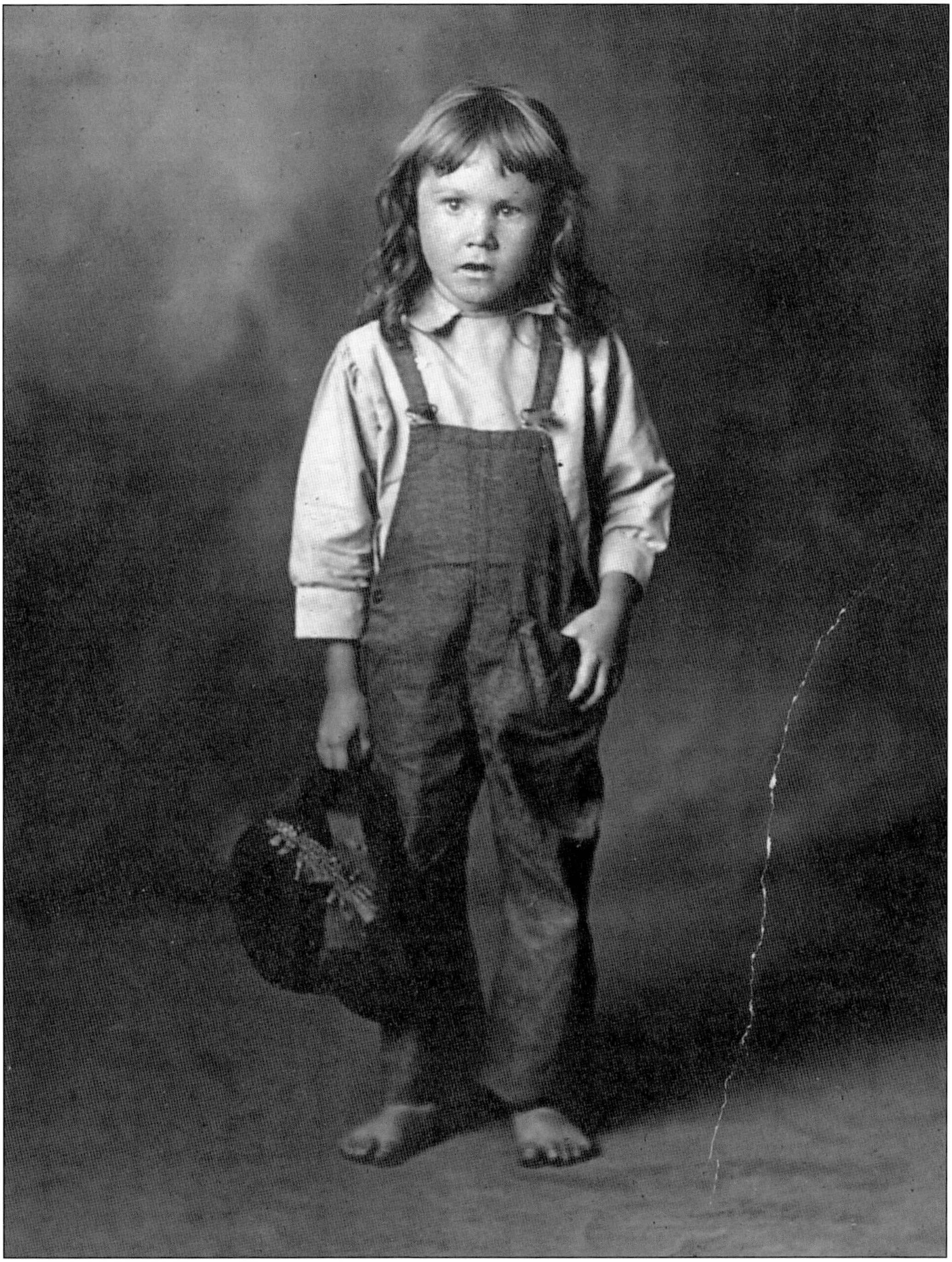

Looking more like a girl than a boy with his larger-than-life hat used to cover up his long red curly hair, six-year-old Orin Benton Holland (1906–1980) poses in a handmade shirt and overalls for a photo at the Pike Studio in Waldron. He is the second son of Nathaniel Lee Holland and was born in a wood-frame house on Church Street in Waldron. As an adult, he measured 5 feet 9 inches in height and never weighed more than 151 pounds. (Courtesy of Ila Rhodes, Fresno, CA.)

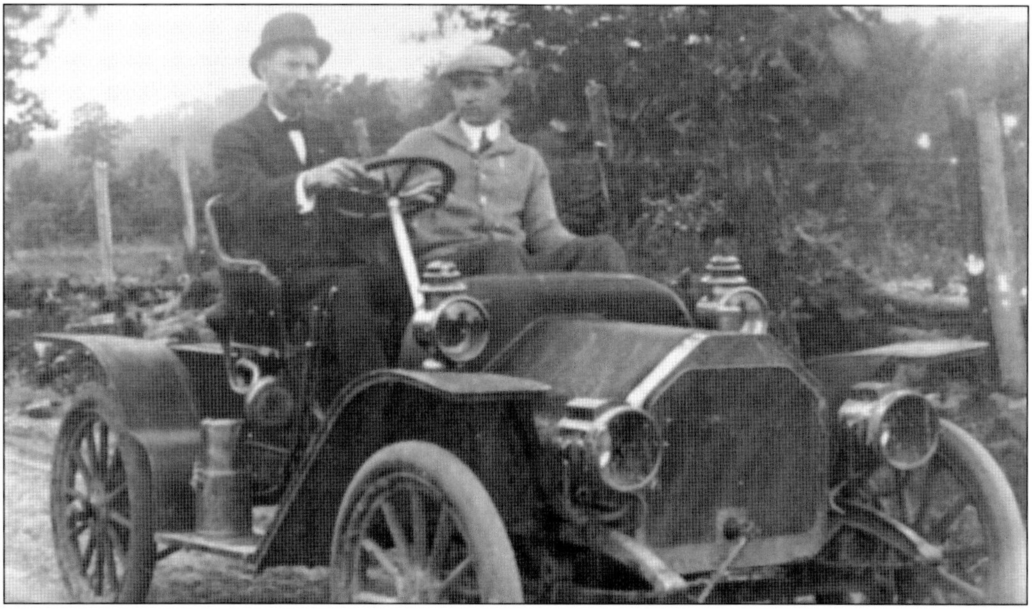

With the advent of the automobile, rural life became less isolated. Free Malone, owner of the Continental Hotel in Waldron, proudly "tools" his friend in a one-seated Metz automobile with a short truck bed in the back in which he is hauling some wood down the dirt road. The meadow in the background has been cleared of field stones and put under the barbed-wire fence surrounding the property. The first automobile in the county was purchased by Jack S. Hill—a two-cylinder Buick. In 1918, there were 192 cars and 4 trucks registered at the courthouse. (Historian's Collection.)

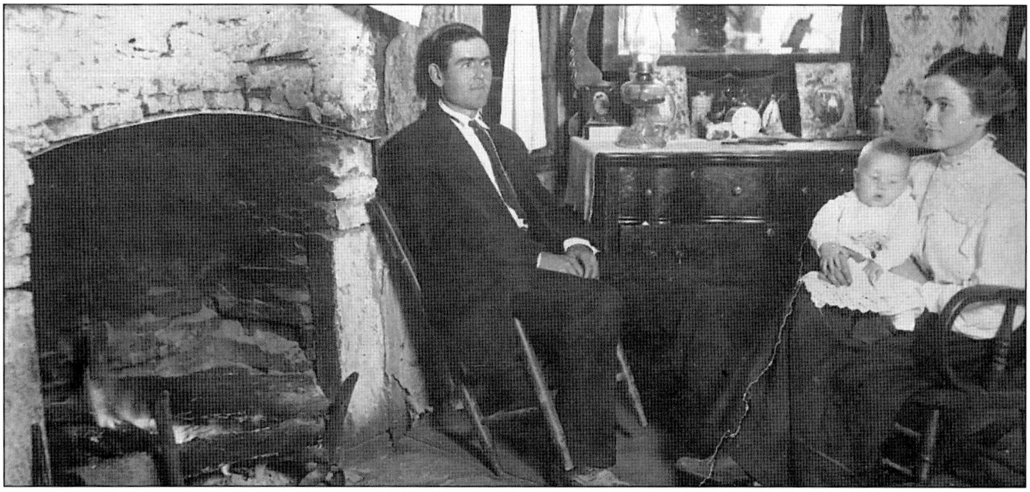

The small rural Blansett home of Jimmy and Cora Thomas Livesay, with baby, Leamon, is representative of the period in this 1913 photograph. The fireplaces were wide, used for cooking as well as heating, and lost about 85 percent of the heat up the chimney. The shovel leaning against it was used for scooping out the ashes from under the firedogs that held the wood allowing air circulation. The lantern on the floor beside the rocking chair was used for light at night to check the animals outside, and the kerosene lamp on the dresser provided the lighting inside. Her beaded purse and flowers and ribbons on the mantel and curtains tastefully decorate the room. (Historian's Collection.)

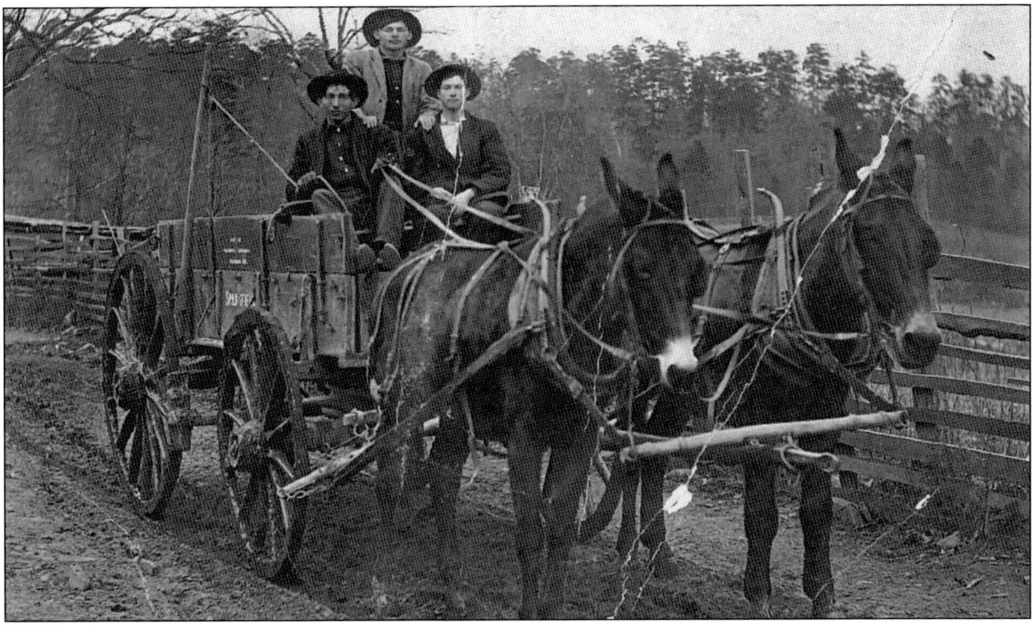

In the early fall morning dew, this pair of mules came to a halt as the driver muttered "Whoa" and pulled on the rope, using the primitive brake shoes that were attached to help slow the wagon down. The timber-covered ridge in the background is typical of a county farm scene and probably helped to supply the material for the wood fence. The names of the three men are not known. (Courtesy of Ila Rhodes, Fresno, CA.)

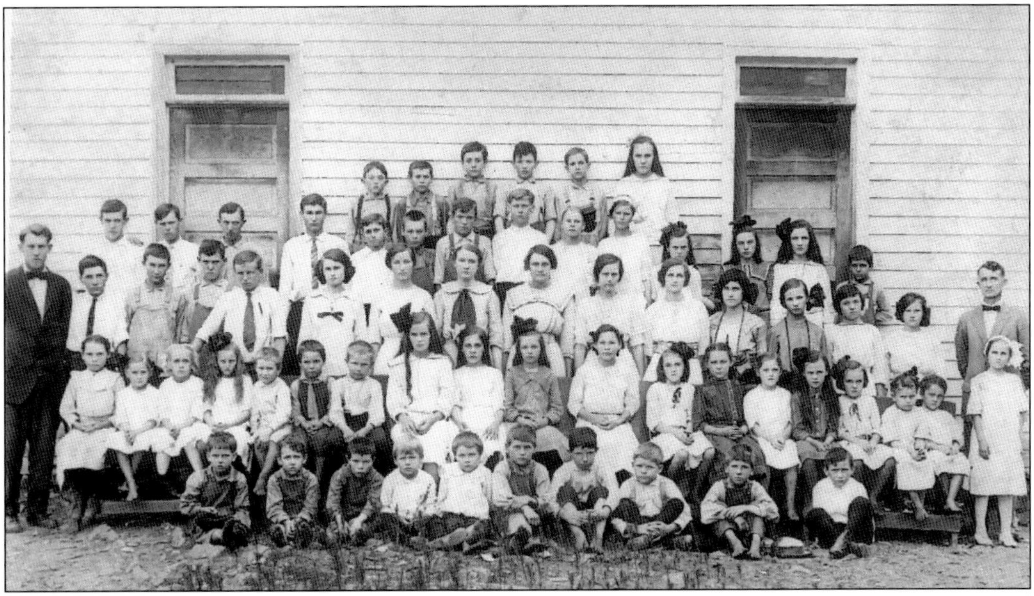

The two-room Centerpoint School, northeast of Waldron, with the ship-lap siding, is pictured here in 1914. The school was heated with a pot-bellied stove and had outdoor toilets, one for the boys and one for girls. To get to school each day, the students walked, often times barefoot, across meadows and fields, and waded through streams. They carried their lunches to school in pails that their parents bought lard in. There were two teachers at this time; however, the rural schools usually only had one teacher for grades one through eight. (Historian's Collection.)

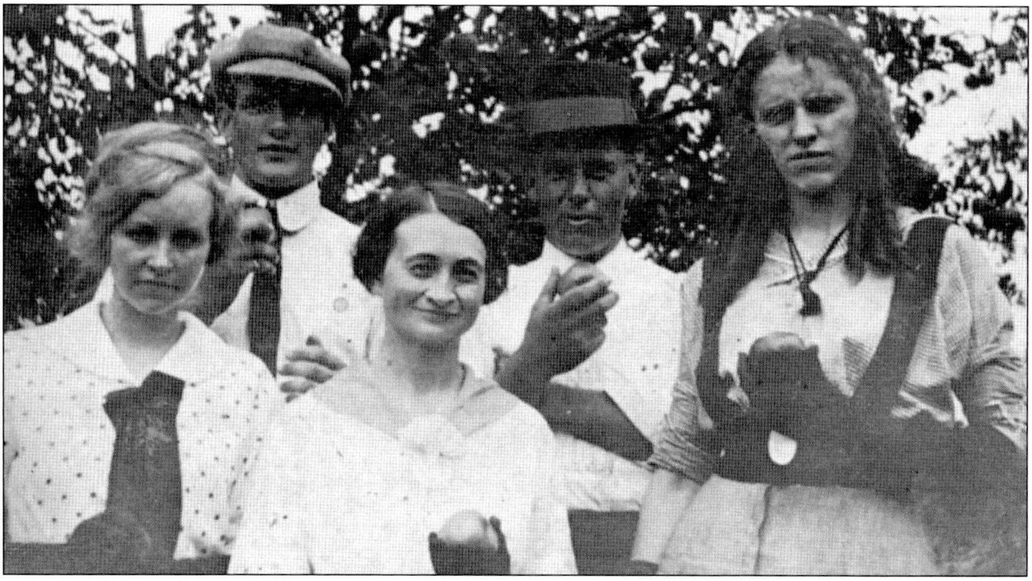

Life in 1915 represented a simpler time, when after church, while walking home, one could happen through an apple orchard and think it fun to taste a few. The cap worn by Ross Gordon (back left) illustrates an Irish influence, but the derby hat worn by Arthur Partain (1884–1944) was the most popular at this time. Katy Kelley (left), Clementine Center (1887–1953, center), and Lena Gordon look lovely in their Sunday attire of the period. (Historian's Collection.)

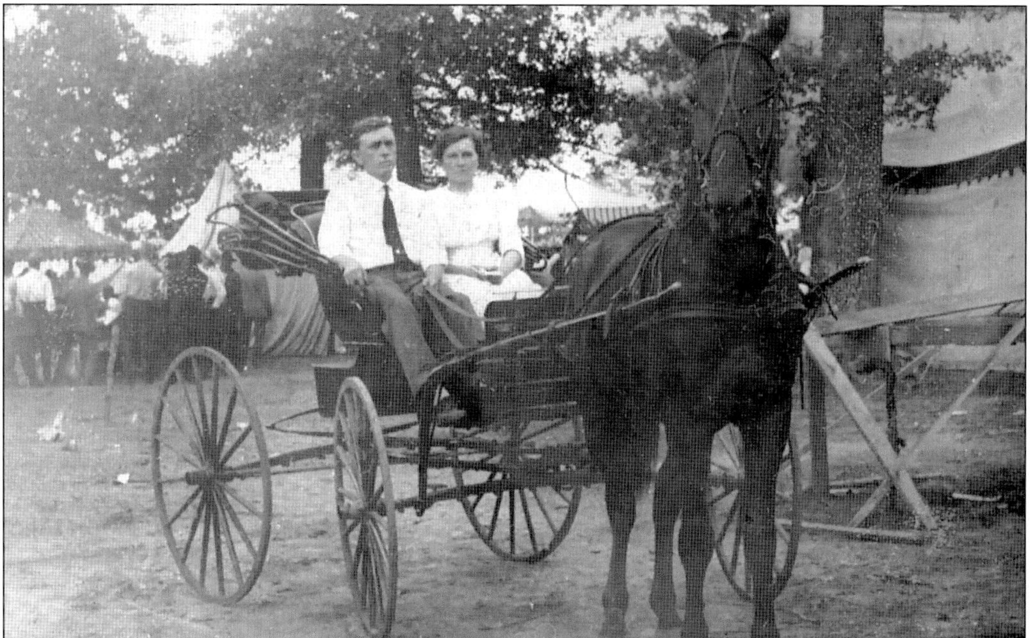

With right ear cocked backward, the young stallion "DanPatch" readies to take his umbrella buggy passengers away from the county fair at a brisk clip. Today, a carriage ride is an expensive pastime, but in 1915, it was still the primary mode of transportation. Pictured are James L. "Jim" Center and Edna Duncan, the daughter of Dr. L.D. Duncan. In 1934, Jim and Edna were shot and killed at their work by a former business partner. (Historian's Collection.)

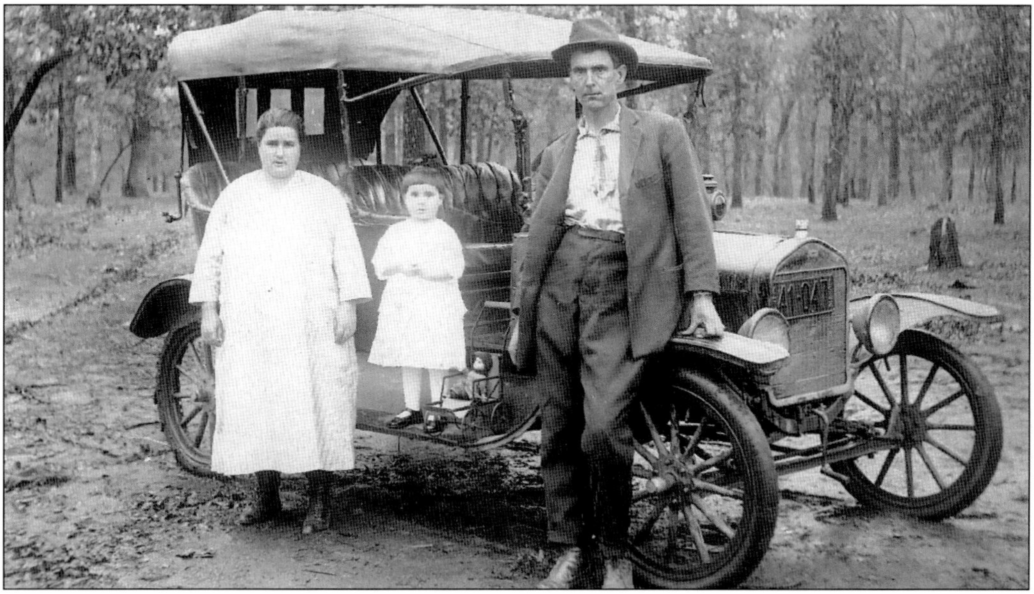

This marvelous new crank-start 1923 touring car, with a ventilating windshield, made light tracks in the wet soil as it came to a stop. These cars came in blue or gun metal grey with a mohair top cover, side curtains, foot and robe rails, and an electric horn. If you bought a blue car, it came with blue wood wheel spokes. A front bumper was optional and could be purchased for $125. Chester Merton "Mirt" Wilson (1887–1949); his first wife, Gertrude Hudson (1892–1923); and little daughter, Ocie Eloice (with her own wheeled buggy for her dolly on the running board) pose beside the new car with the comfortable tufted leather seats. (Courtesy Ila Rhodes, Fresno CA.)

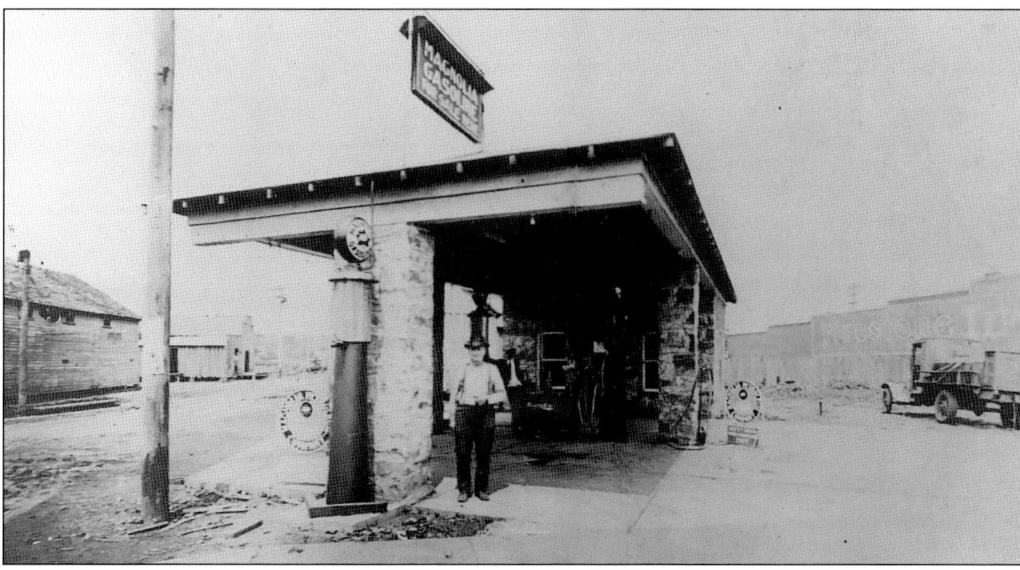

This small native stone Magnolia Gasoline Station on the west corner of Main and Church Streets (now Scott County Bank site) was built between 1910 and 1915, several years before paving of the streets and prior to the building of the red-brick baptist church on the corner to the south, in 1917. The vintage Ford truck in the image had only partially replaced the horse-drawn wagons. The person has not been identified. (Courtesy of William Welch, Tulsa, OK.)

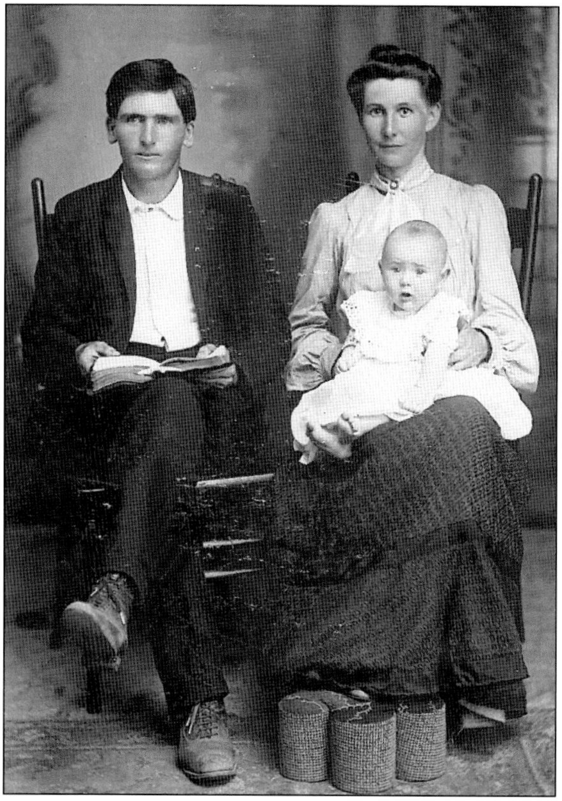

This formal portrait of farmer, Sunday School teacher, and Methodist preacher Thomas Daniel Langston (1883–1918), his wife, Hettie Jane Payne (1876–1952), and his son, Thomas Monroe "Tommy" (1906–1998), is illustrative of the deep spirituality that was present during the building of the communities within the county. It was this spiritual thread that influenced the lives of men, women, and children, building the strong and enduring social fabric of the area. Hettie was the daughter of Wesley Pitsford Payne, who emigrated from Walker County, Georgia, to the Birdsview community. (Courtesy of Della Mae Meredith.)

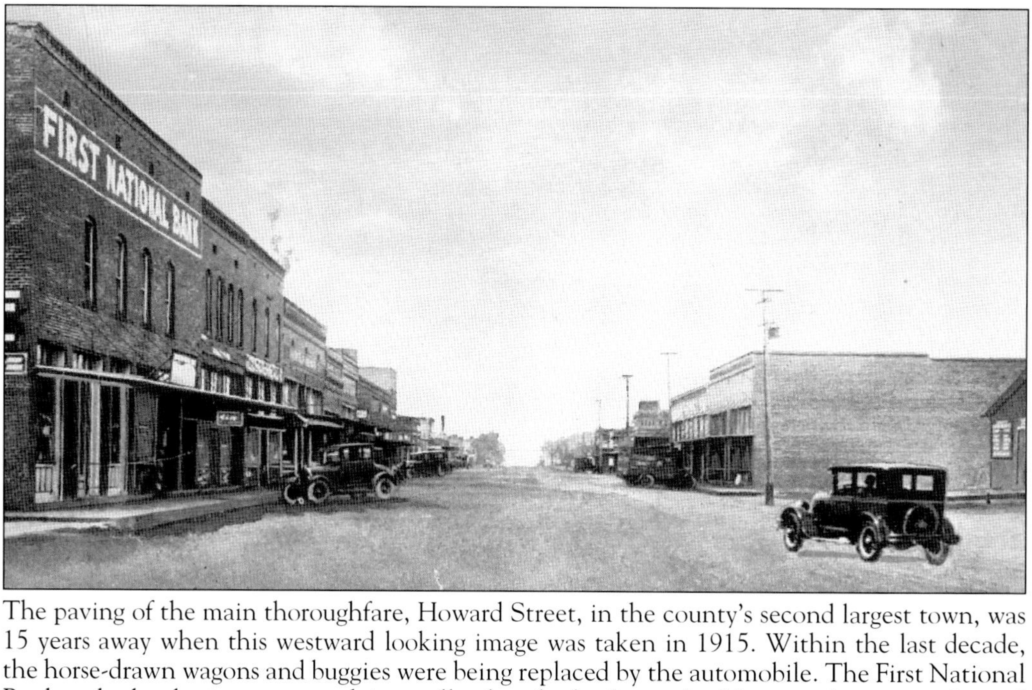

The paving of the main thoroughfare, Howard Street, in the county's second largest town, was 15 years away when this westward looking image was taken in 1915. Within the last decade, the horse-drawn wagons and buggies were being replaced by the automobile. The First National Bank and other businesses were doing well as hundreds of pounds of farm products were shipped by rail. (Courtesy of Harry N. Blackman.)

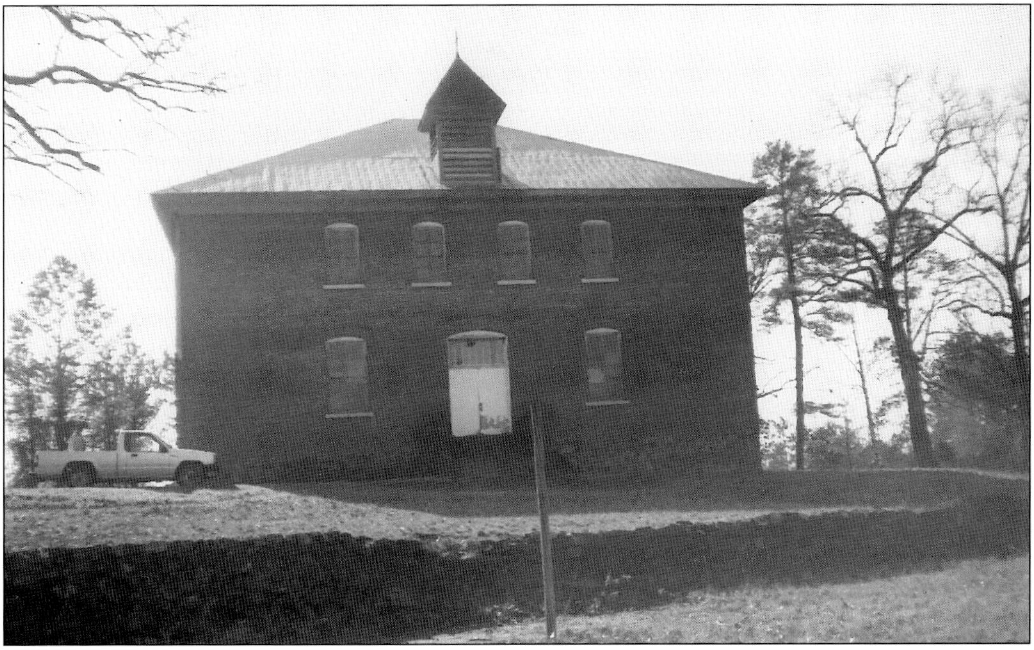

The aged, wood-louvered bell tower perched above the Italianate two-story brick Bates School building proclaims its prominence. In 1917, its large double doors opened to the laughter of the children in this coal mining community near the Oklahoma border. Remnants of the massive coal furnace used to heat the school remain in this structure, though the school closed in the consolidation movement of the 1940s. (Historian's Collection.)

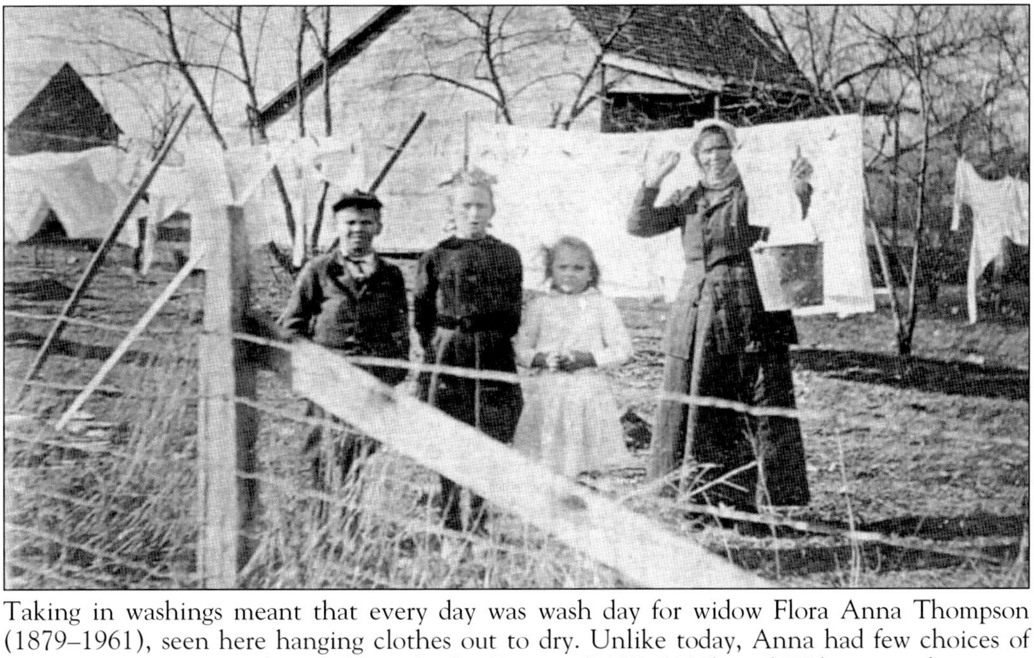

Taking in washings meant that every day was wash day for widow Flora Anna Thompson (1879–1961), seen here hanging clothes out to dry. Unlike today, Anna had few choices of employment to support her children, Letha, Everett (1907–1988), and Wilma, seen here near the six strand wire fence. Anna was the daughter of early settler George Gaden Holland and Elizabeth Penelope Manner. (Courtesy of Ila Rhodes, Fresno, CA.)

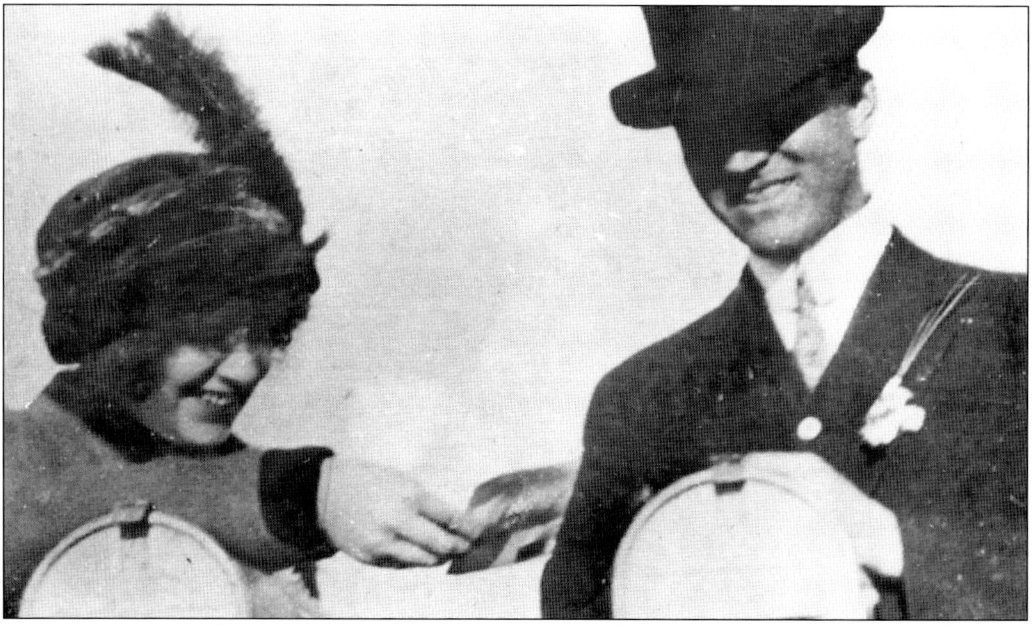

Receiving mail has brought happy smiles to many people like Maude and Leonard Shannon, since the time that postal service was established in the county in 1838. As the postal service grew, mail sacks or mailboxes were placed along the road, and a mail carrier would ride on horseback, mail hack, or car and deliver the mail to the boxes. (Historian's Collection.)

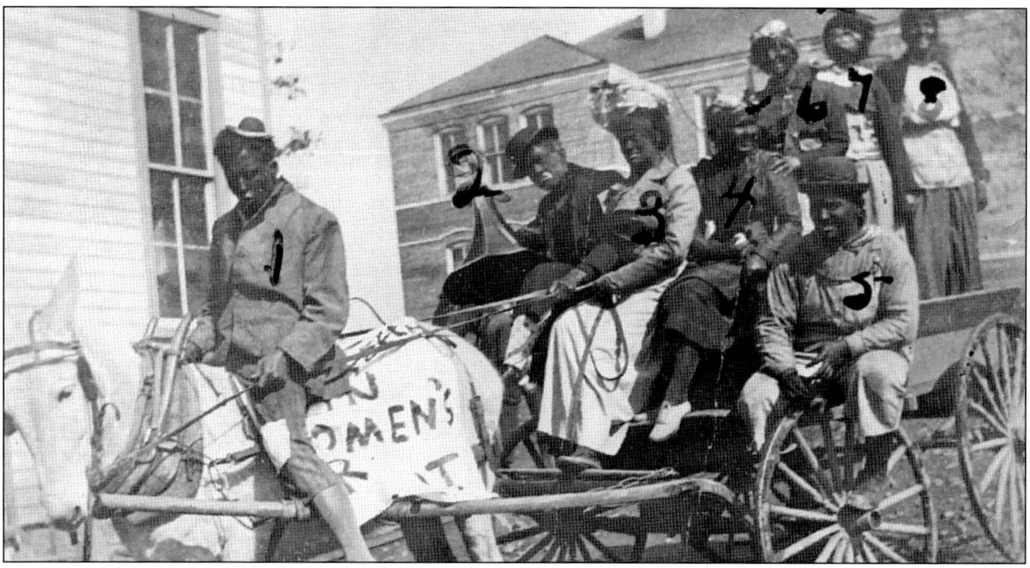

A wagon is filled with white citizens with blackened skin making a public statement for the "rights of women." They grew up during the national women's rights movement of Susan B. Anthony. These individuals are some of Waldron's leading citizens: Milt Bolden (riding mare), Ray Speights (holding megaphone), Clara ?, Chard Forester Davidson, Clarence Vise, Edna Duncan Center, Lex Vise, and John Hart. At the end of World War I, nationally and locally, things began to change in all facets of life. In rural Scott County, however, changes occurred gradually as the population that had risen by leaps and bounds to 14,302 citizens by 1910, was to begin its decline.

Two

Growth and Development 1920–1980

At the beginning of this period, the county continued to depend on its plentiful timber industry, strawberry crops, fruit trees, cattle, and row crop farming. The Depression made a hard life a little harder, but better roads and schools were built as well as some factories. The loss of 7,000 people drove business leaders to work hard developing industry to keep citizens at home; cotton land gave way to pasture land and ranching. The people of the county, with their relaxed, caring lifestyle, are the finest assets the county has.

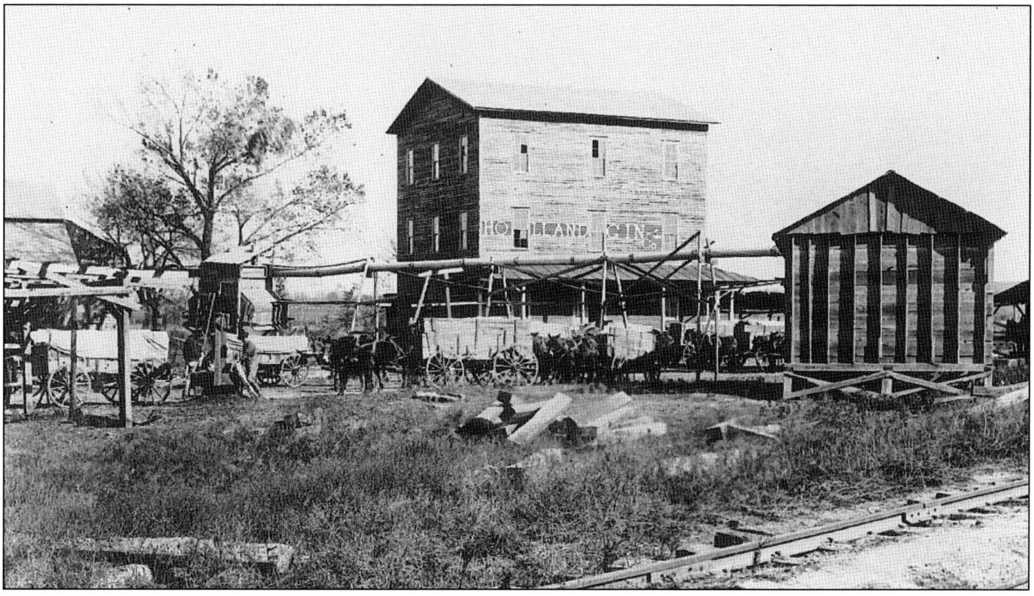

This view depicts life in the fall, when farmers came to the gin. With side-boards on their wagons, three wide boards high and filled with cotton, they lined up to get their cotton ginned at the three-story, steam-powered gin and gristmill of Nathaniel Lee Holland (1875–1942). It is here that the seeds were separated from the cotton and compacted into large bales and shipped to market. The seeds were sold separately to make cottonseed oil. The gristmill was on the second floor, where corn was ground and flour was made. This gin was located near the banks of the south fork of the Poteau River, where the old swimming hole used to be behind the Cedar Mill. From the 1800s to the 1930s, cotton was the cash crop of the farmer. This gin ceased operation when a electric gin was built. It was previously owned by the Castleberrys. (Courtesy of Ila Holland Rhodes. Interview, Kello Holland.)

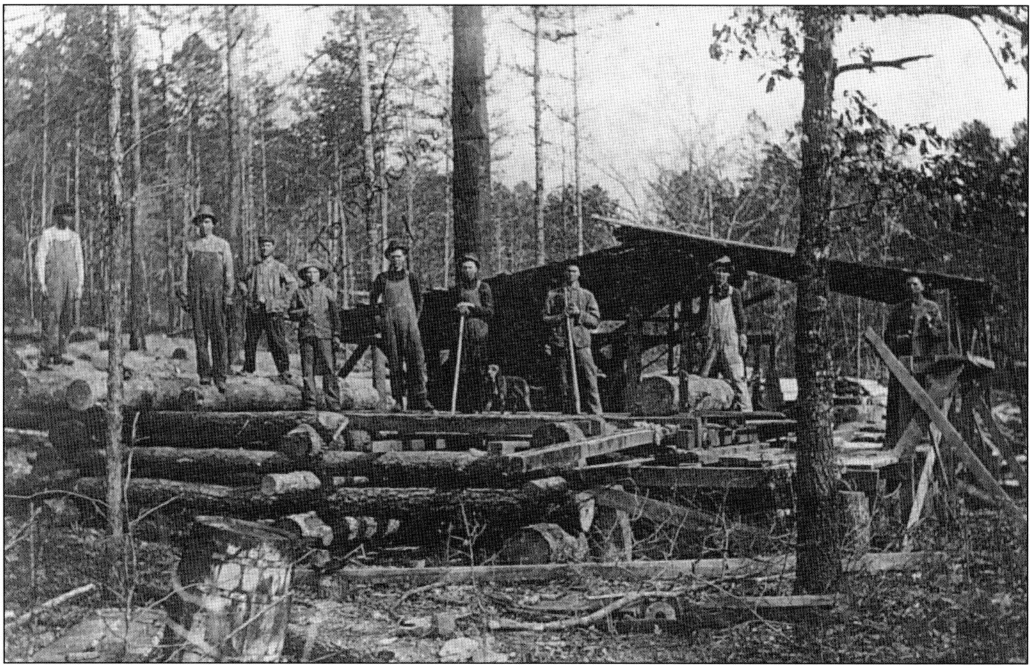

At the House family sawmill, the men in work clothes are standing by stockpiled logs, readying them for sawing. This timber site is near Cold Springs, but the men lived in the Cardiff and Freedom settlements. In almost every community, there was a least one sawmill to harvest the pure stands of tall straight pines and hardwood that covered the many hills of the county. Timber and timber products have been one of the county's greatest economic assets. (Courtesy of Rosemary James.)

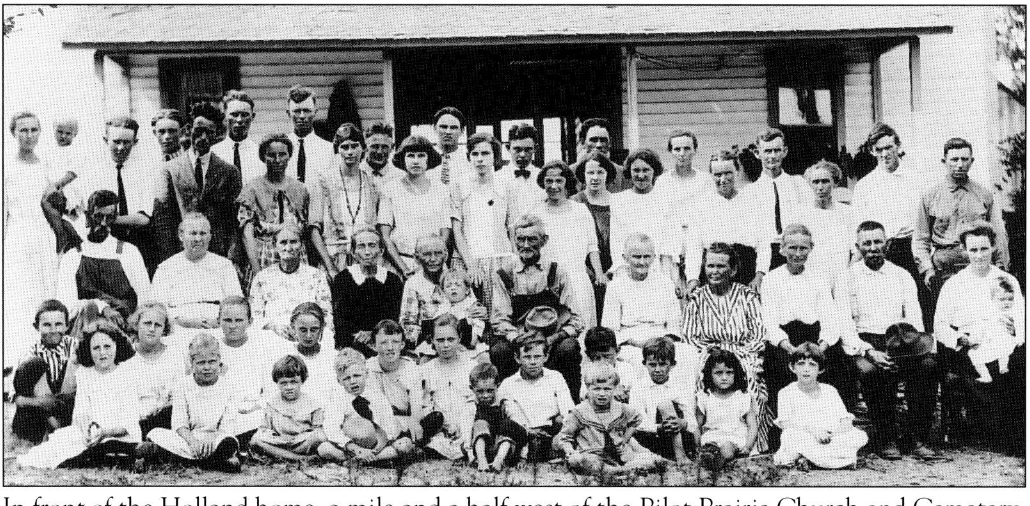

In front of the Holland home, a mile and a half west of the Pilot Prairie Church and Cemetery, is the large extended family of Gaden Holland (1849–1923) and his wife, Penelope Elizabeth Manner (1955–1951). This pioneer family from Alabama were builders and developers of the county, arriving in the 1860s. At this time, Gaden Holland framed 200 acres of land, as well as engaged in the business of ginning cotton. This land still belongs to Holland descendants. Gaden is the son of Rezin Pinkney Holland, born in 1821 in Alabama. (Courtesy of Ila Holland Rhodes, Fresno, CA.)

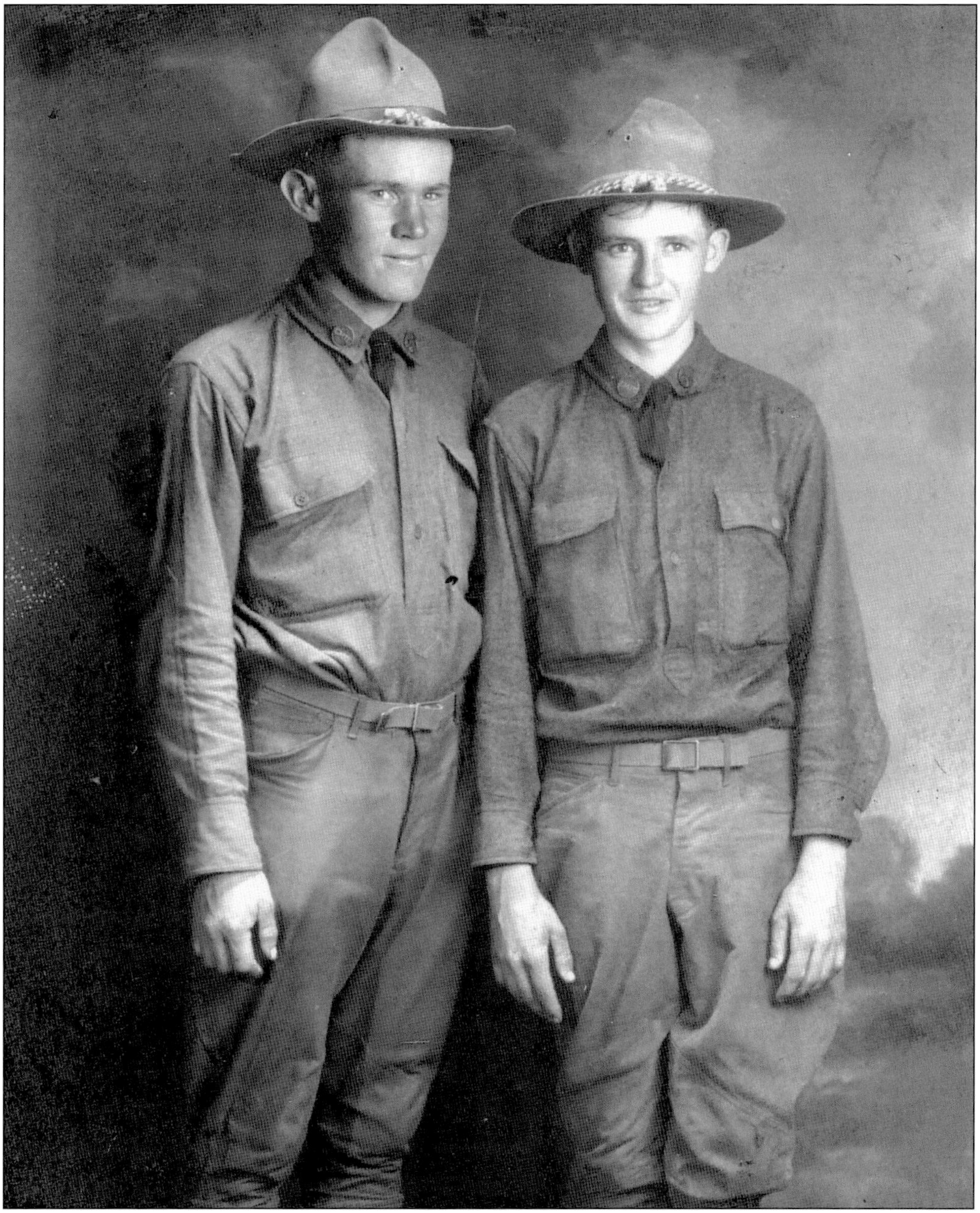

Proudly displaying his World War I Army uniform while stationed at Citizen's Military Camp (a tent city) at Fort Leavenworth, Kansas, is Orin Benton Holland (1906–1980, left) and a friend. He grew up during a period of great nationalism, when in 1917 and 1918, the U.S. sent eight million men to war. He had the opportunity to witness the first uses of the military's new electronic communication devices, the field phone and the radio. Orin's life parallels thousands of men born in the county at this time. He grew up in a Christian home, worked in his father's cotton gin, married early, share-cropped a farm, saved enough to enter the lumber business until the timber played out and then, with the Depression and droughts in the early 1930s, moved to California where he was successful in business. (Courtesy of Ila Rhodes, Fresno, CA.)

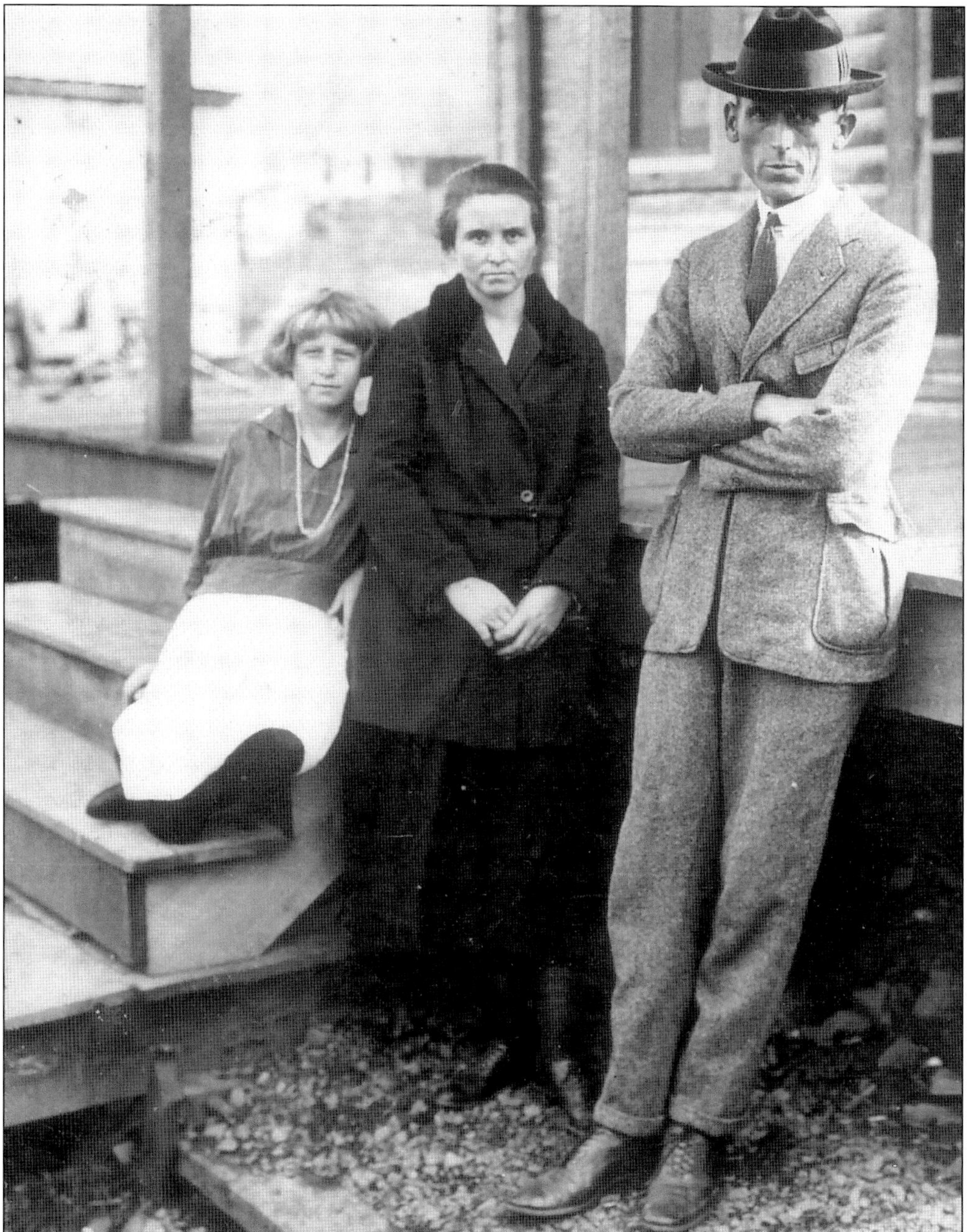

Pictured in this photograph are John Wesley Black (1866–1959) and his wife, Dovie Doley Holland (1893–1983), and daughter, Lora Pauline (1911–1994). One of the county's most industrious and highly respected families, their home also served as the Hon Post Office, where Dovie was the postmaster. He taught in many of the rural schools throughout the county and at Waldron High School, retiring after 39 years in this profession. He also served as county assessor for two terms (1927–1932); in the Arkansas House of Representatives for two terms (1953–1956); as a representative with the Red Cross; and as mayor of the city of Waldron. (Courtesy of Ila Rhodes, Fresno, CA.)

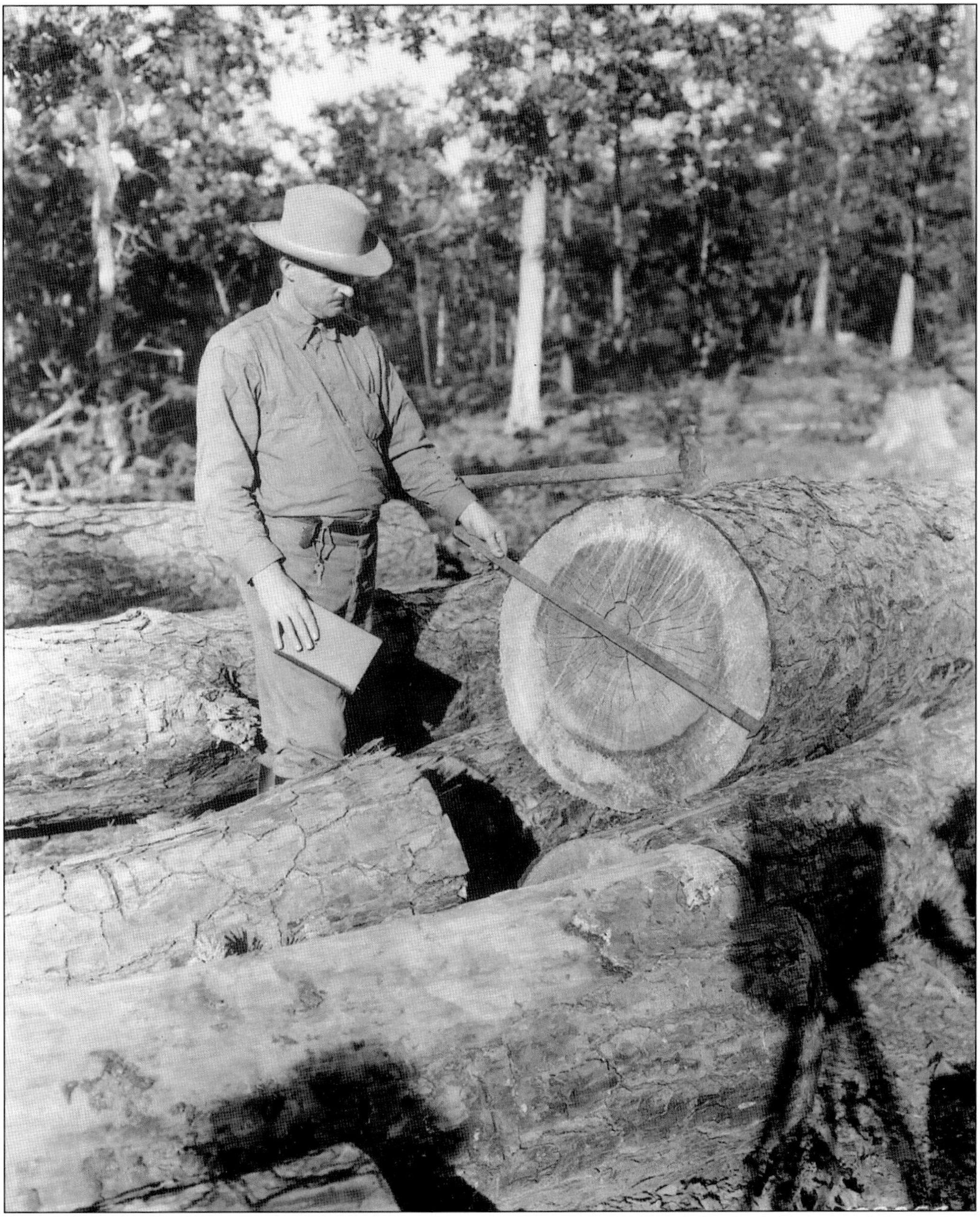

From earliest times, the primitive forest and virgin timber provided shelter, heat, and economic growth in the county. This image of forest ranger Thomas F. Hale scaling pine logs at the lumber town of Forester illustrates the size of the shortleaf pine logs. With the coming of steam-powered engines by 1900, sawmills dotted the landscape. When the lumber played out, they moved to another location, leading to the development of many sawmill settlements where families lived isolated lives in the backwoods of the county. Many farmers became loggers with the advent of commercial logging, thereby progressing from an agrarian community to today's society. (Courtesy of Arkansas History Commission.)

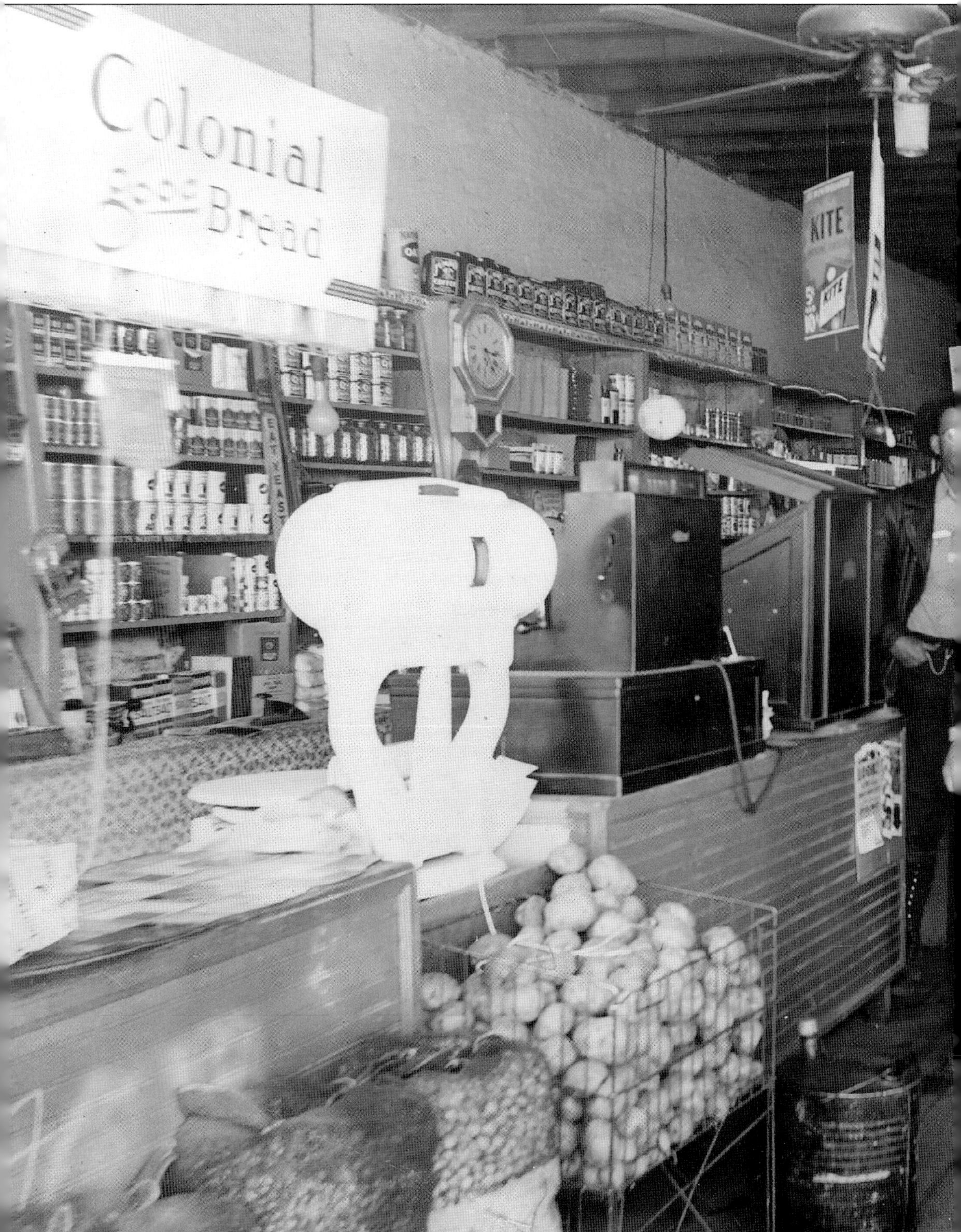
Colonial
Bread
KITE
EAT YEAST

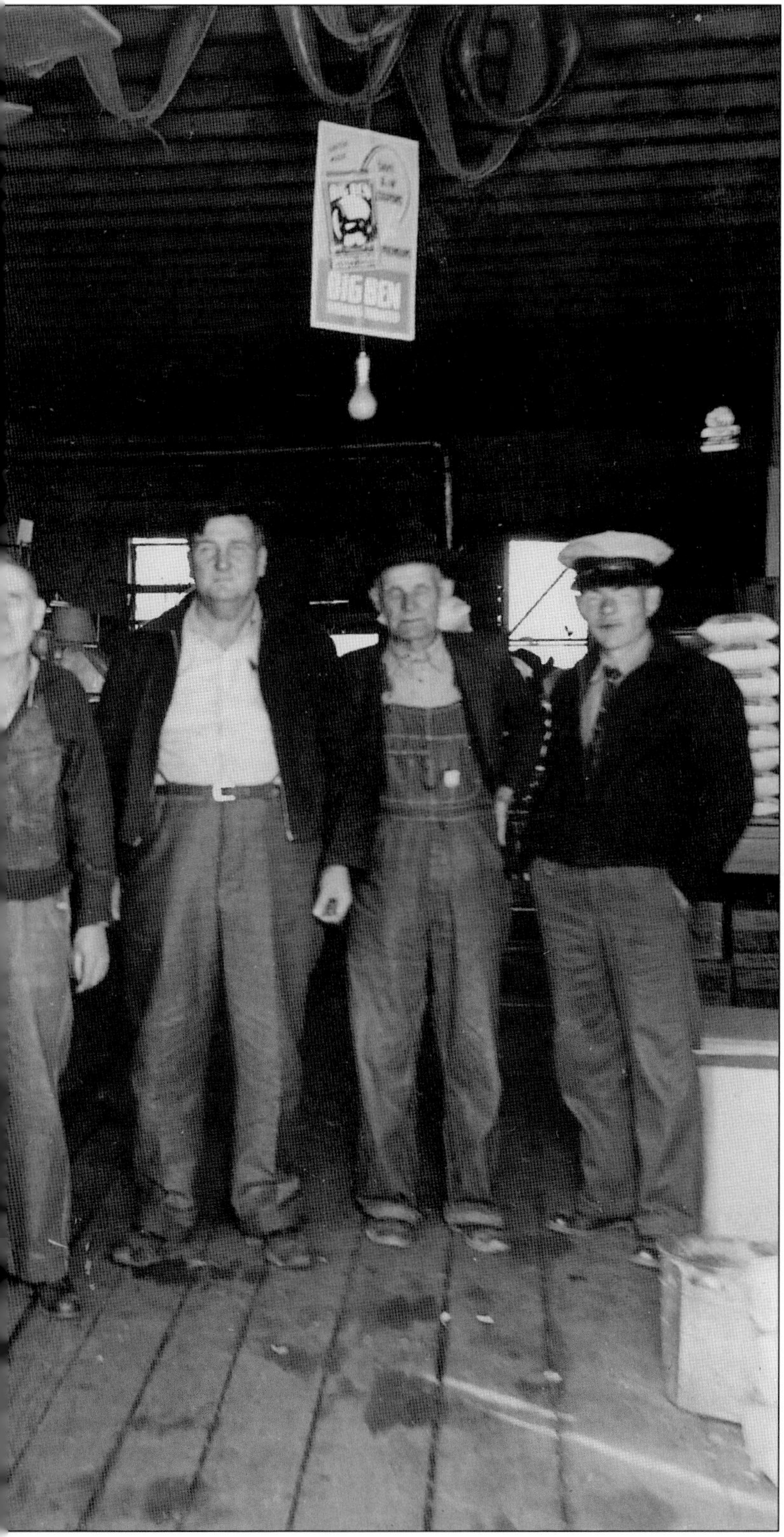

The Waldron Produce Company on Featherston Street in the 1920s and 1930s featured plank floors with wide cracks between the boards. Items pictured include fresh potatoes in a wire basket, a 5-gallon can of black kerosene on the floor, and sacks of sugar, flour, and beans on the table. They sold some groceries, and from the local farmers, they purchased fresh eggs, chickens, cream, and a variety of other produce. Animal hides were also purchased and sold here. Pictured from left to right are as follows: John Harvey, Russell Oliver (who started the business), Russell's brother Henry Oliver, and two unidentified men. (Courtesy of Ann. O. Evans Oliver.)

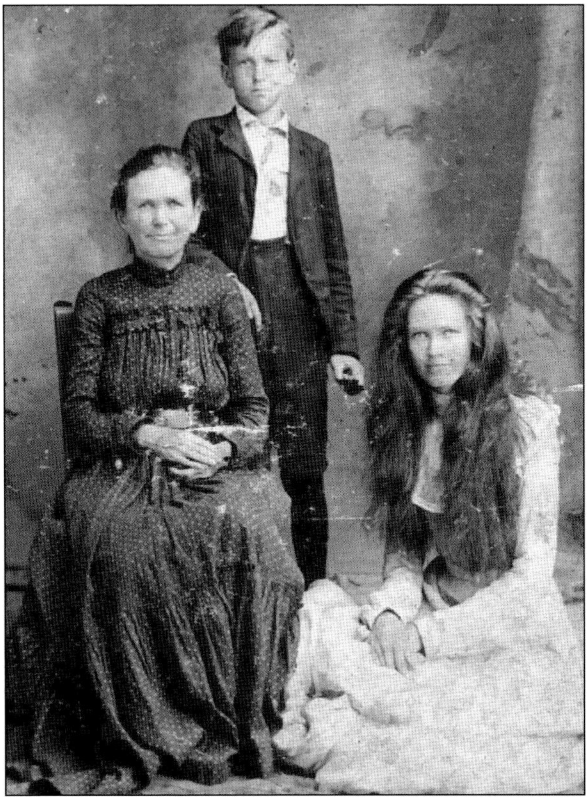

Dressed in her Sunday best is 67-year-old Mary Virginia Black Frizzell (1855–1942) on the left, her son Daniel Boone Jr., and her daughter, Winnie Elizabeth. The independently spirited Winnie wore her hair loose and flowing, a most unusual sight at this time. Prior to moving from Georgia to Arkansas, Mary lost her father and three brothers during the Civil War. She lived near the road where the Union soldiers traveled. Like many, she left her home and desolated Georgia behind and came by boat to Dardenville, Arkansas. She then traveled by wagon to Scott County in the 1870s. (Courtesy of Ila Rhodes, Fresno, CA.)

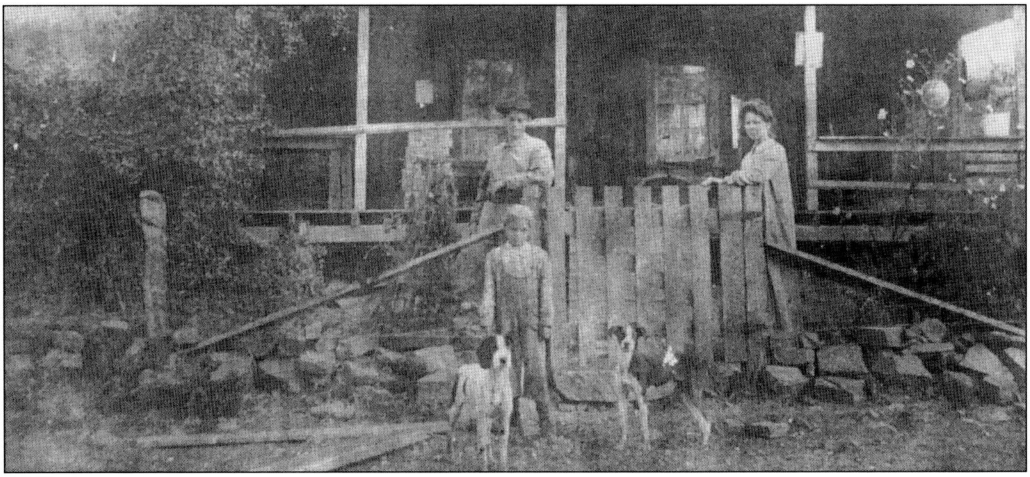

The average family "box" home of rough sawed lumber with board-and-batten vertical siding has a gallery porch across the front, a living room with a stone fireplace on the west, and a main bedroom on the other end. There is a small bedroom and kitchen across the back, and this was a typical home in the county. The sash windows were bought in town and hauled home in the wagon. Good hunting dogs, the pride of young Val Wheeler, were equally as important, as wild game made up a large part of the diet of early settlers. The fenced yard of the home of John Hiram Wheeler and wife, Alice Richmond, had the rocks cleared from the main Greenridge/Cardiff road piled under the bottom strand of wire. (Courtesy of Rosemary James, Waldron.)

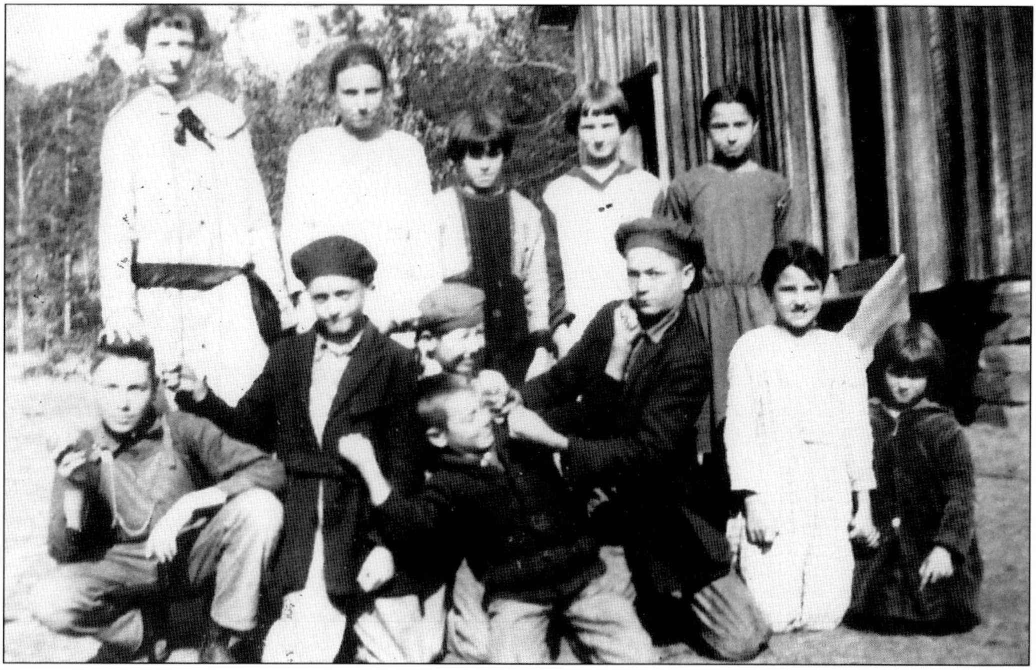

Cross Creek School was a crude one-room schoolhouse built of rough sawed lumber upon a rock pier foundation. This school and community took its name from a creek located about 10 miles west of Waldron on Highway 248 and crosses again south on County Road 10. Pictured from left to right are as follows: Dessie Blackburn, Clara Mills, Lois Hunsucker, Lorene Blackburn, Lora Mills, Estelle Hunsucker, Oliver Hunsucker, Green Blackburn, Grace Mills, and Edith Duncan. The Hunsuckers are the children of Jess and Mandy Hunsucker. (Historian's Collection contributed by Mr. Syler, Arkadelphia, AR.)

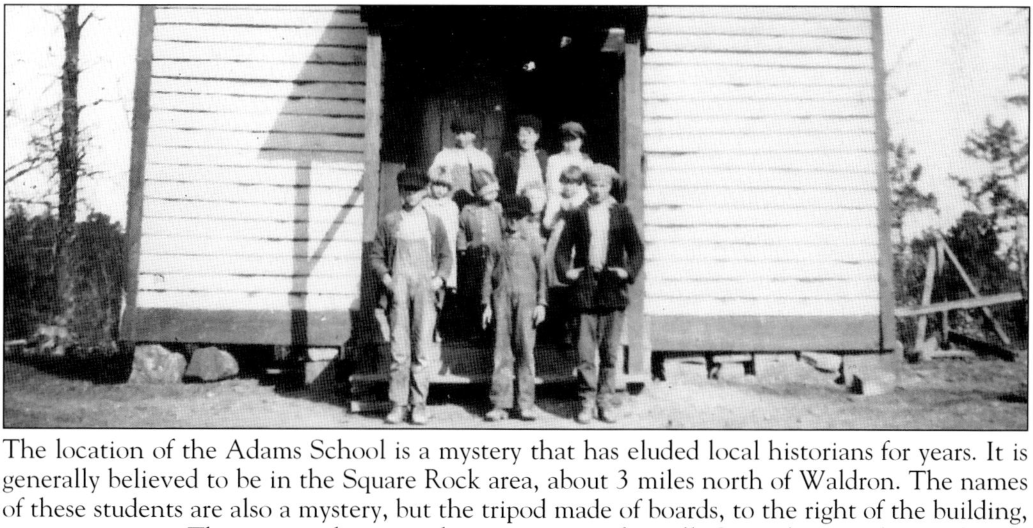

The location of the Adams School is a mystery that has eluded local historians for years. It is generally believed to be in the Square Rock area, about 3 miles north of Waldron. The names of these students are also a mystery, but the tripod made of boards, to the right of the building, is not a mystery. This is a quick way to draw water out of a well. Once the tripod is in place, a pulley is attached to its highest point and a rope is run through the pulley with one end tied to a well-bucket. The other end of the rope is used to lower the bucket down to the water and draw it back to the surface, thus providing students with a fresh drink of water.(Historian's Collection, contributed by Mr. Syler, Arkadelphia, AR)

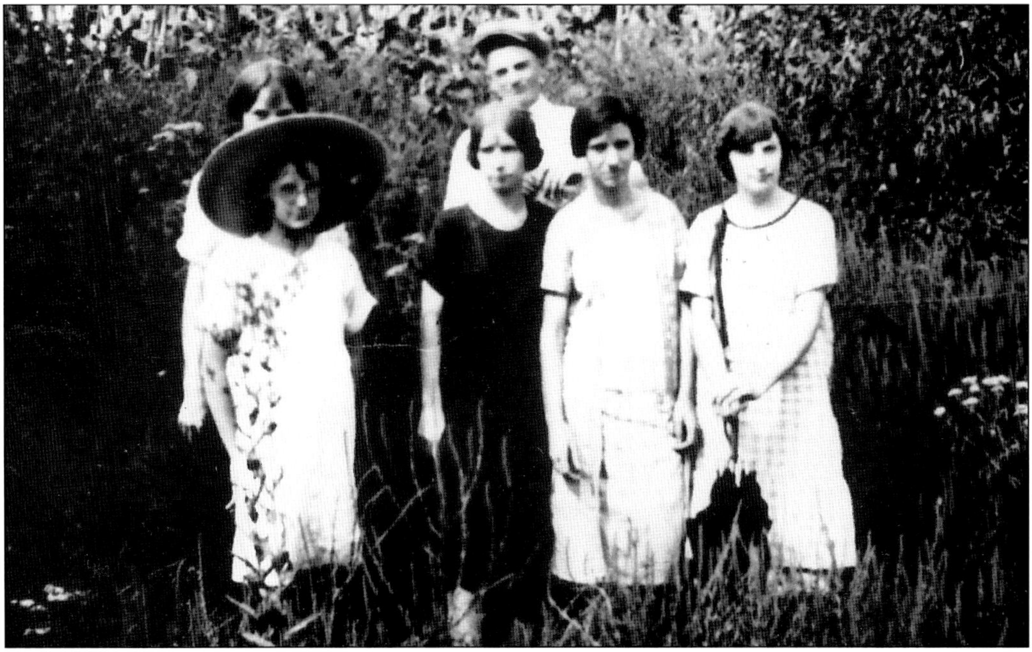

These teenage girls are seen strolling leisurely along the countryside in 1925, in the Lower Centerpoint community west of Waldron, on a Sunday afternoon. Pictured from left to right are as follows: Gladys Hullender, Ruth May, Opal Taff, Millard Hullender, Melba Taff, and May Hullender. There is quite a difference in the life of a teenager 75 years ago compared with that of today. (Courtesy of Allen Syler, Texarkana, AR.)

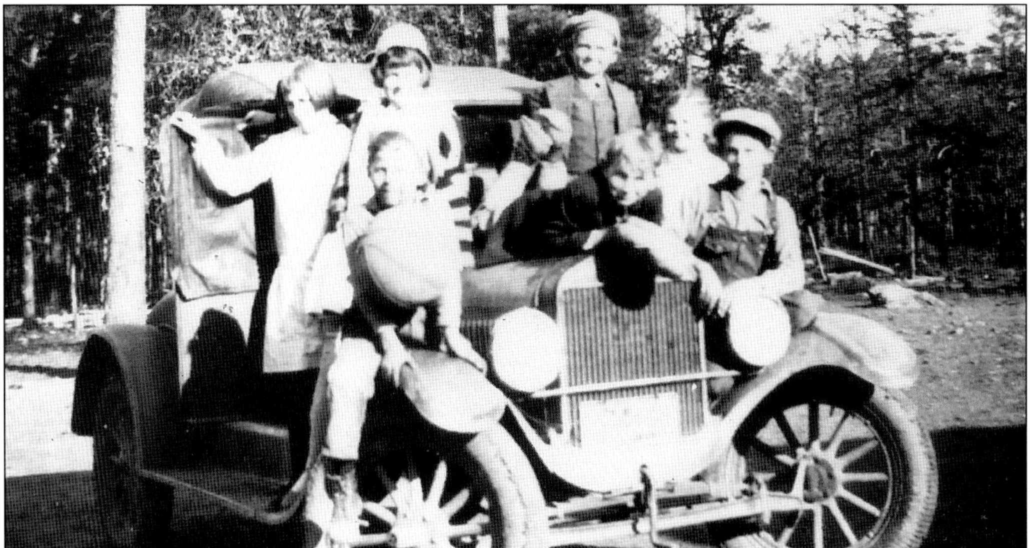

This 1927 image of seven children on the running board, fenders, and hood of the vintage crank-start Ford car was taken on the dirt road in the Lower Centerpoint Community west of Waldron. Pictured from left to right are as follows: Louie and Glenn Plummer, Clara May and Denver Jones, Mangus Newman, Jewell Cline, and Opal Grisby. (Courtesy of Allen Syler, Texarkana, AR.)

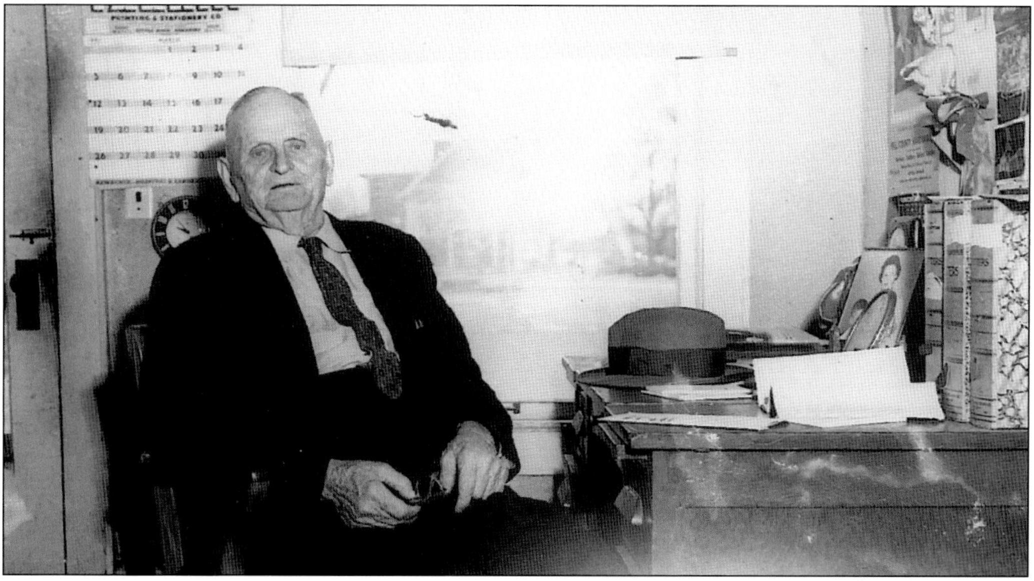

An unpretentious wooden desk in a small cubical for an office was sufficient for John E. Chambers, the chancery judge of the 14th District, which included Scott County. He was appointed by Arkansas Act 18 in 1927, elected in 1931, and served until 1948. He was a self-made man, a Mason, an Odd Fellow and Knight of Pythias. He graduated from Vanderbilt University, was admitted to the bar, and opened a law office in Danville, Arkansas, in 1901. (Courtesy of Johnny Chambers, Danville, Arkansas.)

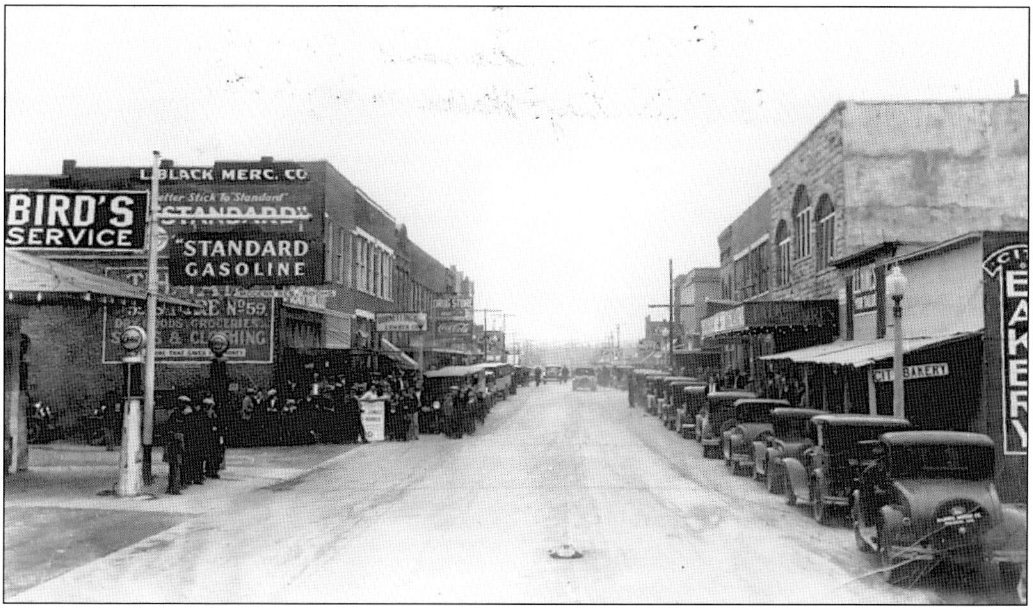

Nearly every Saturday, Main Street was lined with two-seated Ford automobiles bought from the Bates and Williams business west of the courthouse for just under $500. The children clamored to visit the "talking picture" show at the Pines Theater (third building on right). Gasoline cost about 6¢ a gallon, and business was booming in 1910 as the county had reached its population zenith of 14,302 citizens; however, by 1920, it had begun its downward spiral. (Historian's Collection.)

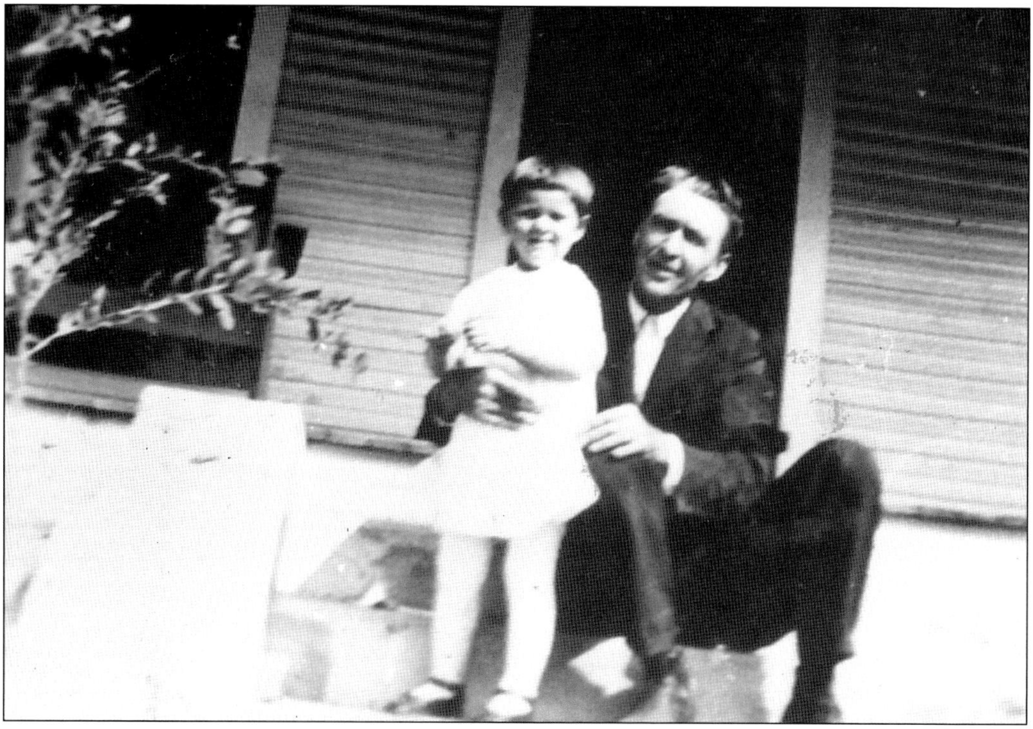

Enjoying life on the front steps of his home east of Waldron is W.G. Farnsworth with his granddaughter, Anne. He owned and operated the Farnsworth Grocery on Main Street in Waldron in the 1920s. (Historian's Collection.)

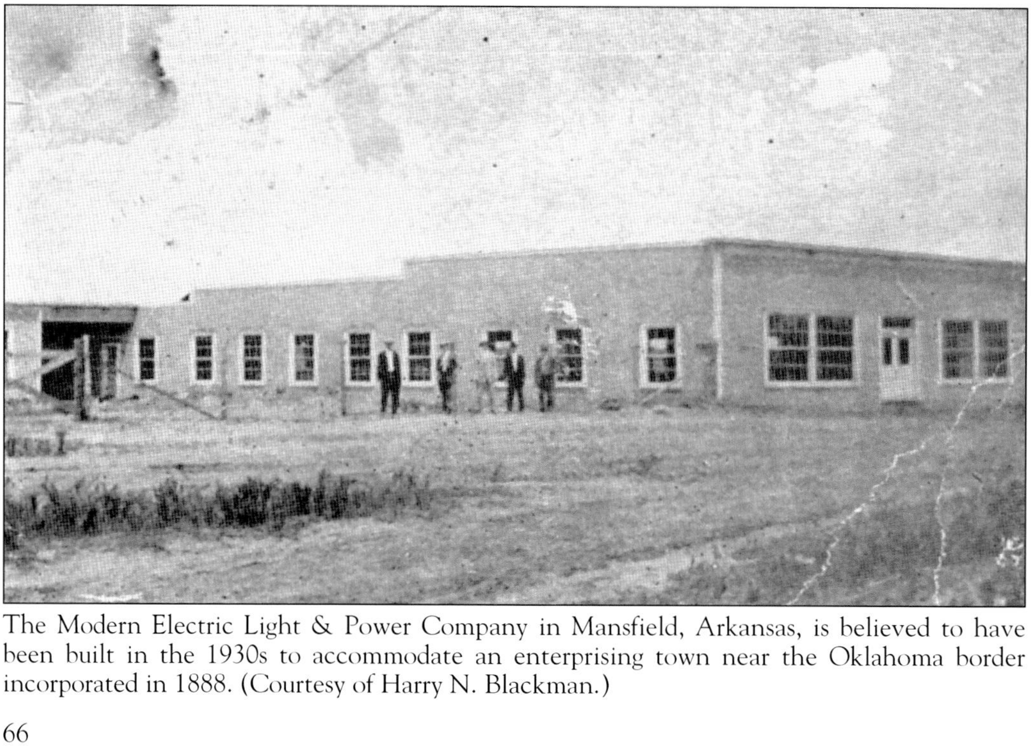

The Modern Electric Light & Power Company in Mansfield, Arkansas, is believed to have been built in the 1930s to accommodate an enterprising town near the Oklahoma border incorporated in 1888. (Courtesy of Harry N. Blackman.)

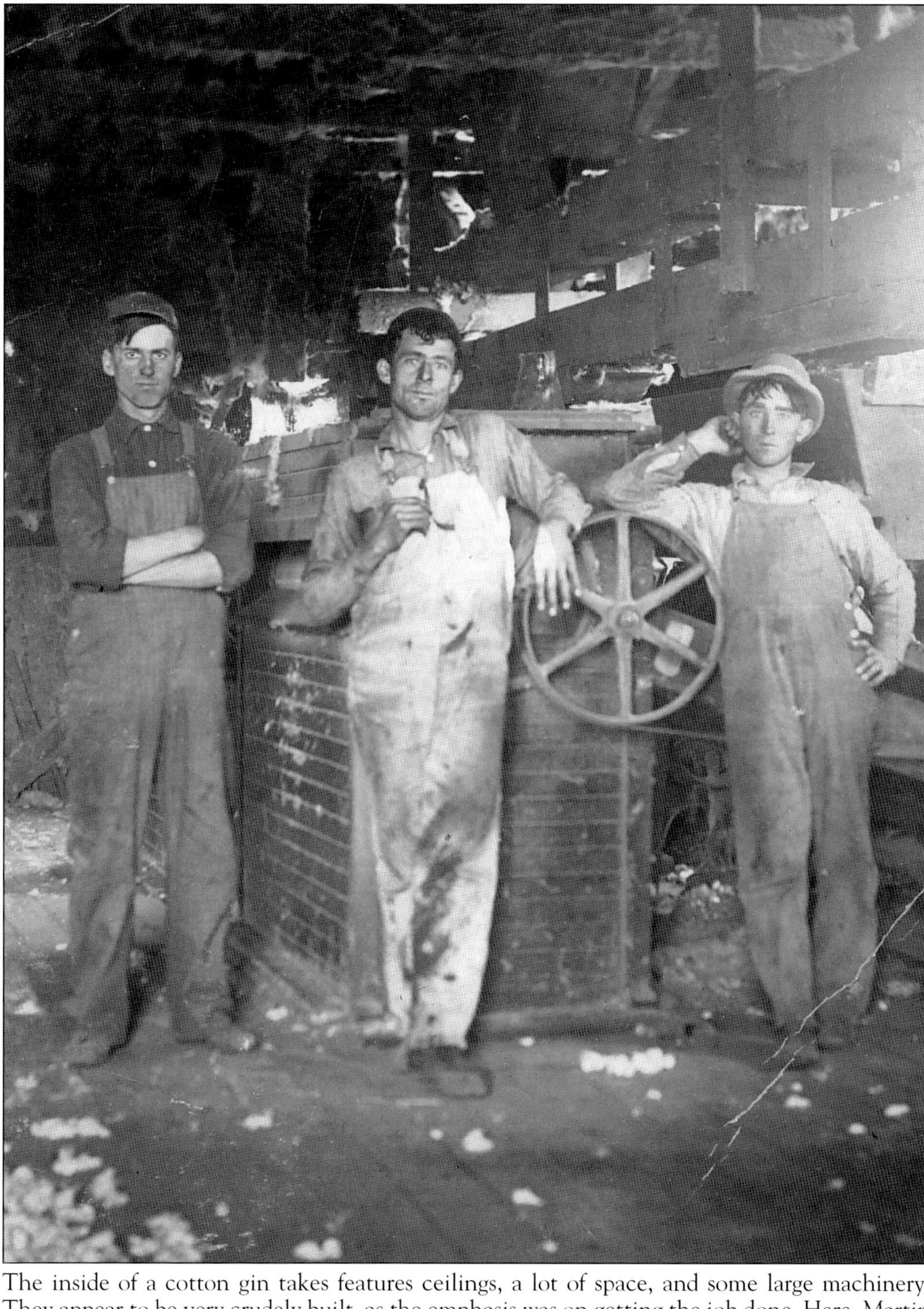

The inside of a cotton gin takes features ceilings, a lot of space, and some large machinery. They appear to be very crudely built, as the emphasis was on getting the job done. Here, Martin Ruthloff (right) and his co-workers enjoy a break from work for a photo opportunity. Martin lived in the Boles community in 1920, but it is not known whether or not this gin is in that area. (Courtesy of Ila Rhodes, Fresno, CA.)

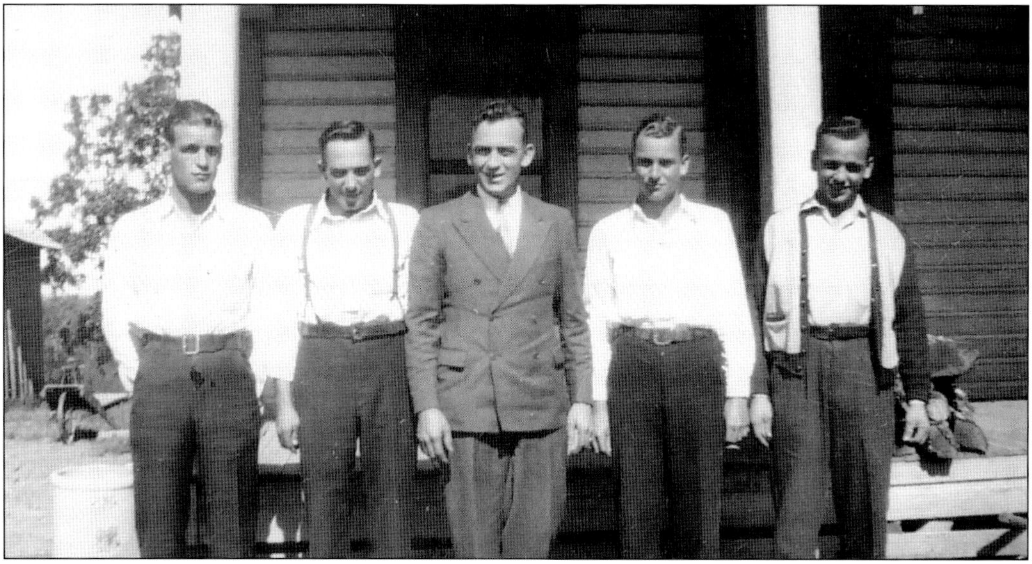

This 1939 picture features the Center boys from California visiting their cousin. The storage house on the left has vertical rough sawed board-and-batten siding and was constructed around 1890, as was the house, but it shows some updating. To the left of the house is an interesting wheelbarrow used for the movement of firewood from the woodpile to the front porch. From left to right, the men are as follows: Ed Rhyne, Levi Center, Glen Center, William Cranford Center, and Leo Center. (Historian's Collection.)

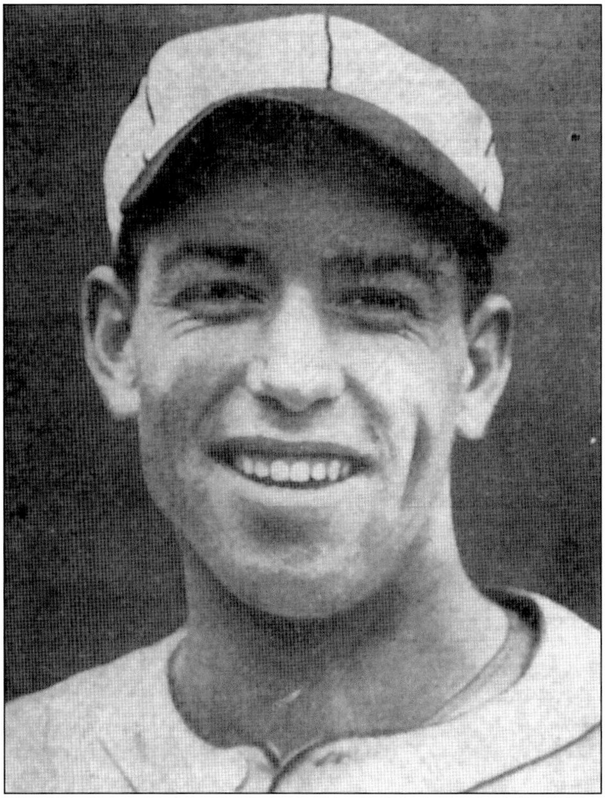

Captured here are the ready smile and twinkling eyes of the famous baseball Cardinal pitcher Paul "Daffy" Dean (1913–1981). He and his brother, baseball great Dizzy Dean, were born in Lucas, Arkansas, on land originally belonging to Scott County, in a primitive farm home. His father had little money, and the family moved around picking cotton. In 1930, when the Depression hung over the country like a cloud, it was in a cotton field near Houston that Paul signed his first baseball contract. By 1934, he and Dizzy had each pitched two winning games in a World Series. About "Daffy" Dean, his wife, Dorothy Sandusky, said, "He was a quiet man . . . loved his family and was blessed with innate intelligence . . . he and 'Diz' excelled in all sports, not just baseball." (Historian's Collection.)

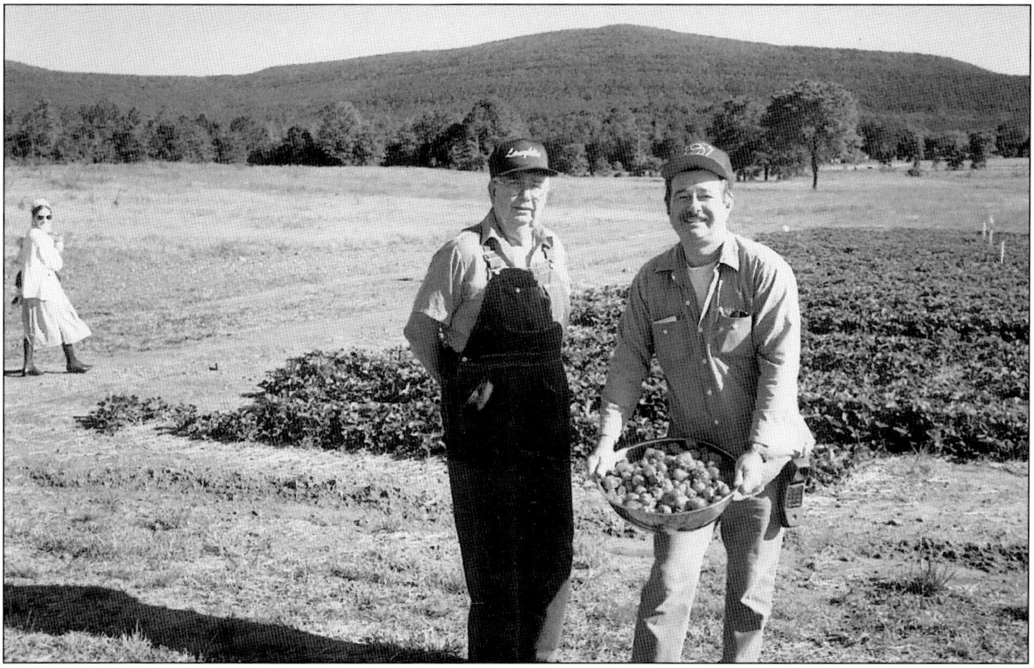

The pine and hardwood covered Poteau Mountain provides a fitting backdrop for the wide green valley floor and the luscious strawberry patch where an Amish lady strides to a row to begin picking. In the foreground, in customary overalls, are descendants of pioneer Plummer settlers Denver Plummer (left) and his son, Paul, proudly displaying the large berries produced on the Berry Hill Farm west of Waldron. In the 1930s, money was hard to come by on the small rural farms, and strawberries were the primary cash crop. (Historian's Collection.)

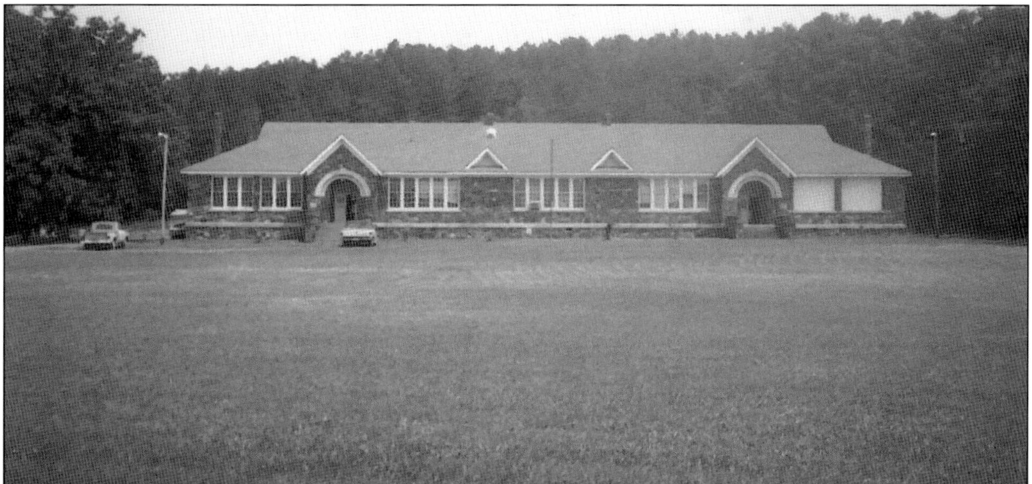

Pictured here is the peaceful image of the native stone Parks School built on wide, flat, grassy land with a tree-lined hill in the background. This school was built in the broad Fourche LaFave Valley, in the southeast part of the county, in the 1930s by the Public Works Administration. For nearly 40 years, it has been lovingly cared for, and today it serves as the Parks Community Center. (Historian's Collection.)

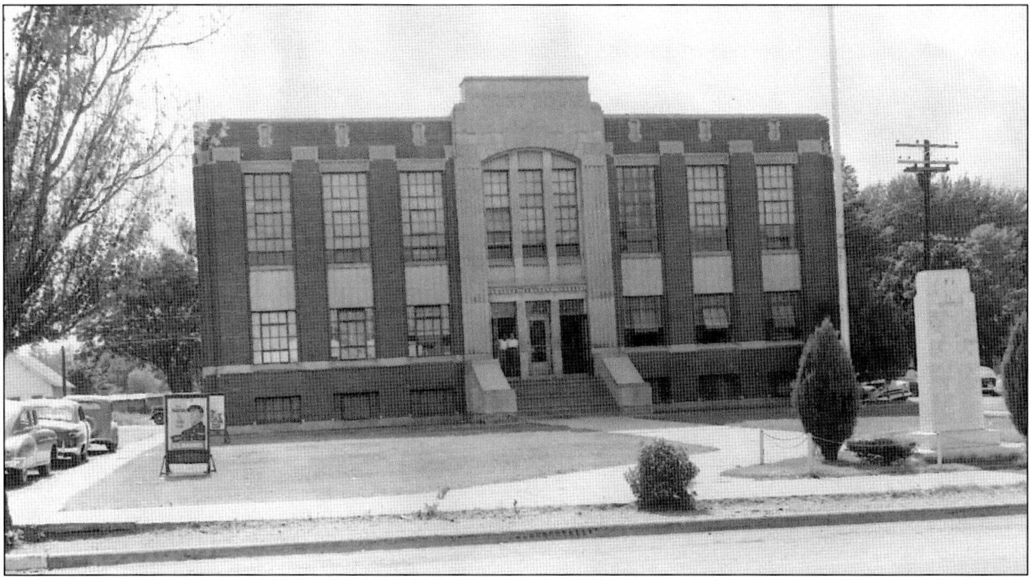

In 1935, this modern courthouse stood in stark contrast to the more ornate buildings in the early part of the century. It was the eighth courthouse, the others being destroyed by fire. All but the first two were built on the same site. The World War I and II monument in the foreground by the flagpole has two evergreen shrubs acting as sentinels. Today the courthouse is empty and awaiting restoration funds. (Historian's Collection.)

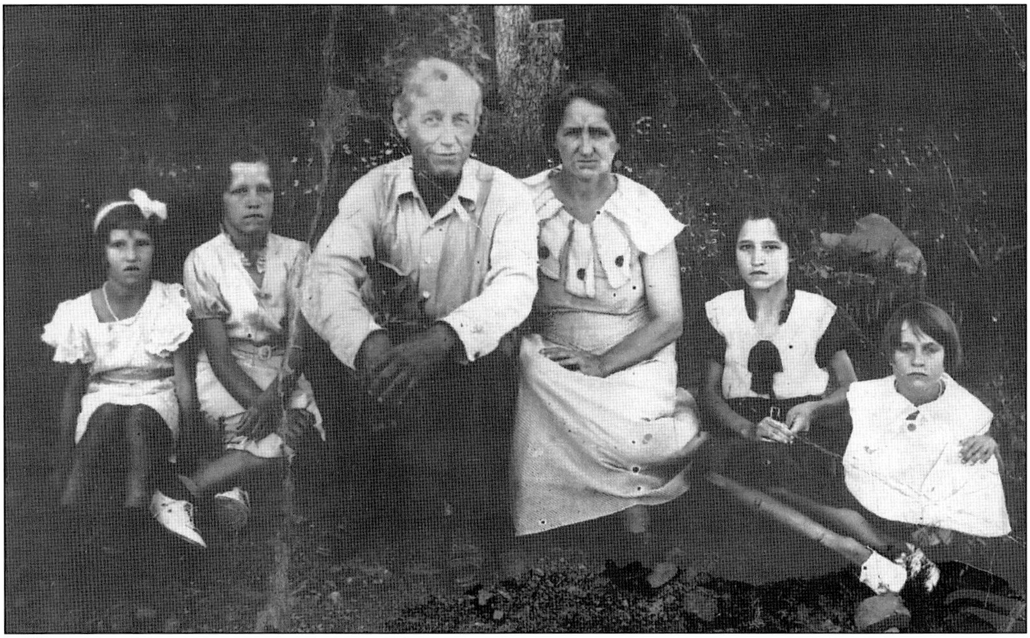

Seated on the ground and on pieces of wood is the family of a rural school teacher and farmer, C.E. Wade. Pictured from left to right are the following: Wanda, Juanita, C.E., his wife, Pearl Kennon, Lella, and Syble Wade. Their farm was 14 miles east of Waldron in the Mt. Moriah community, on which the Conservation Corp (C.C.) camp was later located. He taught at the Keener School when it was consolidated, Mt. Moriah School, and Little Texas School, as well as other rural schools. (Courtesy, Juanita Wade Holland.)

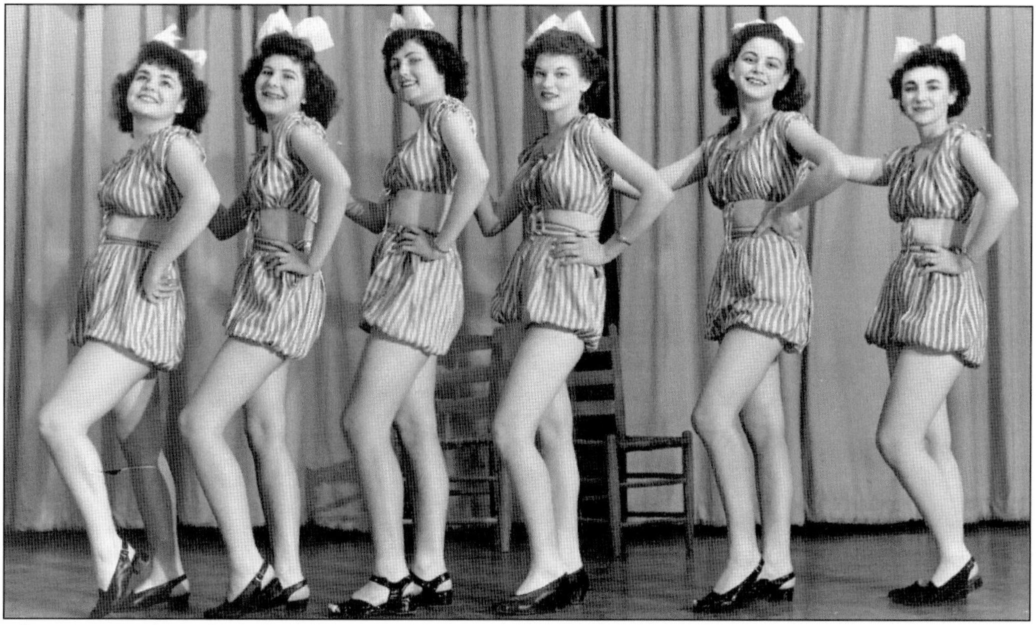

They put on their dancing slippers and tripped the light fantastic to the tune of "Put Your Little Foot Right There." In their midriff blouses, with bows in their hair and wearing bloomer-type shorts, they rehearsed for the Waldron High School musical *Corn's A Poppin'*. Pictured from left to right are as follows: Johnnie Faye Hinkle, Thelma Lee Payne, Melbalene Franklin, ? McCutchen, Janice Hawkins, and Margaret Plemmons. (Courtesy of Lou Nell McCraw Davis, Lamar, AR.)

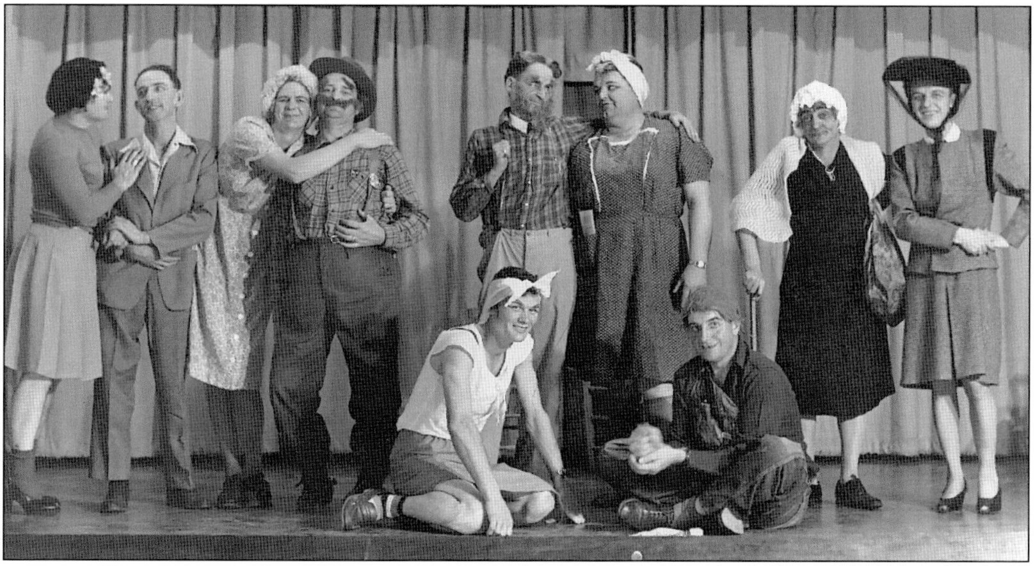

This theatrical production, featuring an all male cast at the Waldron High School, was patterned after the *Beverly Hillbillies*. Pictured from left to right are as follows: unidentified, Lindsey Windham, unidentified, unidentified, John Wesley Black, Orbin Little, James Cox, and Orville Goodner. Seated on the floor playing the children, from left to right, are the following: Joe Bob Austin and Glen Abbott. (Courtesy of Lou Nell McCraw Davis, Lamar, AR.)

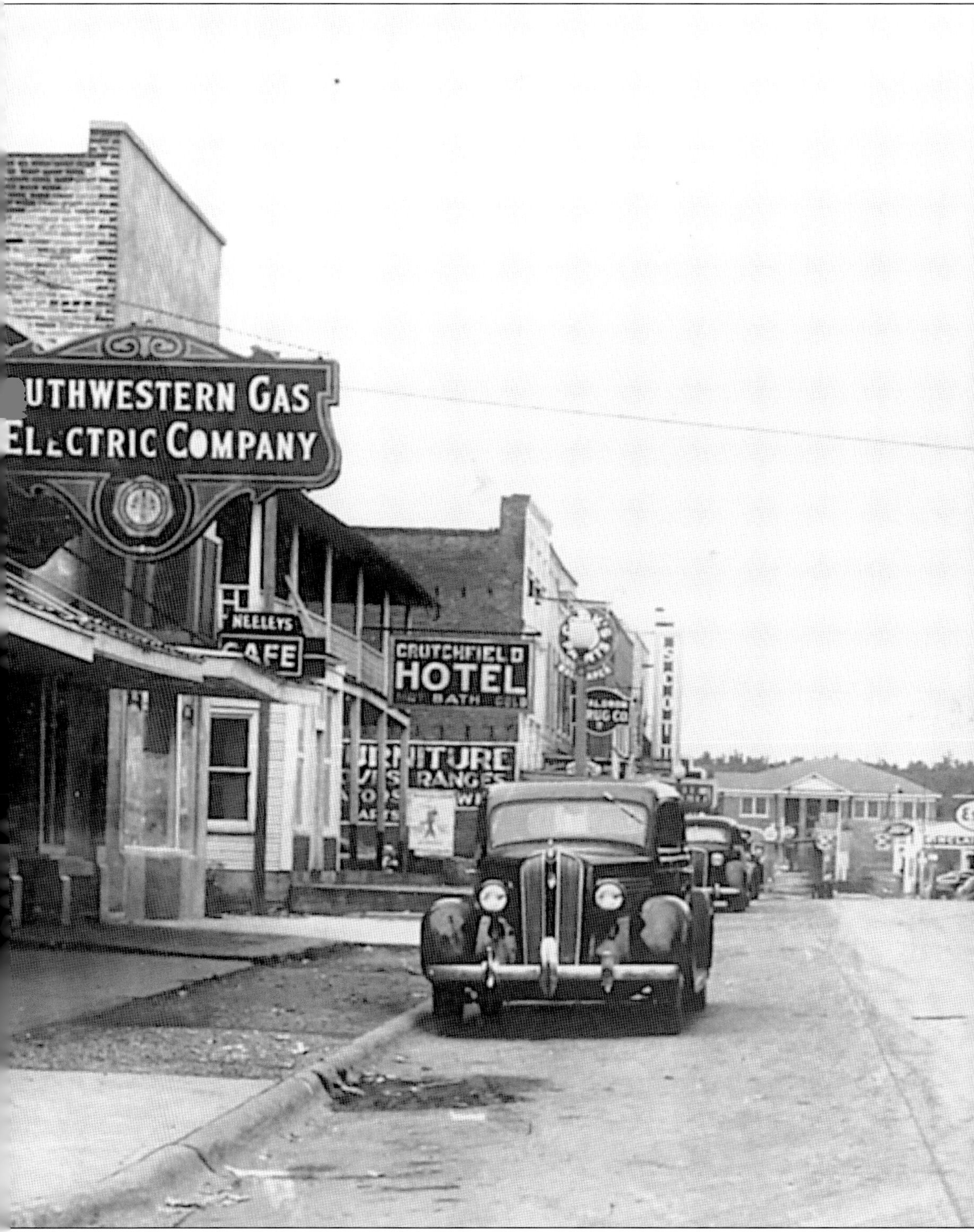

Livestock no longer roamed Main Street, and a few blocks were paved in the 1930s, leaving some sidewalks a high step from the street. This photo was taken looking south from the east

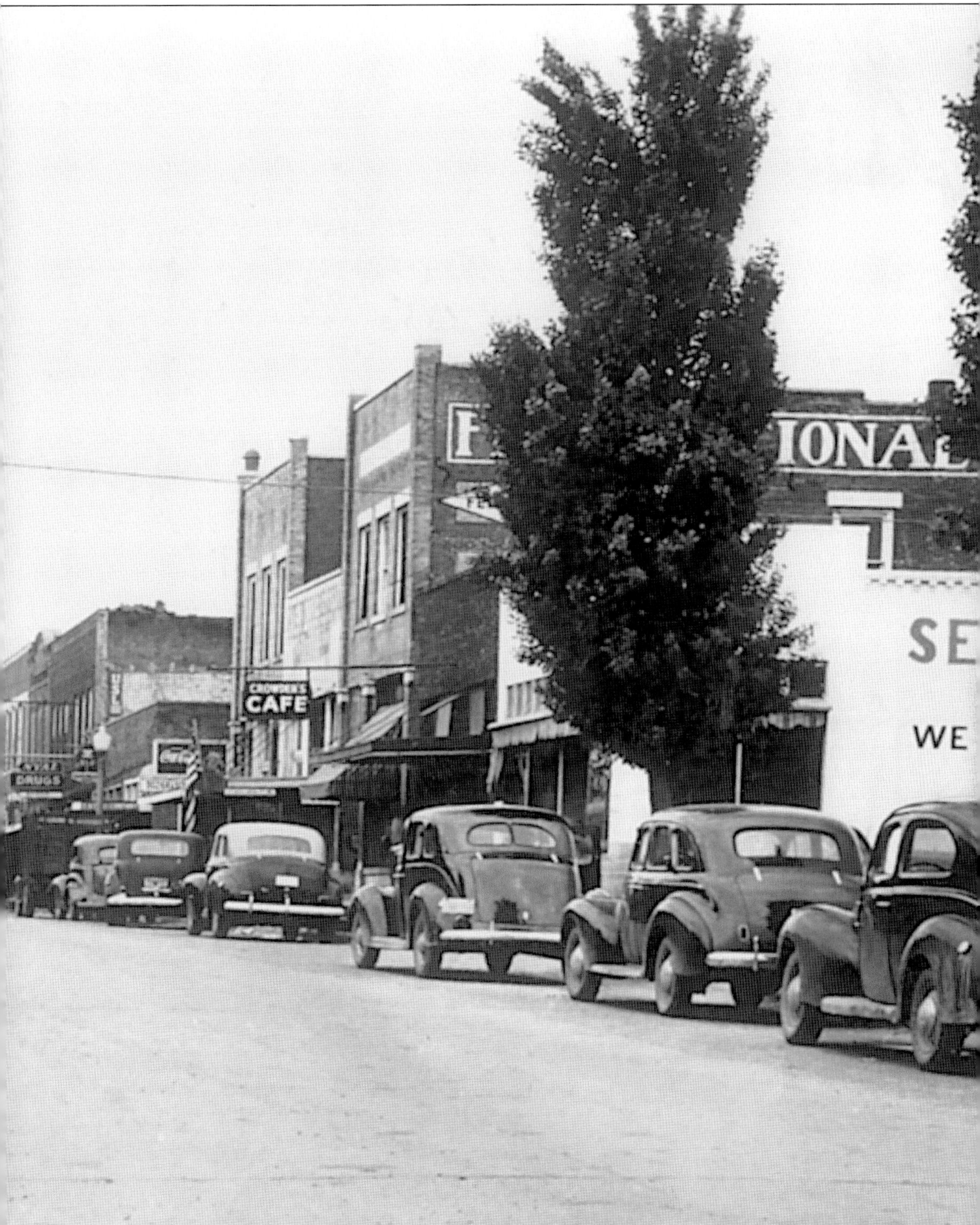

corner of Second Street to the Baptist Church built in 1917. Unfortunately, this fine building was torn down in the 1980s. (Historian's Collection.)

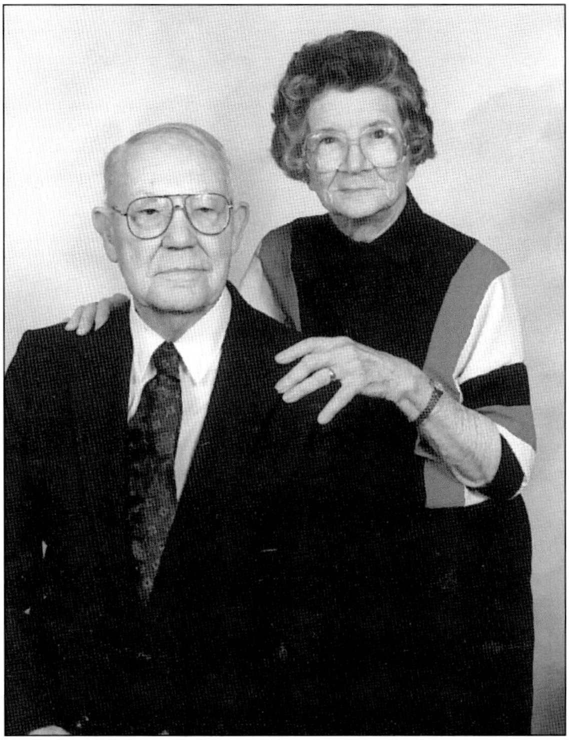

Waldron's celebrated football coach, Lecil Richard "Tom" Sawyer, and helpmate, Vera Martin, married in 1934, just four years after he came to Waldron as a history teacher and coach. He was the fourth coach ever to grace the football field here and carried the team to state championships in 1948 and 1949, as well as being undefeated in 1939, 1940, 1948, and 1949. He was hired as a school superintendent in 1934 and filled the post for 40 years, after which he served as mayor of the city of Waldron for eight years.

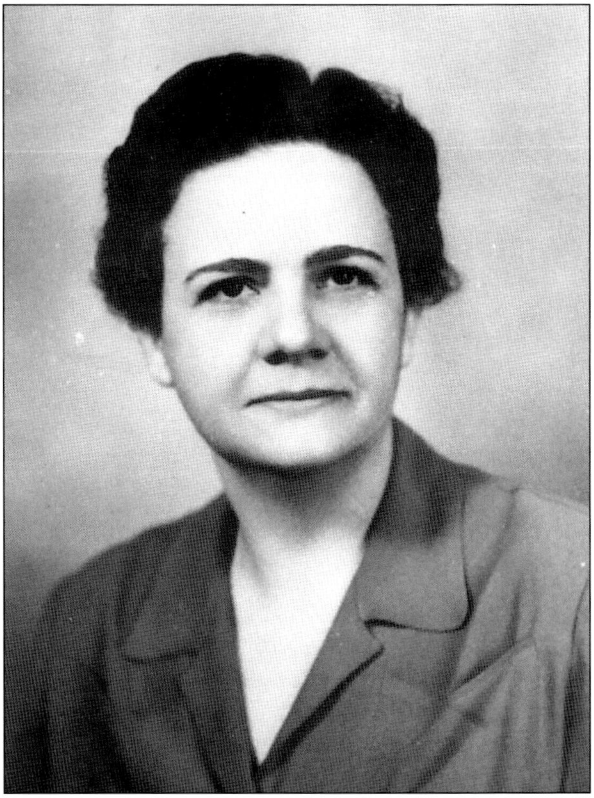

Dr. Florence Clyde Chandler (1901–1987), with her penetrating dark eyes and neat, cropped dark hair, was born in the small community of Oliver, west of Waldron. In a day when women had a hard time being recognized for their work, she became a world-renowned botanical geneticist working with the Merck Chemical Company, the Boyce Thompson Institute for Plant Research, Inc., and the New York Botanical Gardens. She was the daughter of W.F. and Nannie Chandler. (Courtesy of Steve Demarest, Arvada, CO.)

Enjoying his enlistment in the United States Navy at the end of World War II is 19-year-old Truman Cecil Cross. He was born in Scott County in 1926 to John R. Cross and Edna Mae Ferguson. His father served in World War I in the 59th Infantry of the 4th Division and died in 1926. His mother died three years later, leaving he and his two sisters, Elva Edna and Virginia, orphans to be reared by his aunts and uncles. After World War II, Truman spent his work life in the oil fields of Texas. (Historian's Collection.)

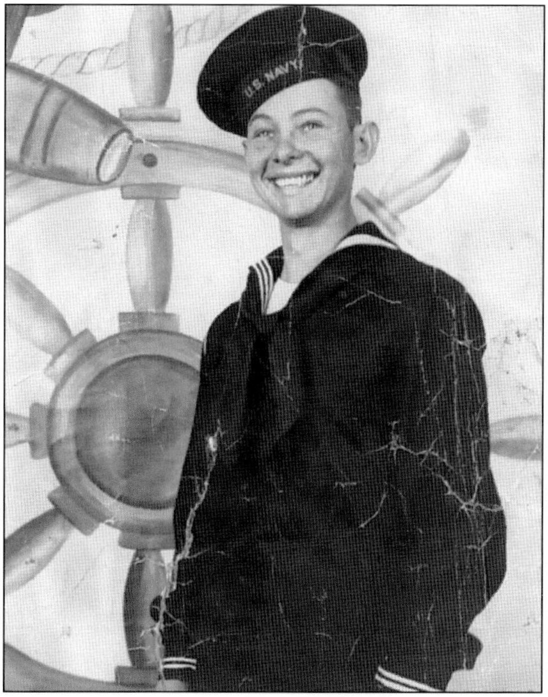

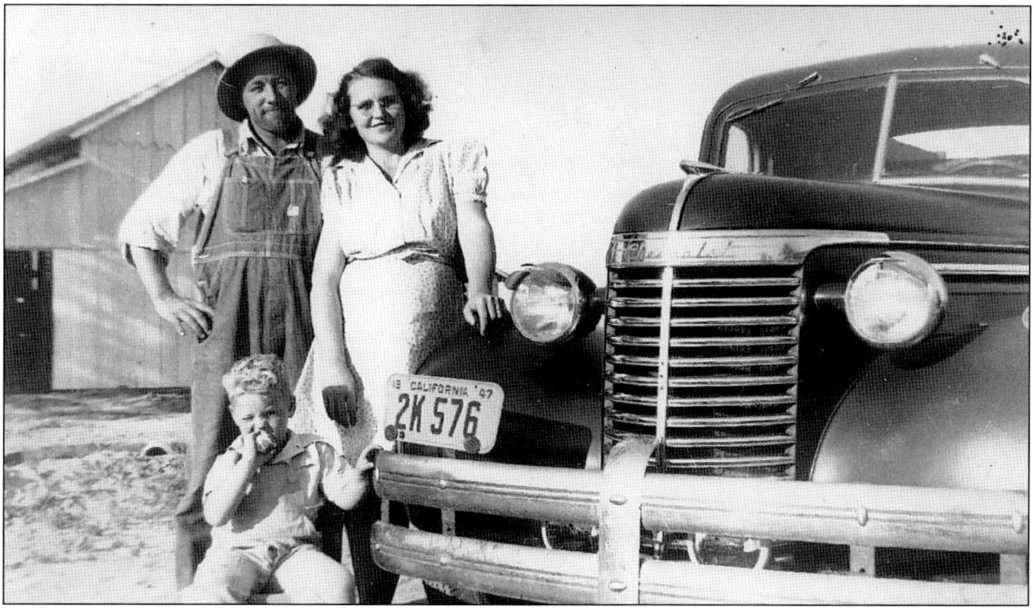

Like many families, Haskell and Elaine Sliger and their sons left their farm in the Cauthron community in Scott County and traveled to California in the 1930s in search of work. Haskell did not relinquish his Arkansas clothing, the overalls, or love of farming, as the barn in the background indicates. On November 14,1939, at Hansford, California, while traveling home, tragedy struck this family. Another car collided with them and killed their eight-year-old son, John D. Sliger. Also, like many, they worked the crops, prospered, and soon were able to "see the USA in a Chevrolet" as the popular singer, Dinah Shore, used to sing on the Chevrolet television commercials in 1947. (Historian's Collection.)

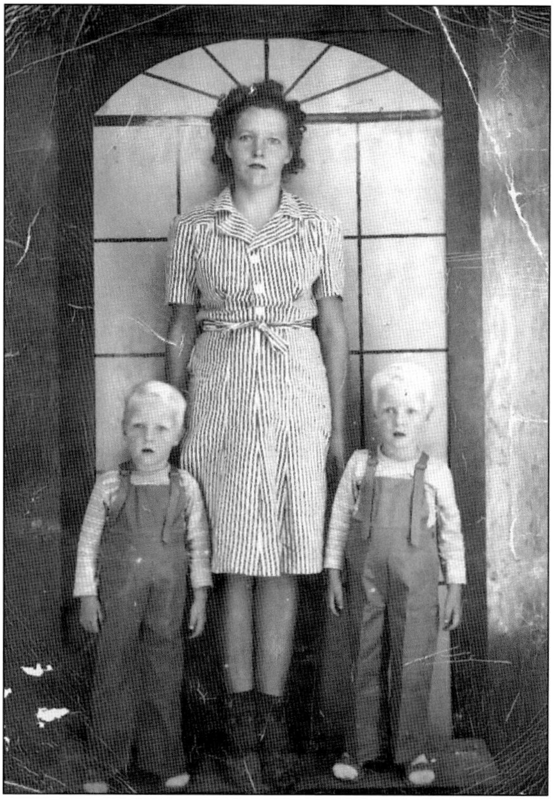

Posing for pictures the day she left California to return to Waldron is the former Scott County Tax Assessor, Juanita Holland and her two sons, Lindy (left) and Randy. Like many from the county, they had gone west looking for work on the large fruit and vegetable farms and the cotton gins. Her husband, Kello, worked by the hour for Kim Brothers Company, owner of many fruit orchards. He was able to save up $1,000 in six months and thought he was doing well. They lived in a labor camp—an old granary made into a house. She remembered that World War II ended while they were in California and that they returned in 1947. (Courtesy of Juanita Holland.)

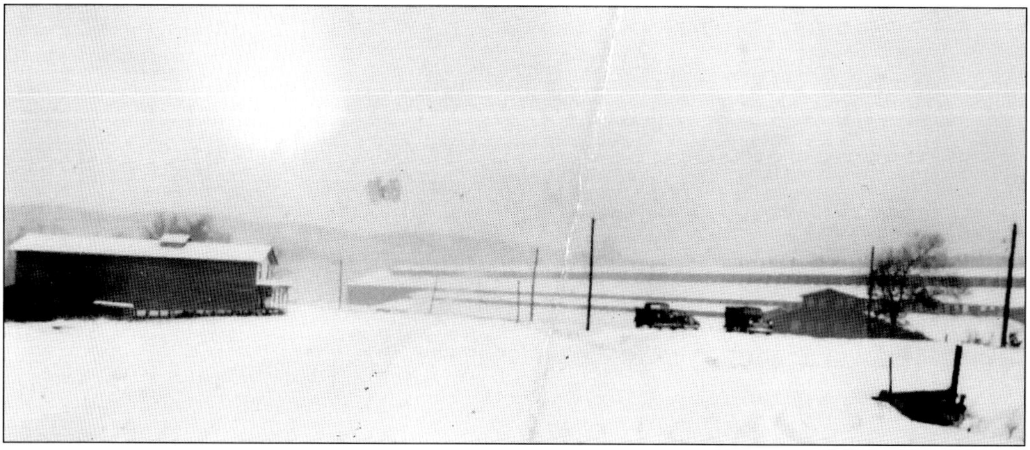

This snow-covered scene on Main Street (looking north) shows the lumber mill town of Forester in the southeast part of the county. It was established by the Caddo River Lumber Company in the 1930s and operated 20 years. It was a self-sufficient community, dedicated to all phases of work connected to a huge lumber mill operation that could put out three million board feet a month. On the left is the theater, on the right is the planing mill, and in the background are the lumber sheds. The lumber was essential to the war effort, and workers were exempt from the draft during World War II. At the close of the war in 1945, the Dierks Lumber and Coal company bought the mill and town with 2,000 acres of land. In 1950, Forester had a population of 1,306 people, but two years later, having exhausted the timber, it went into rapid decline and soon ceased to exist. (Courtesy of Arkansas History Commission.)

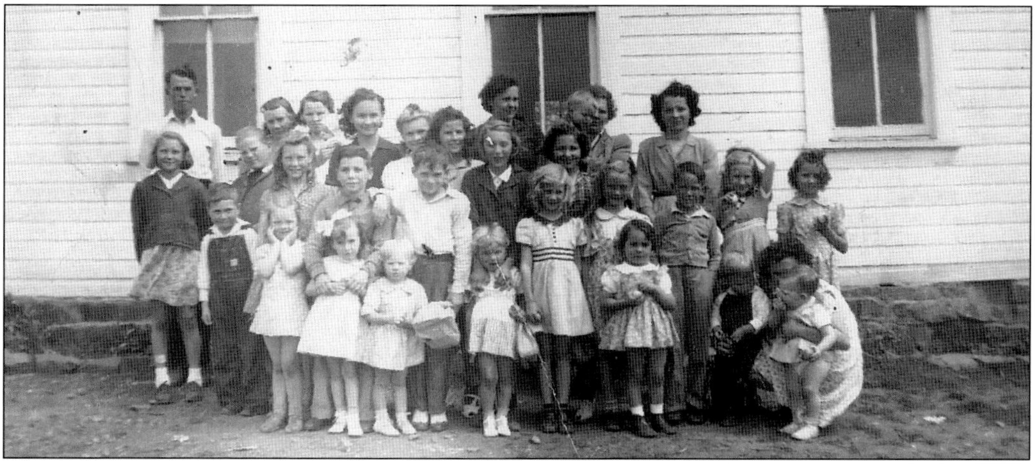

Captured after an Easter egg hunt at the Lone Elm country schoolhouse are images of students and parents. The school was located 5 miles east on the Birdsview Road past the Birdsview Church to a few yards west of the home of Otis Ammons. Here, the water was drawn from a well, and the teachers built fires in the winter in a pot-bellied stove and served as janitors. Pictured from left to right are as follows: (front row) Junior Lee, Ethel Fay Kelly, Shirley Ammons, Alla Merle Langston, unidentified, unidentified, and Ritta Dean Lee; (middle row) Doris Taff, Mary Lee, Billy Ammons, Jimmy Duncan, Betty Taff, Blondina Woodall, May Ruth Kelly, Bernard Gerald Langston, unidentified, and Buddy June Lee; (back row) Delmer Langston, Lois Ammons, Annie Langston holding son, Tommy Junior; Bernice Ammons, Marcine Taff, Della Langston, Irene Lee, Em Taff holding Louise, and Glynn Lee. (Courtesy of Della Meredith.)

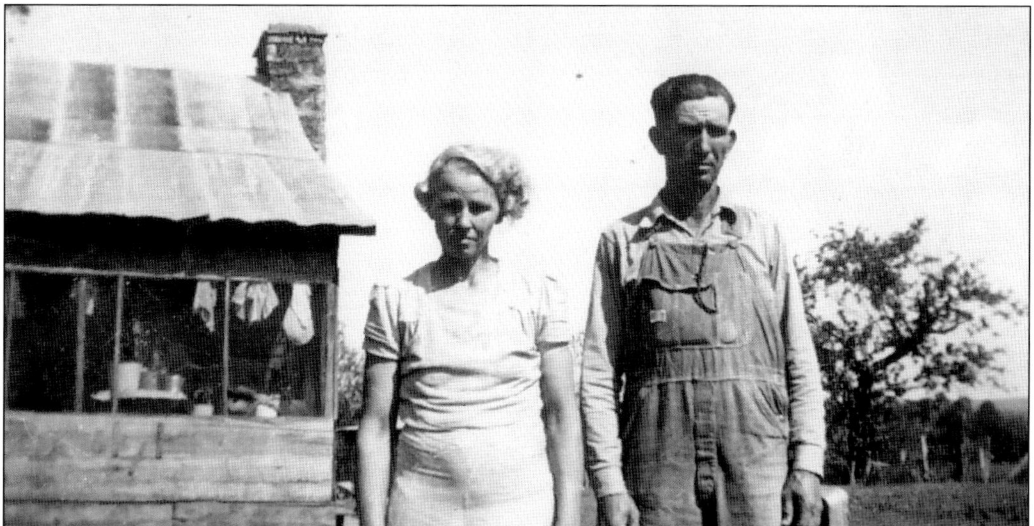

A few yards from the log barn is the old house, which had a "dog-trot" in the middle and three fireplaces. The house shook from the vibrations of music and square dancing on many a Saturday night. This is a view from the screened porch on the back of the house. The broad axe marks can be seen on the hand hewn foundation oak logs notched to fit other logs. This house was used for almost 100 years. Annie F. Johnston, commonly known as "Bobbie," and Thomas Monroe Langston, both second generation Scott Countians, made a living from the land all of their lives and reared their children on this farm. (Courtesy of Della Meredith.)

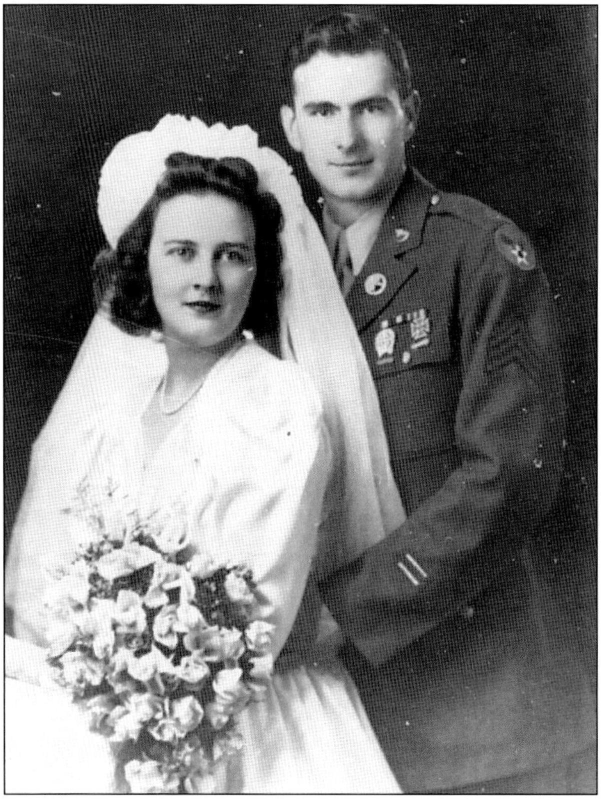

World War II provided the opportunity for lovely concert pianist and composer, Anne Shannon, to meet her husband, Steve Demarest. They were wed on November 25, 1944. She was born in the west front room of the historic Farnsworth house on East Church Street in Waldron. (Historian's Collection.)

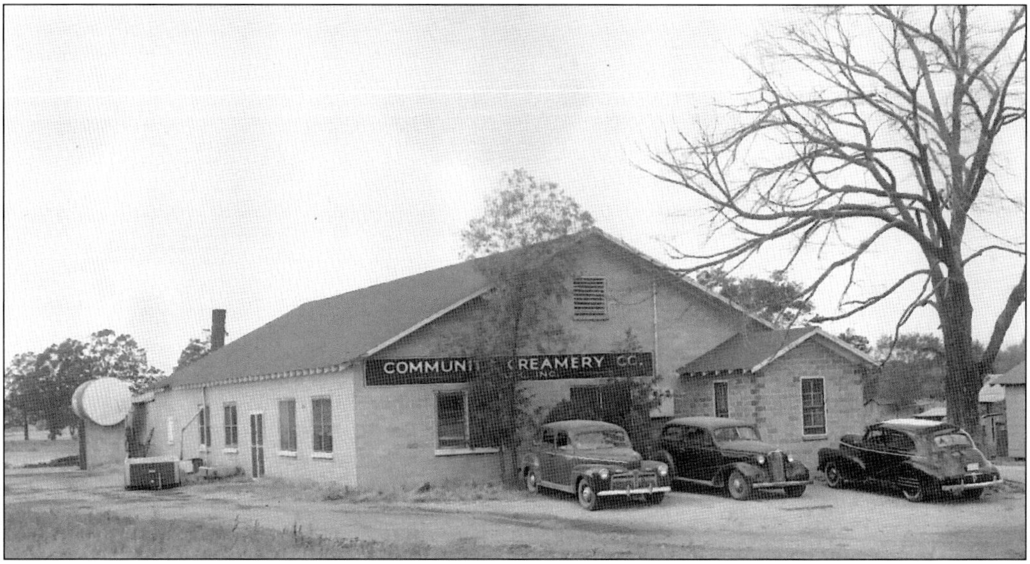

The Community Creamery and Cheese Plant was in business from 1942 to 1957, and it employed several people. This concrete block building is now the home of Sims Building Materials on south Main Street in Waldron. The large built-up tank next to the building on the rear left of the image was filled with whey, and the farmers could come by and get it free of charge to feed their pigs. Mr. Steve Hunt was employed there for several years. In 1945, 131,000 pounds of butter fat was sold by the county farmers. (Historian's Collection.)

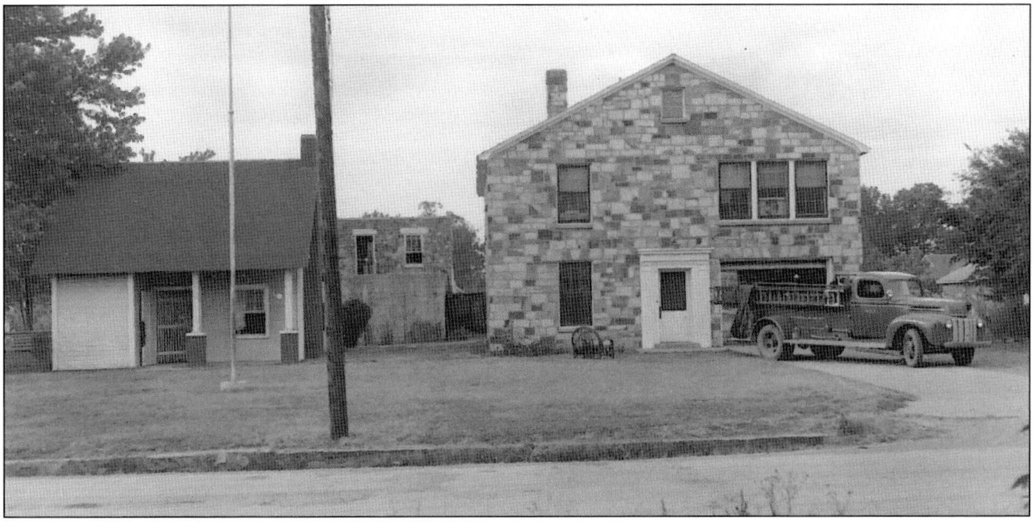

The small, white dollhouse-like building (left) behind the flagless flag pole and in front of the plain two-story building (center) is actually the office and water filtering plant, processing water from Square Rock Lake for the city of Waldron. The two-story natural stone building with the ladder fire truck is the city's fire station, now an apartment house. (Historian's Collection.)

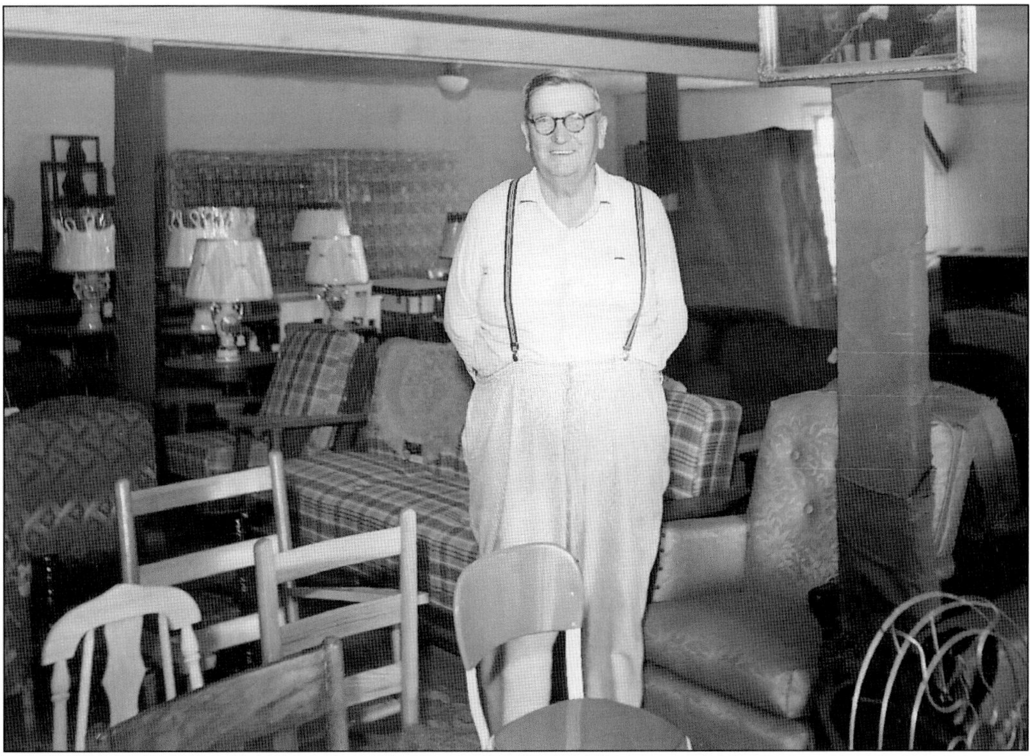

Standing in his furniture store is Henry E. Oliver (1892–1979). This store was located where the parking lot for the Scott County Health Department is today, and it was facing Danville Street. Henry is the son of a pioneer settler of the Brawley community, John C. Oliver, and moved to Waldron in 1922. (Courtesy of O.Ann Evans Oliver.)

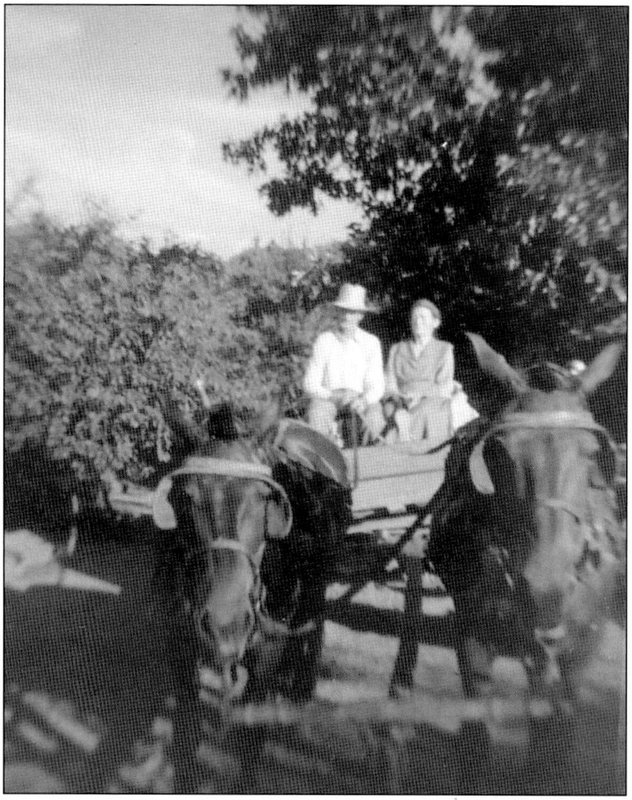

"Patsey" and "Bonnie," the trusty team of horses hitched to a wagon, travel down a country lane almost hidden by the trees to take N. Brown Stewart and his wife, Nora, to town on Saturday. The were going to sell their milk, eggs, and farm produce and to buy items not produced on the farm such as sugar, coffee, and flour. It was a common sight in the summer for women to shade themselves with an umbrella. From simple beginnings in the early 1800s until a century and a half later, this mode of travel was still being used in rural Arkansas. (Courtesy of Bernice Nunn Collection.)

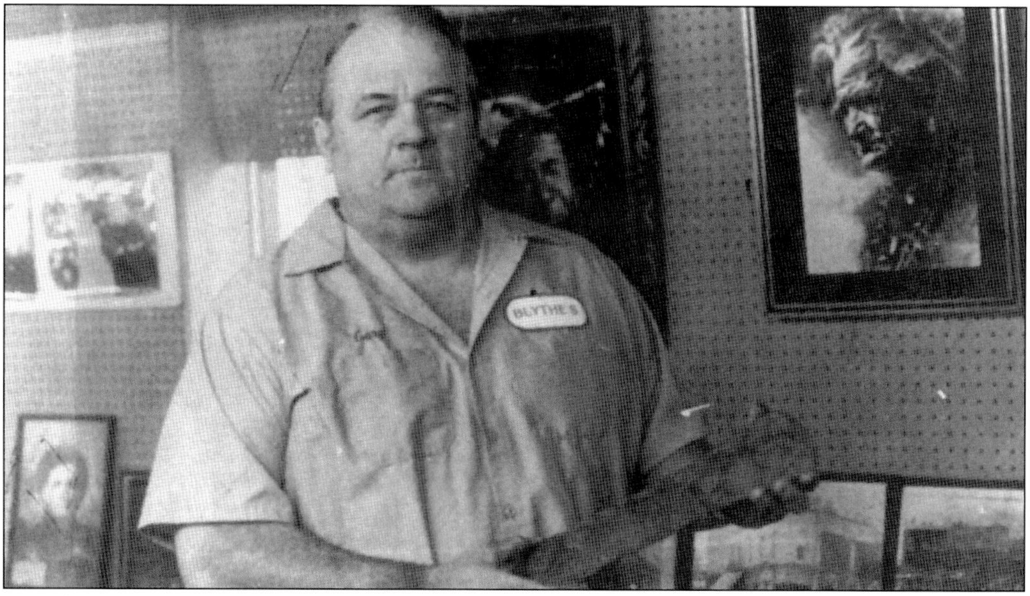

Standing in front of a photo gallery, holding one of many Indian artifacts, is Gary Blythe in his private museum north of Waldron, founded in 1954. His large collection of American Indian artifacts includes stone knives, pipes, scrapers, drills, celts, axes, metates, hammerstones, projectile points, and historical documents—a testament to his life-long interest in history and archaeology. (Historian's Collection.)

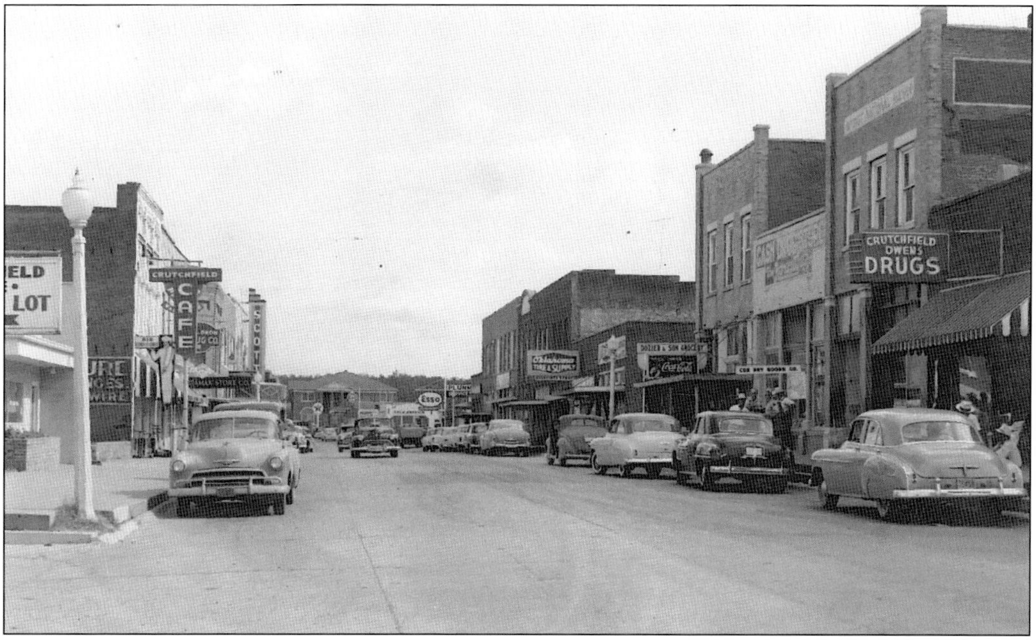

The Waldron Main Street scene (looking south) had changed very little since the young men of the county had returned from two world wars. On the left, the Crutchfield Hotel had been torn down, and a new restaurant and parking lot had been built on the site of Waldron's first business, a tavern, operated by William G. Featherston in the 1840s. (Historian's Collection.)

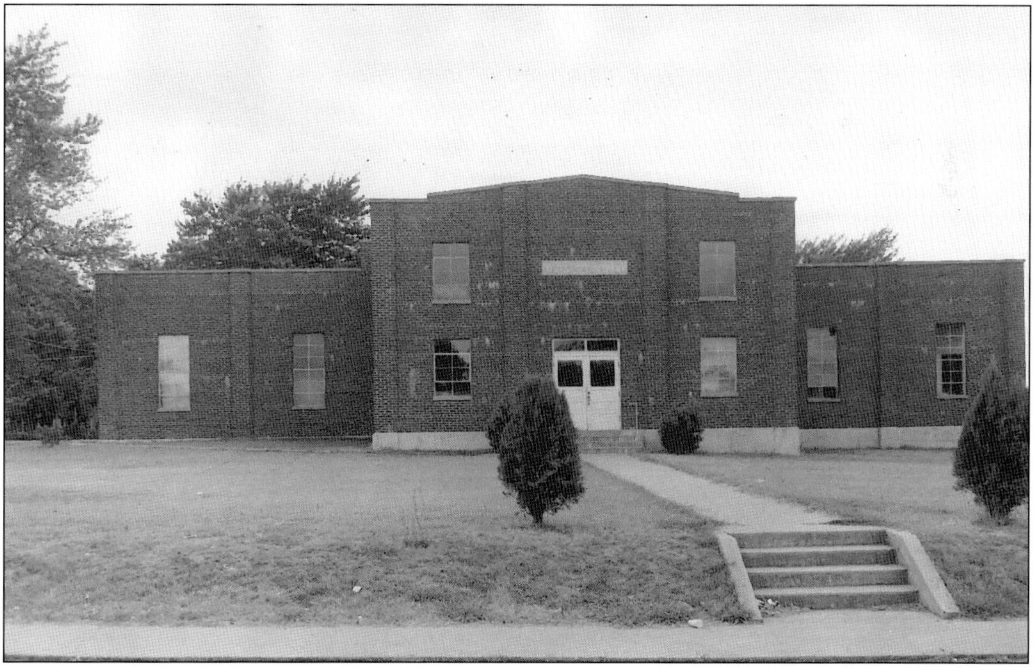
The Memorial Hall fronting Main Street in Waldron, a block north of the courthouse, was built by the efforts of veterans returning from World War II and local citizens. It has been used as a community building and for business, voting, and social activities. It is situated on the site of the old Union Hotel. (Historian's Collection.)

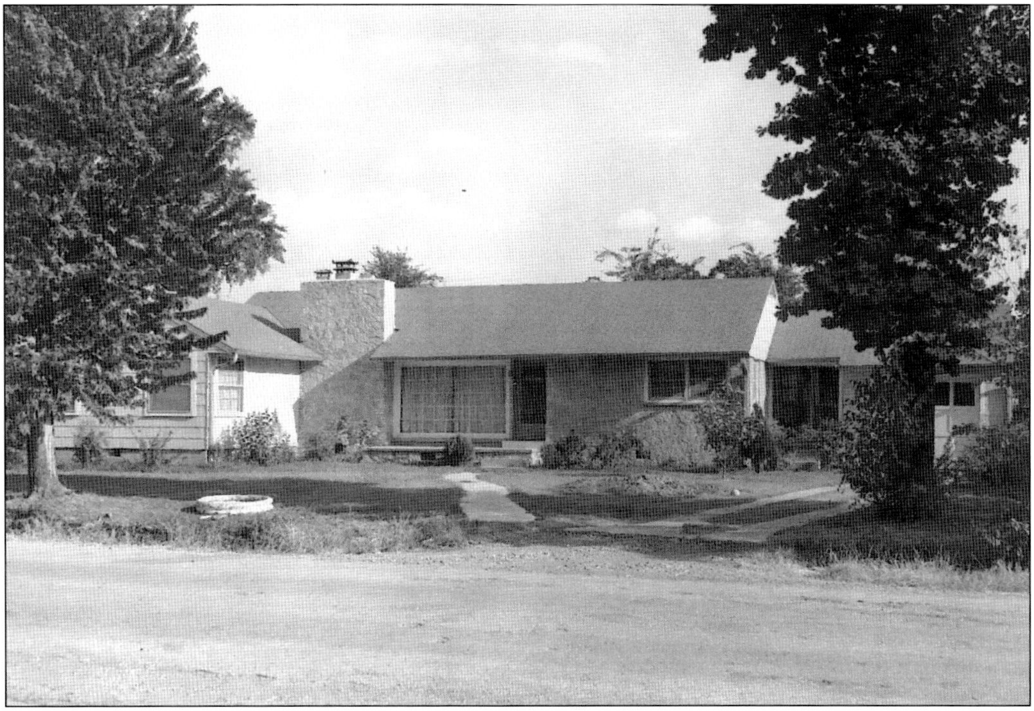

The home of Ralph and Mary Francis Hinkle Meyers on West Fourth Street exemplifies the many new homes being constructed in Waldron. Ralph Meyers was a businessman in Waldron, having owned the Meyers Auto Supply as early as 1938. (Historian's Collection.)

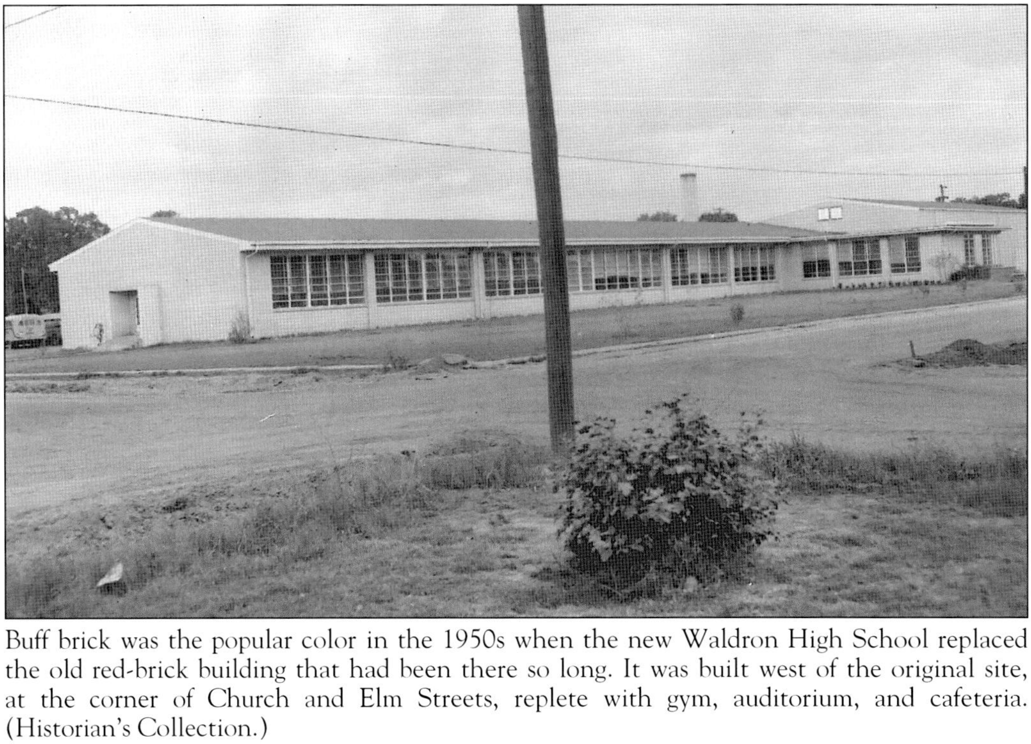

Buff brick was the popular color in the 1950s when the new Waldron High School replaced the old red-brick building that had been there so long. It was built west of the original site, at the corner of Church and Elm Streets, replete with gym, auditorium, and cafeteria. (Historian's Collection.)

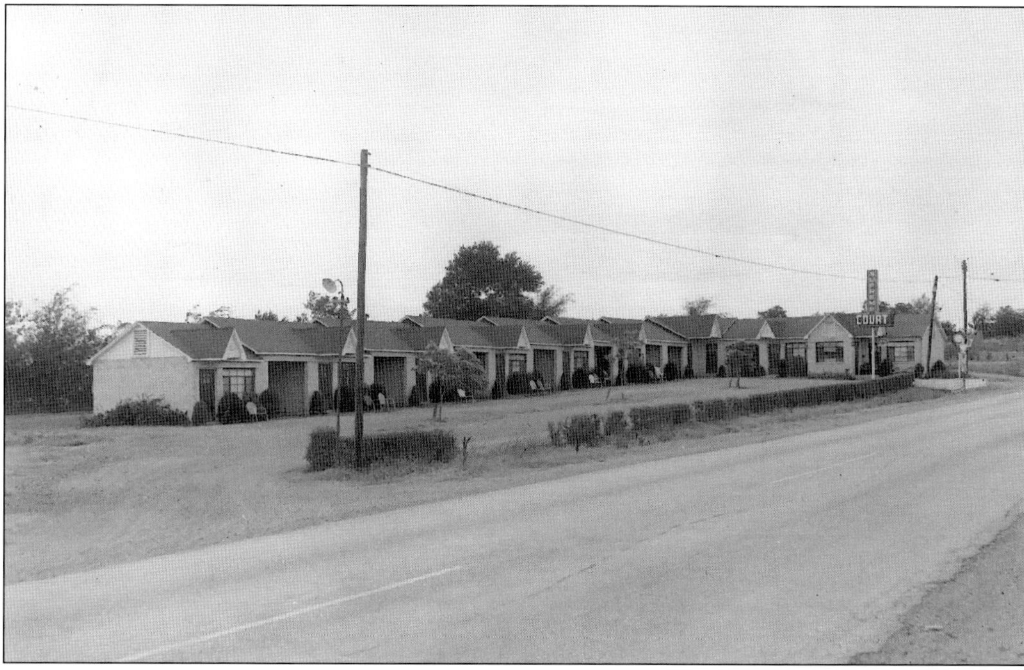

The post–World War II era saw an increase in automobiles, and with Highway 71 now paved, it led to the opening of a number of tourist courts like the Supreme Court, north of Waldron. It was constructed of buff brick with eight rooms to rent to the travelers passing by. The motor court, or a motel as we call it today, where one could drive his car to the door, brought about a rapid decline in the hotel business. (Historian's Collection.)

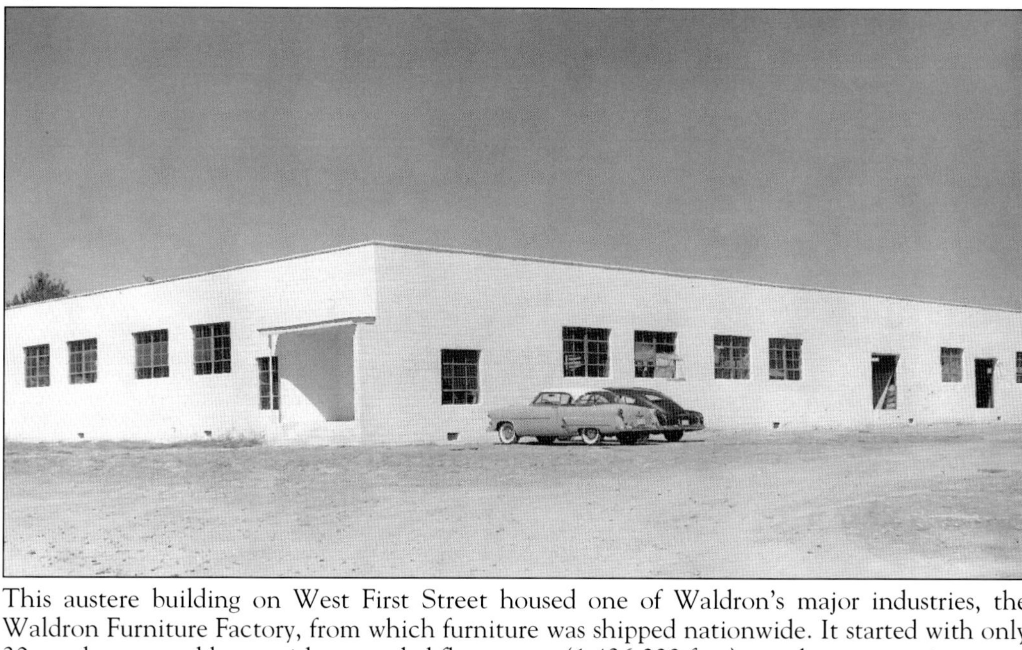

This austere building on West First Street housed one of Waldron's major industries, the Waldron Furniture Factory, from which furniture was shipped nationwide. It started with only 30 employees, and later, with expanded floor space (1,436,000 feet), employees were increased to 336 with a weekly payroll of $45,000, greatly enhancing the economic life of the county. (Historian's Collection.)

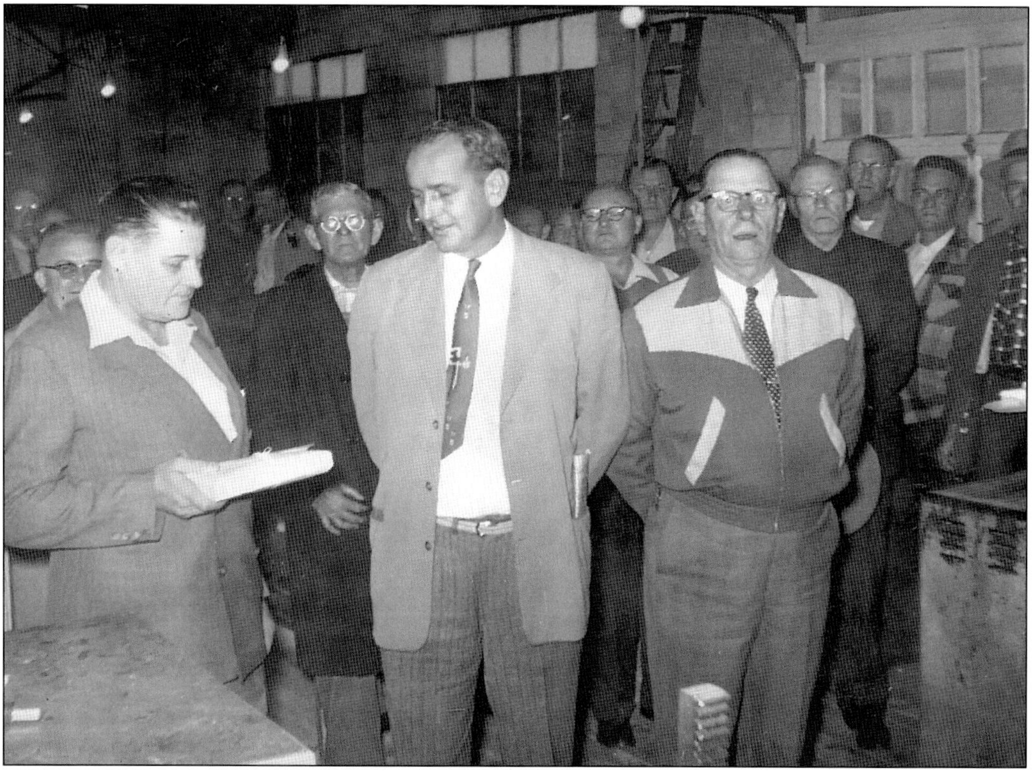

Manager Paul Rush (left) presents an award to Kenneth Oliver (center) and Ted Audas (right) inside the Waldron Furniture Factory as others look on. Ralph Meyers is directly behind Mr. Rush, and he, Kenneth Oliver, and County Judge John McCraw were the local business leaders instrumental in bringing this industry to Waldron. (Courtesy of O. Ann Oliver, Waldron.)

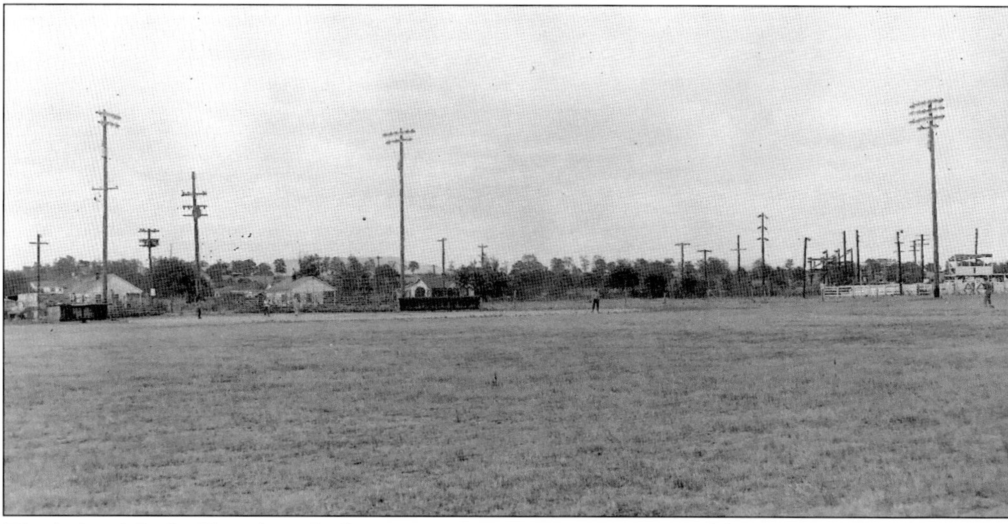

The lighted Sodie Davidson Park was a great improvement to Waldron as children could enjoy ball games, swimming, and picnicking. The land for the park was donated by Charlye Forester Davidson in honor of her husband, who was a University of Arkansas quarterback early in the century. (Historian's Collection.)

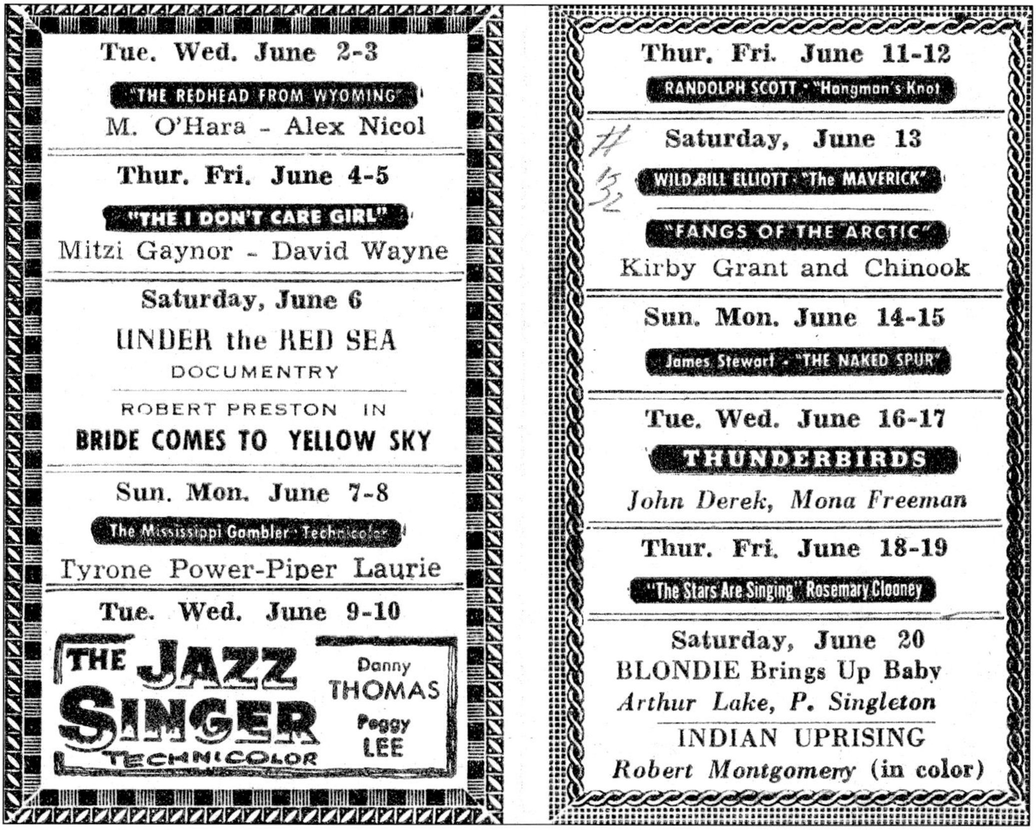
Tue. Wed. June 2-3
"THE REDHEAD FROM WYOMING"
M. O'Hara - Alex Nicol

Thur. Fri. June 4-5
"THE I DON'T CARE GIRL"
Mitzi Gaynor - David Wayne

Saturday, June 6
UNDER the RED SEA
DOCUMENTRY

ROBERT PRESTON IN
BRIDE COMES TO YELLOW SKY

Sun. Mon. June 7-8
The Mississippi Gambler - Technicolor
Tyrone Power-Piper Laurie

Tue. Wed. June 9-10
THE JAZZ SINGER
TECHNICOLOR
Danny THOMAS
Peggy LEE

Thur. Fri. June 11-12
RANDOLPH SCOTT - "Hangman's Knot"

Saturday, June 13
WILD BILL ELLIOTT - "The MAVERICK"

"FANGS OF THE ARCTIC"
Kirby Grant and Chinook

Sun. Mon. June 14-15
James Stewart - "THE NAKED SPUR"

Tue. Wed. June 16-17
THUNDERBIRDS
John Derek, Mona Freeman

Thur. Fri. June 18-19
"The Stars Are Singing" Rosemary Clooney

Saturday, June 20
BLONDIE Brings Up Baby
Arthur Lake, P. Singleton

INDIAN UPRISING
Robert Montgomery (in color)

By the mid-20th century, the population continued to decline, but from the big screen at the Scott Theater in Waldron (formerly the Pines), cares could be forgotten while listening to Rosemary Clooney belting out "The Stars are Singing," watching Tyrone Power play cards in the *Mississippi Gambler* or watching James Stewart in *The Naked Spur*. (Historian's Collection.)

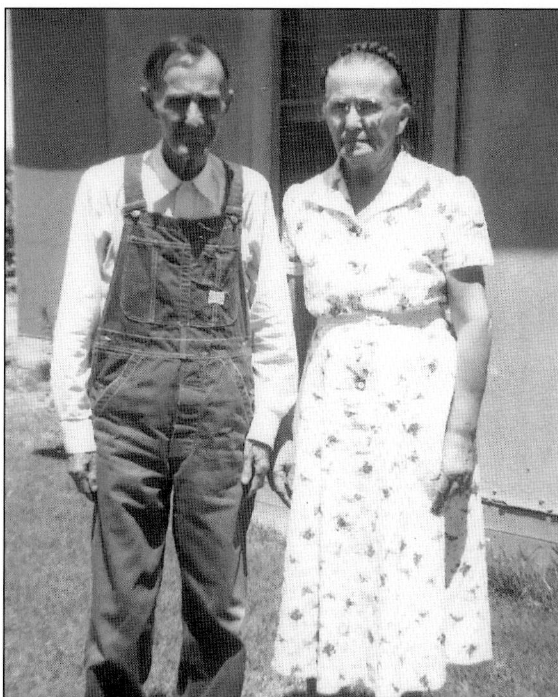

In their later years, Dick and Annie Brooks, born in the 1870s, are illustrative of small rural farmers in the county with simple tastes, who have devoted many years to the soil and to each other. She is the daughter of pioneer Andrew J. Roland of the now-extinct Cardiff settlement. (Historian's Collection.)

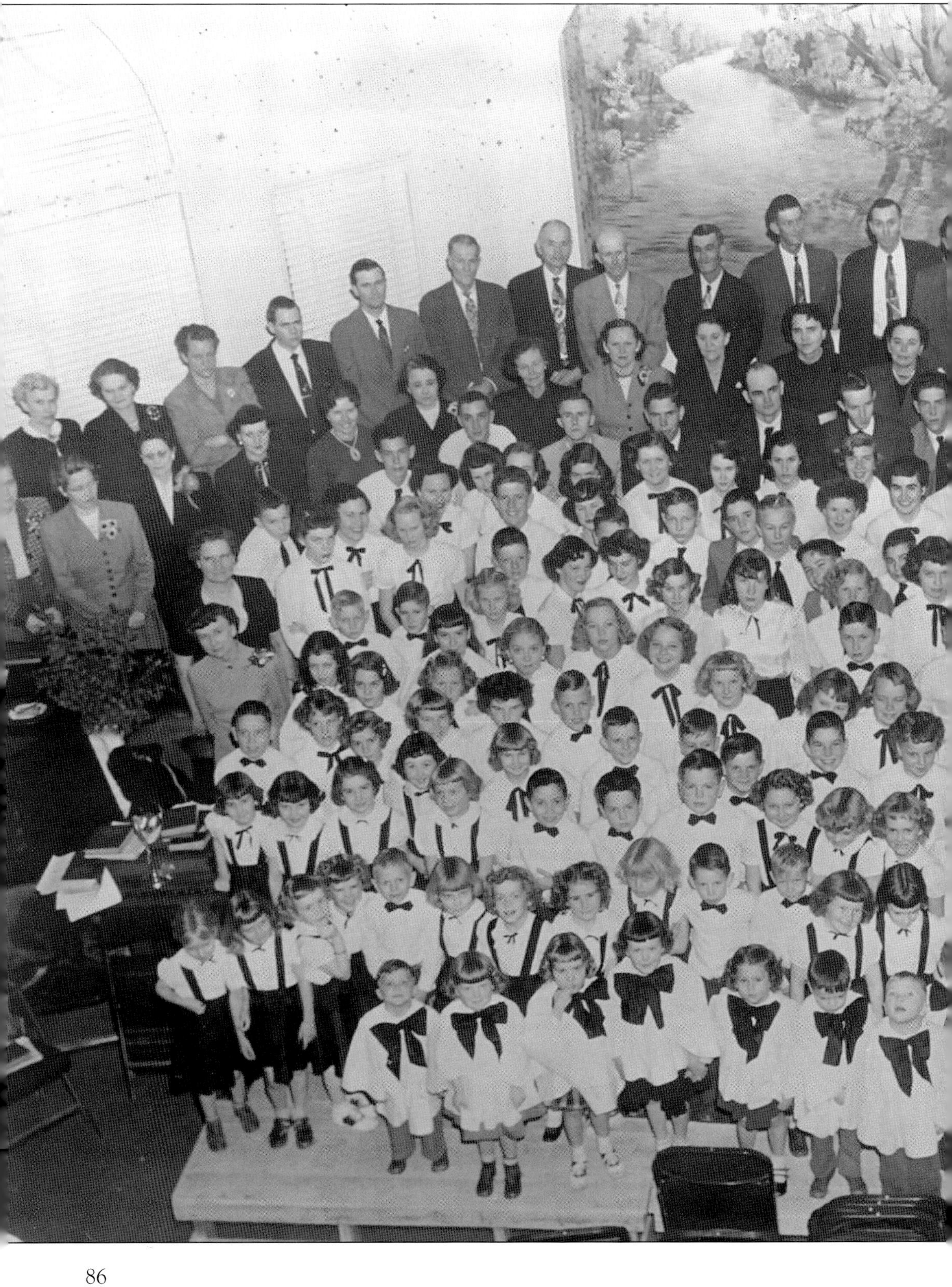

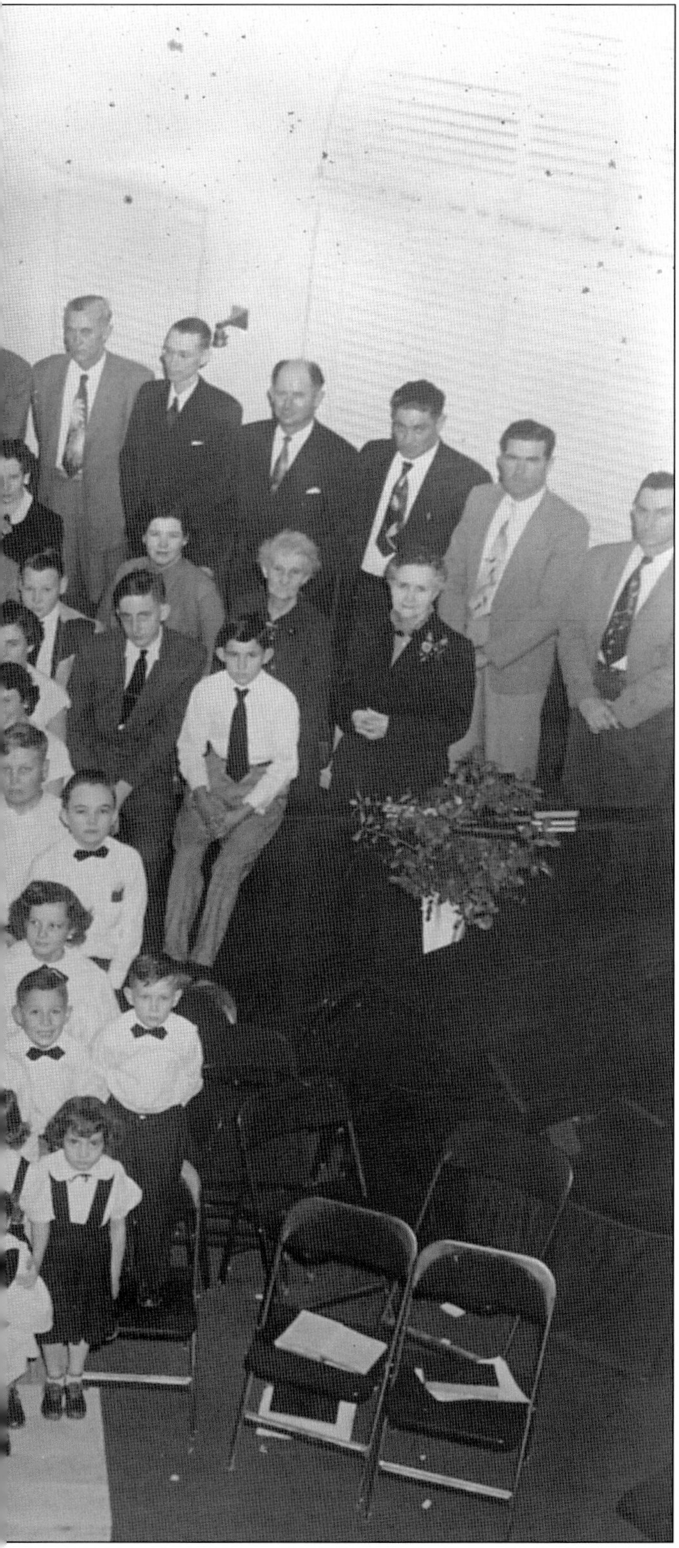

The music programs of the First Baptist Church in Waldron, Arkansas, have always been of superior quality. The 1950 Yuletide choir was no exception. The choir director included voices from all age groups—the primary to the adult members. In this image, you may recognize people from many walks of life, businessmen, public school teachers, Sunday school teachers, and civic leaders. A pause to reflect upon the large number of youth in this image brings to mind the sharp contrast with this church today. Unfortunately, there has been a sharp decline in the number of young people attending church within the past 25 years, not only in this church but in churches across America. (Courtesy, O. Ann Oliver)

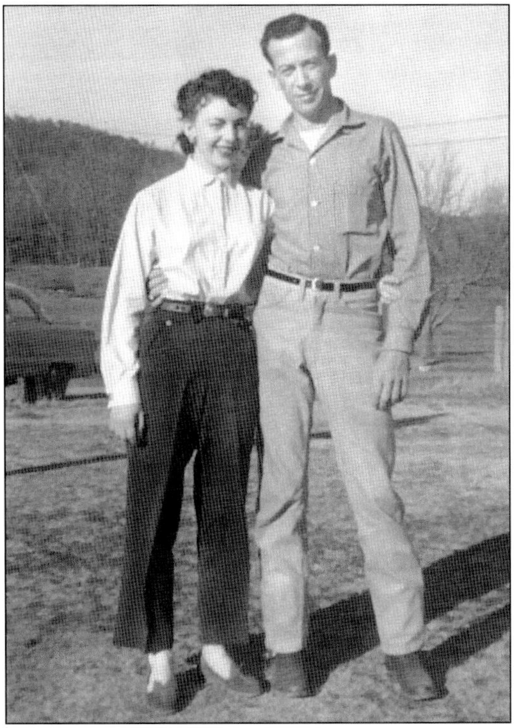

The pine tree–covered rolling hills are typical of the landscape east of Waldron on the Self farm. The land behind the couple shows evidence of earlier clearing and fruit tree planting, while the electric pole on the extreme left proclaims the coming of electricity to the rural area. This was the first visit to Arkansas for Iowa-born Virginia Mae Peet with the man who became her husband, James Alvin Eugene Self, the son of Arvil Self of the Greenridge community. The ankle length, flared leg slacks worn by Virginia gave way within in a few years to the wider flare of the bell-bottom slacks. They had a daughter who was born and died in 1956 in Muskogee, Oklahoma, and a son, Bryce W. Self, born in Tahlequah, Oklahoma, who is currently employed by the Peninsula Christian Center at Redwood City, California. (Courtesy of Bryce W. Self.)

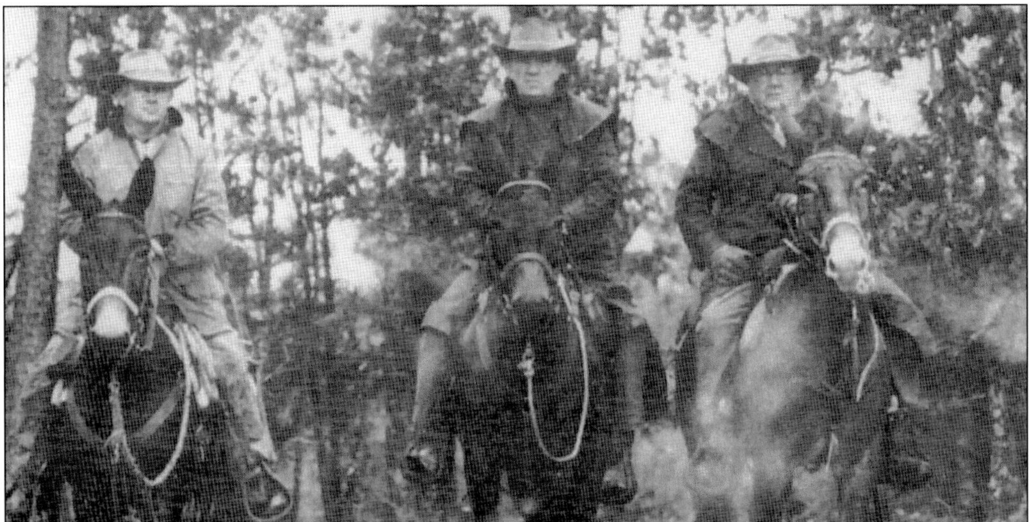

Reminiscent of the desperado days in the county when outlaws were heading for the border on their Rasputin mules is the image of Judge William R. Wilson (center), Joe Huie (right), and Dick Huie (left). William R. Wilson is fondly remembered as "Billy Roy." He is a graduate of Waldron High School, a loyal Democrat, and was appointed to a federal judgeship by President Bill Clinton in 1993. These three "hard looking cases" are symbolic of the 1800s, when farmers throughout the county plowed their fields with a gun in easy reach, and many were murdered for various reasons. Political tensions were elevated to such heights after the Civil War, and so many murders occurred that the governor had to send troops as a show of force that these actions were not to be tolerated. (Courtesy of Judge Wilson.)

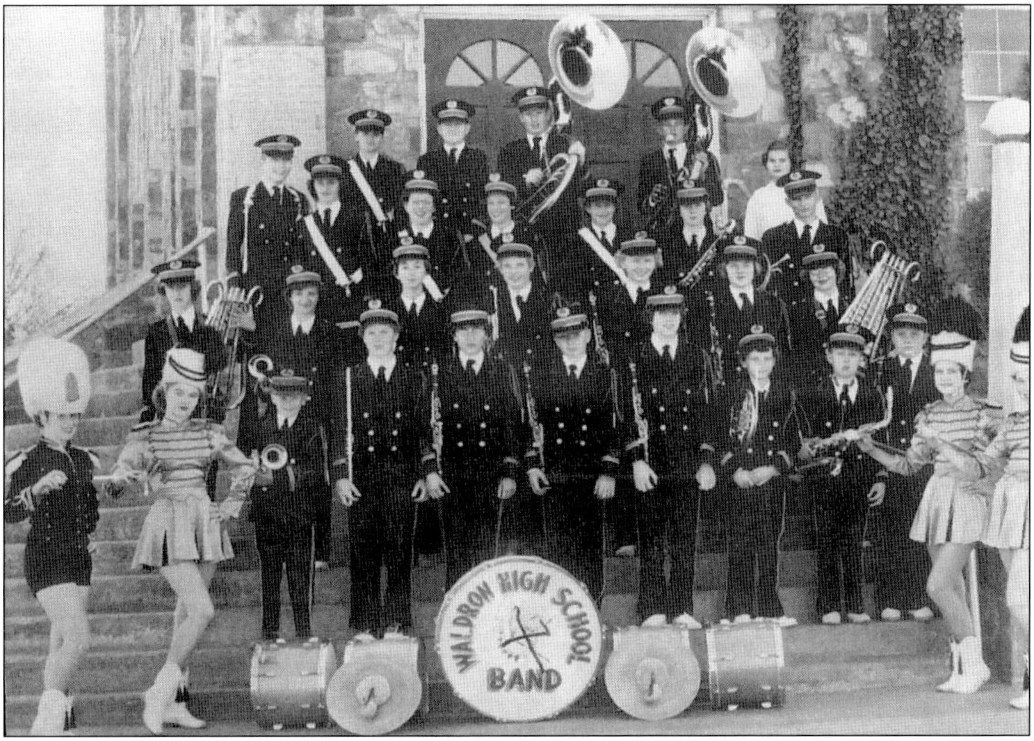

The Waldron High School Band poses across from the school grounds on the steps of the Nazarene Church for the 1955 school yearbook image. In comparison with today, they were a small band, but powerful when they played their alma mater, "Oh Waldron High we'll sing your praises tonight . . ." Pictured on the bottom left is the drum majorette, Helen Marie May, and majorettes, Nancy Baber, Sharon Jackson, and Becky Rackley; and at the top row, upper far right with the bass horn is Bennie Newberry, and the teacher (in white blouse) is Ms. Ann Hudgens. Helen Marie May is the daughter of Ms. Lorene May. She married Mr. Johnny Ward and resides in Waldron. Bennie Newberry is the son of Harvey Lester Newberry and Gertrude Rhyne, and after retiring from El Paso Natural Gas Company, he returned to make his home in Waldron. (Historian's Collection.)

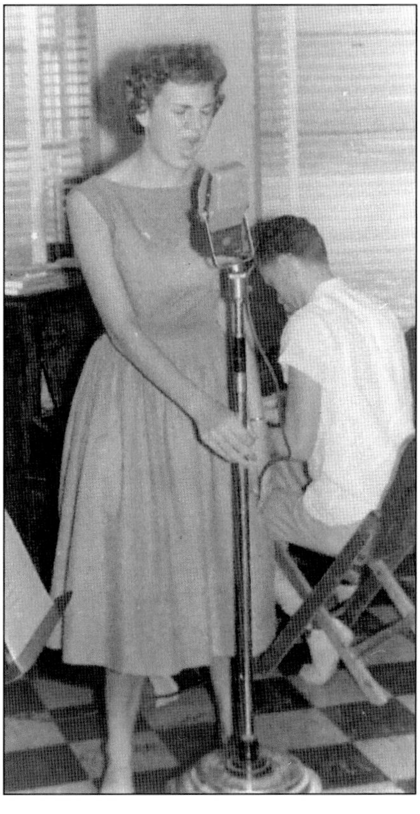

Holding onto the microphone belting out the "St. Louis Blues" in a recording session while in college at Russellville, Arkansas, is the musically talented Lou Nell McCraw of Parks, Arkansas. Accompanying her at the upright piano on the diamond designed black and white tile floor is Ronald Fields. (Courtesy of Lou Nell McCraw.)

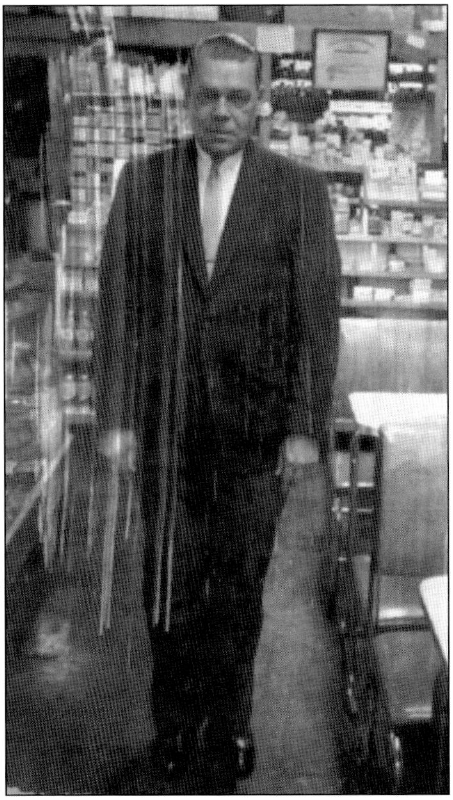

This image is of James Maurice Harvey (1902–1975) standing near the counter in the Waldron Drug store. It was established by his father, James M. Harvey, in 1906, on the east side of Main Street, next door to the Bank of Waldron. The Harveys, a highly respected family, compassionately served the people of the county for 60 years. (Historian's Collection.)

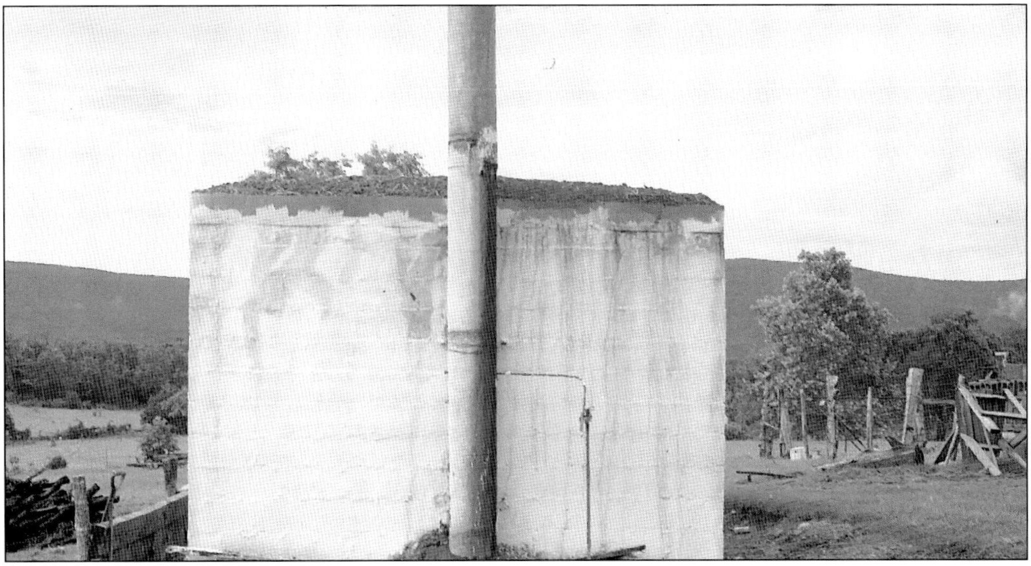

This round object with a smoke pipe built to the south of Poteau Mountain (in background) is a farm charcoal burner constructed to utilize cull hardwoods and convert the residue to a marketable product. The idea was developed by Commissioner (Rev.) John Evans with the Poteau River Soil Conservation District as a part of the woodland conservation effort. A commercial project was generated from this idea and has been used for the past 40 years. (Courtesy of O. Ann Evans Oliver.)

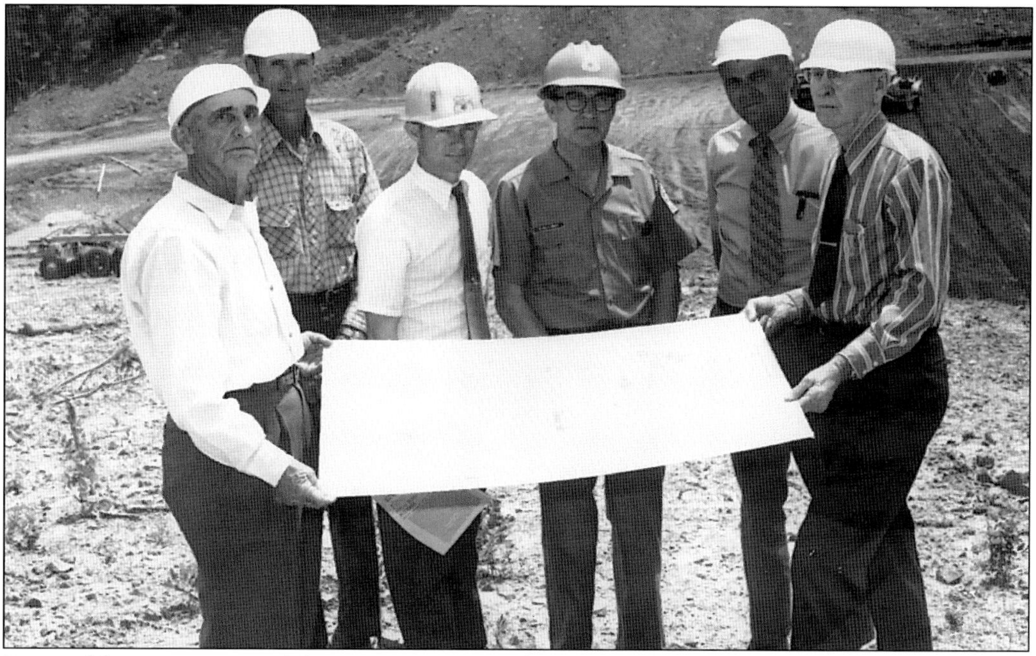

Pictured here are some of the men reviewing plans to establish a series of watershed lakes to catch excessive rainwater instead of allowing it to flow into waterways, subsequently flooding the area. Rev. John Evans (far right) traveled extensively in the 1960s, working with different governmental agencies to establish this program and served as chairman of the Poteau Watershed Improvement District. Other local citizens commissioned by a chancery judge to serve as commissioners in the early stages of this program were John Kopf, Willie Denton, O.H. Strickland, and Winton Ray Nelson. (Courtesy of O. Ann Evans Oliver.)

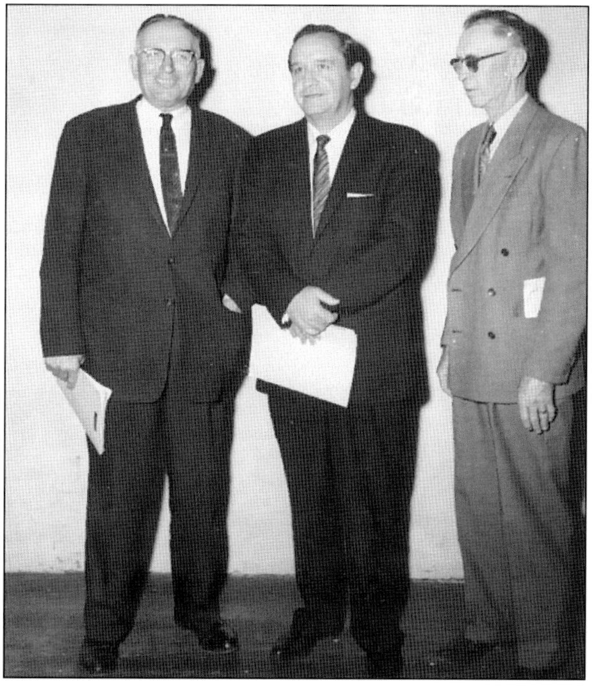

This image reflects the early conferences necessary to establish the Poteau River Watershed District flood prevention program. Captured during a conference are, from left to right, as follows: Dr. Church, Governor Orval E. Faubus (served from 1955 to 1967), and Rev. John E. Evans. (Courtesy O. Ann Evans Oliver.)

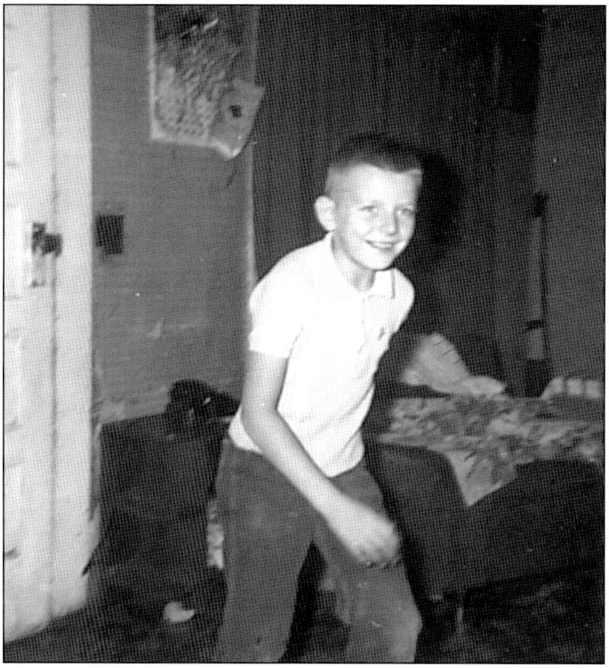

Young Mike Gray is working off Thanksgiving Dinner by showing off the latest dance craze, the "twist." During this time, the revolutionary musical artist Elvis Presley also had a popular song "Come on Baby, Let's Do the Twist." A common phrase heard during this time was "Twist and Shout." Michael Dee Gray is the son of J.W. Gray Jr. (Historian's Collection.)

STATEMENT

BANK OF WALDRON

WALDRON, ARKANSAS

SEPTEMBER 30, 1963

ASSETS

Loans and Discounts		$1,597,728.54
Federal Reserve Bank Stock		4,500.00
Banking House		1,500.00
Furniture and Fixtures		8,400.00
Other Real Estate		12,800.00
Cash and Due from Banks	$1,341,157.77	
U. S. Government Obligations	1,173,947.25	
State, County and Municipal Bonds	730,543.78	
Obligations of Federal Agencies	74,375.00	3,320,023.80
		$4,944,952.34

LIABILITIES

Capital	$ 50,000.00
Surplus	100,000.00
Undivided Profits	209,298.58
Reserved for Taxes	10,200.00
Interest Collected—Not Earned	7,279.72
Deposits	4,568,174.04
	$4,944,952.34

The oldest financial institution in the county, The Bank of Waldron, opened its doors in a corner room of the Continental Hotel in 1901. Shortly thereafter, the bank built a two-story building two doors south, at the corner of Main and Danville Streets in Waldron, where they remained for many years. They have enjoyed continued success for almost a century and are looking forward to servicing the citizens of Waldron in the 21st century. (Historian's Collection.)

Seen here is a formal portrait of Byron Scudder (B.S.) Hinkle (1893–1973), former beloved county agent and state representative. Mr. Hinkle is remembered in baggy trousers, with a worn felt hat and smoking a pipe. He traveled over the county for years tending to sick animals and offering advice on bettering the farmers plight. When Lake Hinkle was built, it was named in his honor. He is the father of local residents Juanita Hinkle and Mary Frances Myers, highly respected ladies. Juanita resides in the family home. (Historian's Collection.)

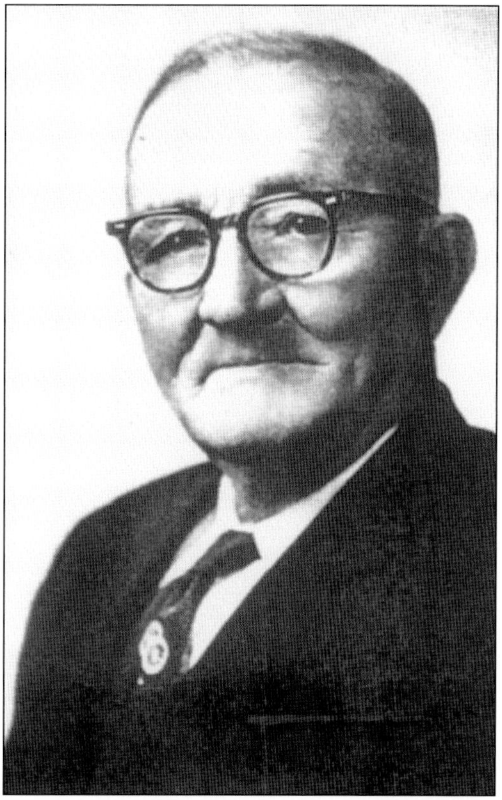

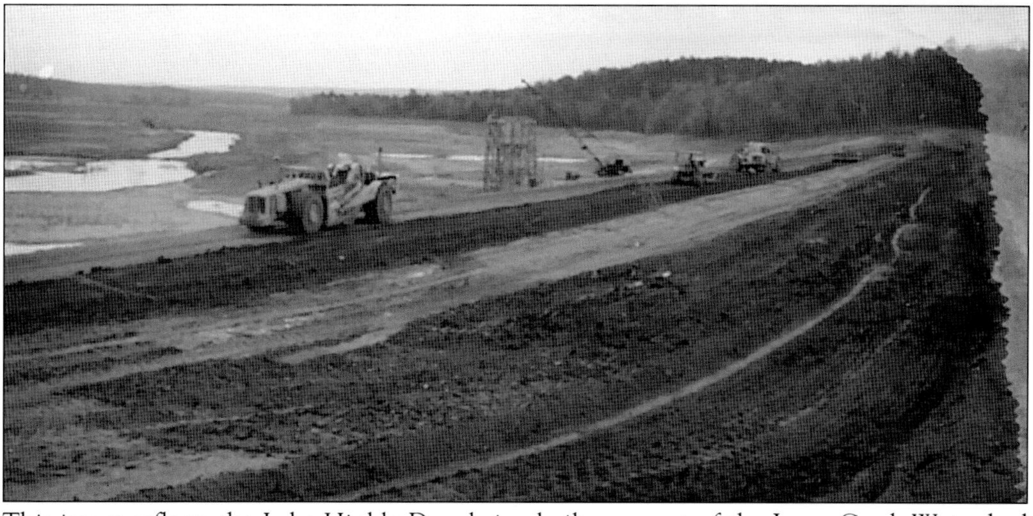

This image reflects the Lake Hinkle Dam being built as a part of the Jones Creek Watershed Development project. It is a multi-purpose flood-detention recreation structure in the Poteau River Watershed. It was built by local project sponsors in cooperation with Arkansas Game and Fish Commission, U.S. Forest Service, and Soil Conservation Service. Locals can enjoy fishing for crappie, bass, or channel catfish, and swimming or camping at a nearby recreation area. It was named for B.S. Hinkle and dedicated on October 15, 1971. The dam is 76 feet high, has a water surface of 965 acres, has a flood storage area of 5,000 acre feet, and drains 7,162 acres. (Courtesy of O. Ann Oliver.)

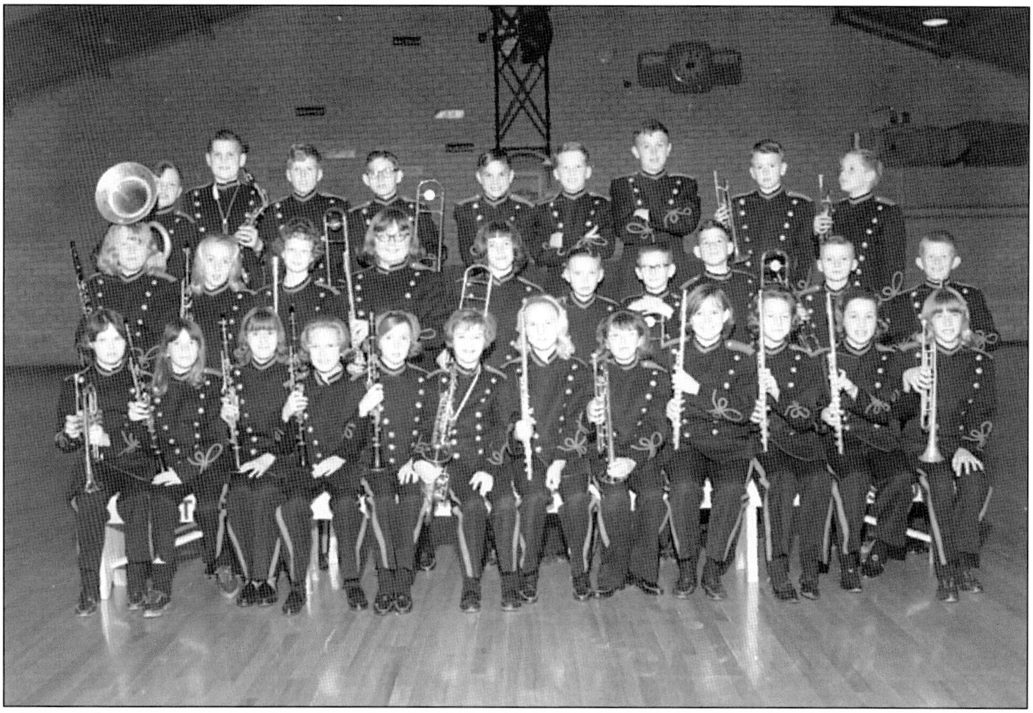

The Waldron Junior High Band poses with their instruments on the gleaming hardwood floor of the gymnasium. This band worked hard marching and playing their instruments to prepare for the Waldron Senior High Band, where they would have the honor of marching at halftime at football games, and in 4th of July and Christmas parades. (Courtesy of O. Ann Oliver.)

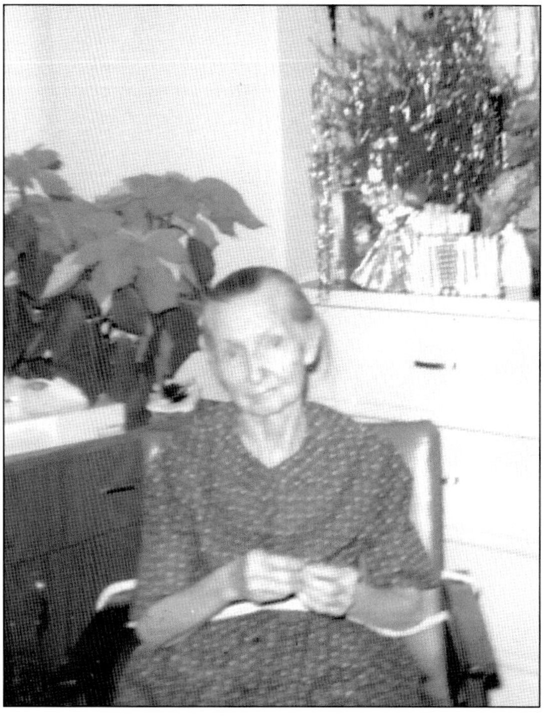

In the later years of her life, Hattie May Mitchell spends Christmas at the Pinewood Nursing Home in Waldron. This gracious lady was a stockholder in the Bank of Waldron and wife of a former Mayor "Seab" Mitchell. She is a second generation Scott Countian having been born in the county in 1882. (Historian's Collection.)

Three

Reaching for Y2K 1980–1999

The images in the following pages provide a view of how far we have come, as we reach for the year 2000—a new millennium. In many ways, the people of rural Scott County have changed little, in spite of the advent of the automobile, railroads, airplanes, space travel, radio, television, the internet, fast food restaurants, new homes, and greater economic advantages.

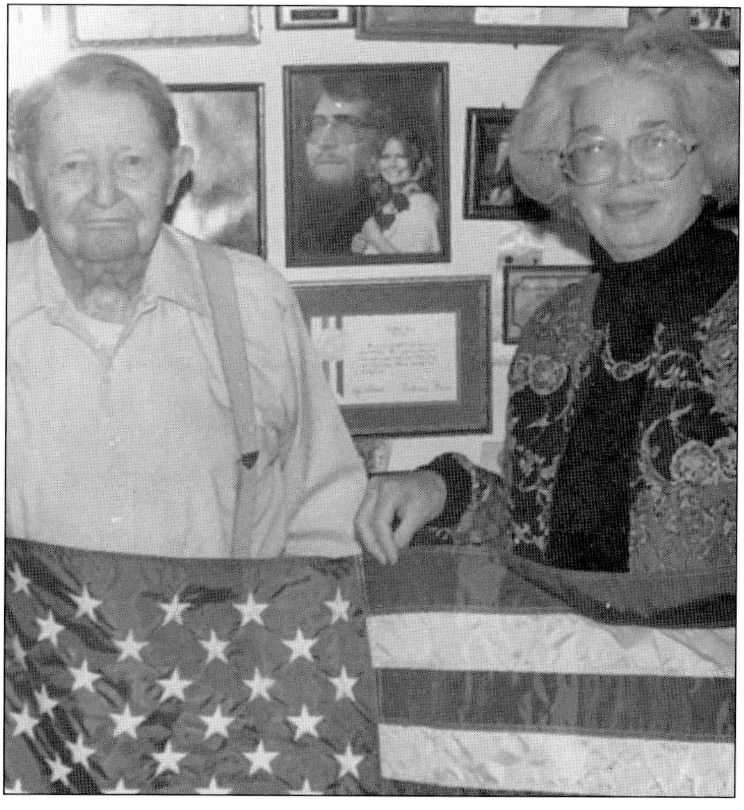

Positioned in front of a wall filled with family pictures and certificates, Oscar Lee Cauthron is the active 103 year old who resides a short distance from the original Cauthron home site. He is the great grandson of Walter Cauthron, in whose home the first county seat was established in 1833. Holding the American flag with him is historian Wanda M. Gray. (Courtesy of Ron Mullenax, Historian's Collection.)

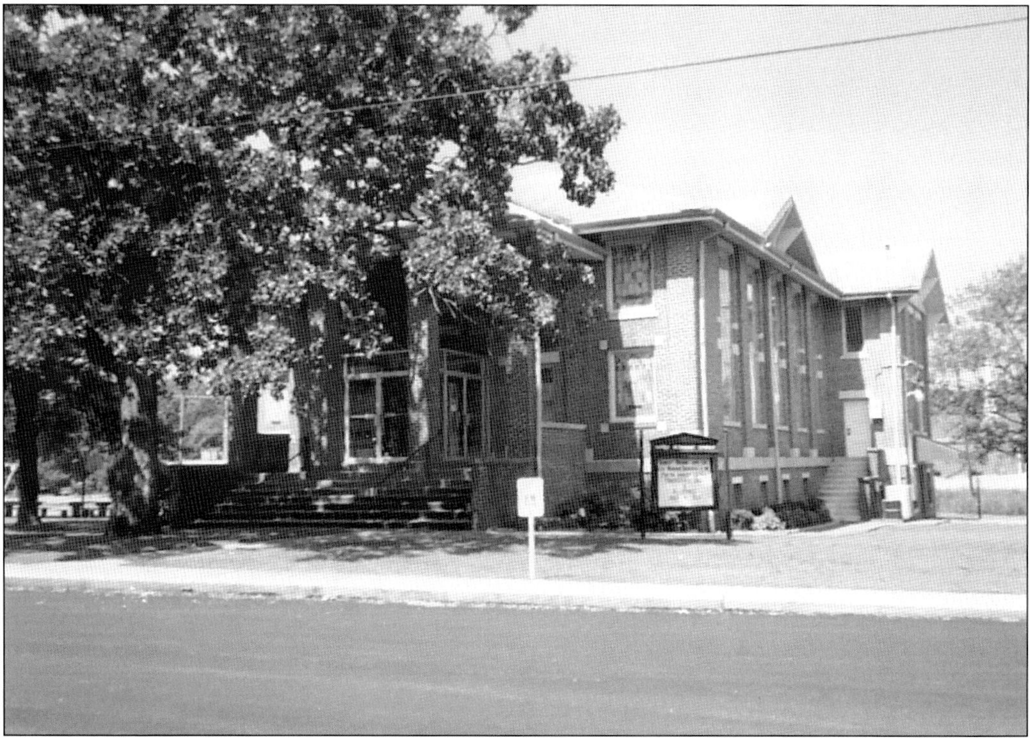

This majestic red-brick Methodist church building, with memorial stained-glass windows in the sanctuary, has actively endured for 80 years. It was built in 1920 across the street from the original church and organized in 1869. Five acres were donated in 1870 by A.C. Bernie of Fort Smith for a parsonage, church, and cemetery. The founder of Waldron, W.G. Featherston, is buried in this small burial ground, which has long been inactive. (Historian's Collection.)

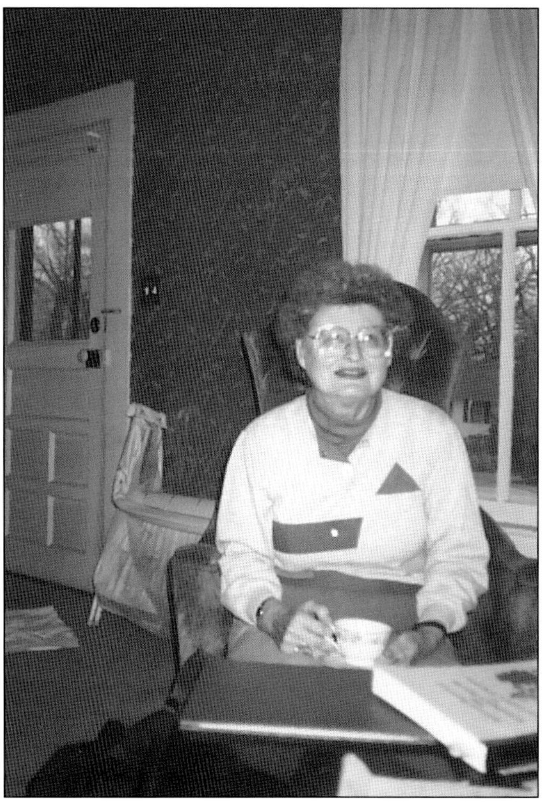

Caught relaxing, Reba Nell Bethel Bergman enjoys refreshments while attending the Heritage Day Reception for Chief John Ross of the Keetoowah Band of Cherokee Indians at the historic Farnsworth House. Of Cherokee heritage, she is also a descendant of murdered pioneer settler James Monroe Bethel and his son, Henry Clay Bethel, and his son, Virgil Bethel. As organist of the Methodist church in Waldron, she furthers the musical heritage of the family. (Historian's Collection.)

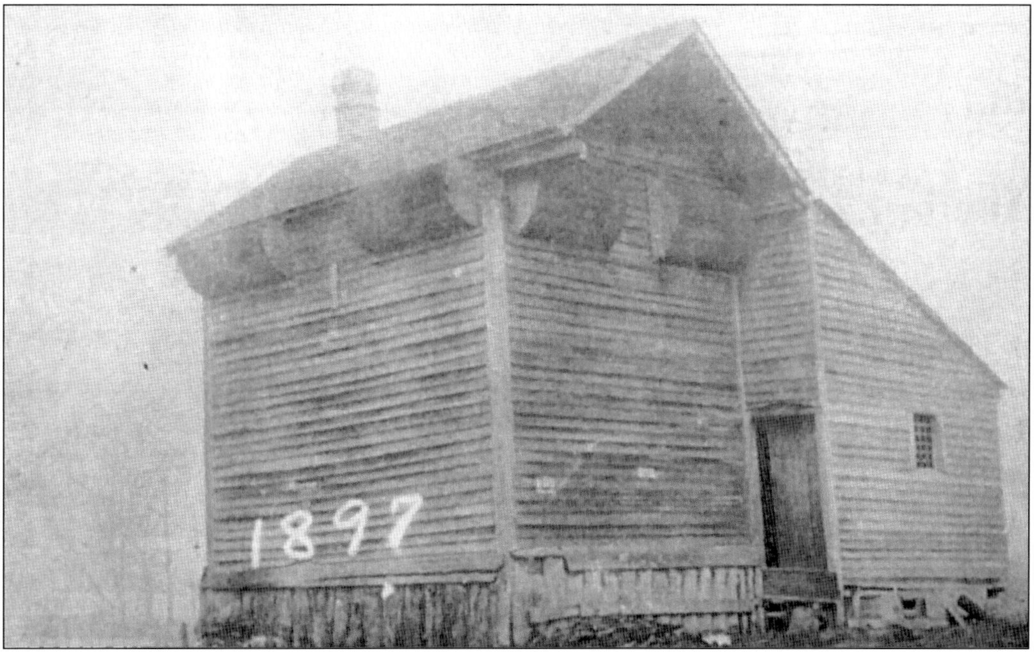

This crude, wooden-framed jail was plagued with jail breaks and had sheriffs tolerant of Saturday night drunks. It was torn down in 1905 and replaced with a stone building, under the Judge W.A. Bates' administration in 1907. The building still stands and houses the Historical Society. When the 1934 courthouse was built, it had a jail on the third floor that was used for about 50 years. (Historian's Collection.)

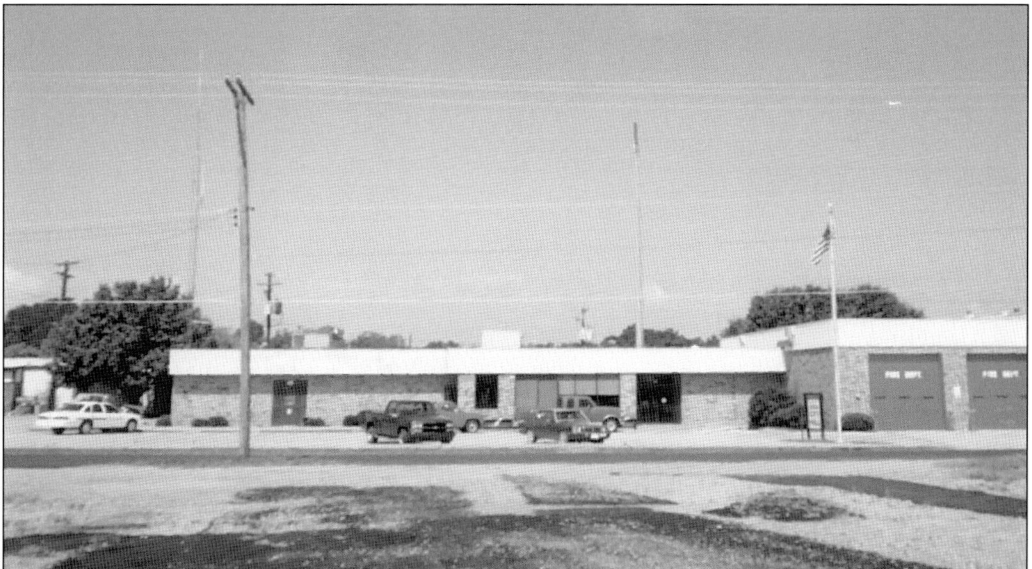

From the old jail to the new one in the Waldron City Hall, this variegated red and white brick building with the flat roof was built under the Major L.R. Sawyer administration. Behind the brown door on the left is the jail, which is leased to the county. It fronts east on Featherston Street, and the vacant lot east of City Hall was the home of the last cotton gin in the city. (Historian's Collection.)

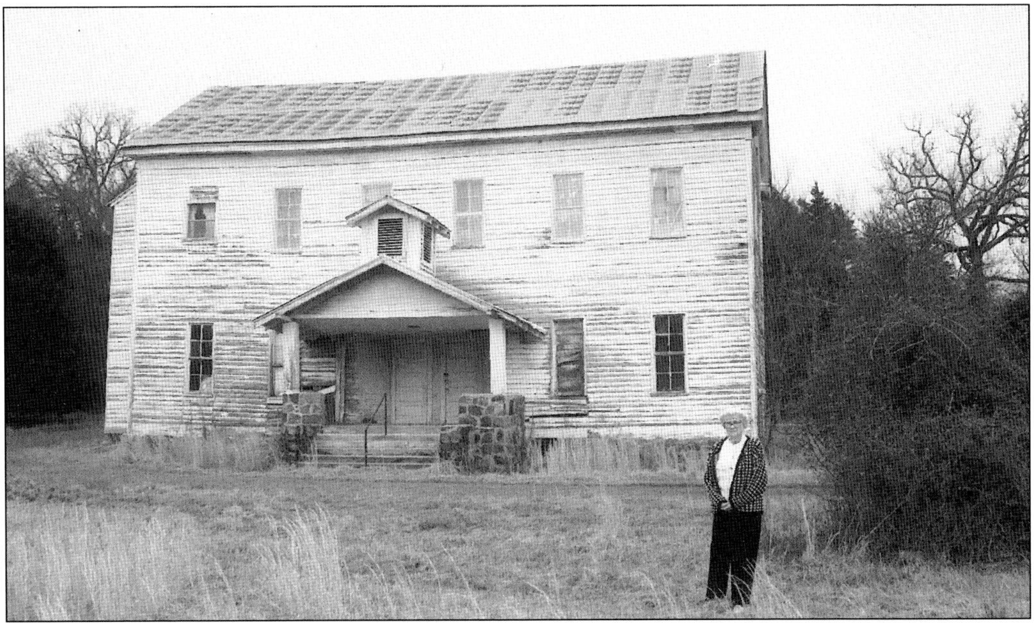

This early-20th-century, two-story Cauthron School was once the only high school in the county. Anne Shannon Demarest returned to visit places of her childhood in 1980. Since the school consolidation era of the 1940s, the first floor has been used as a community center, and the second floor has been the home of the Cauthron Masonic Lodge. This fine old structure is in need of care and maintenance to see it through the next century. (Historian's Collection)

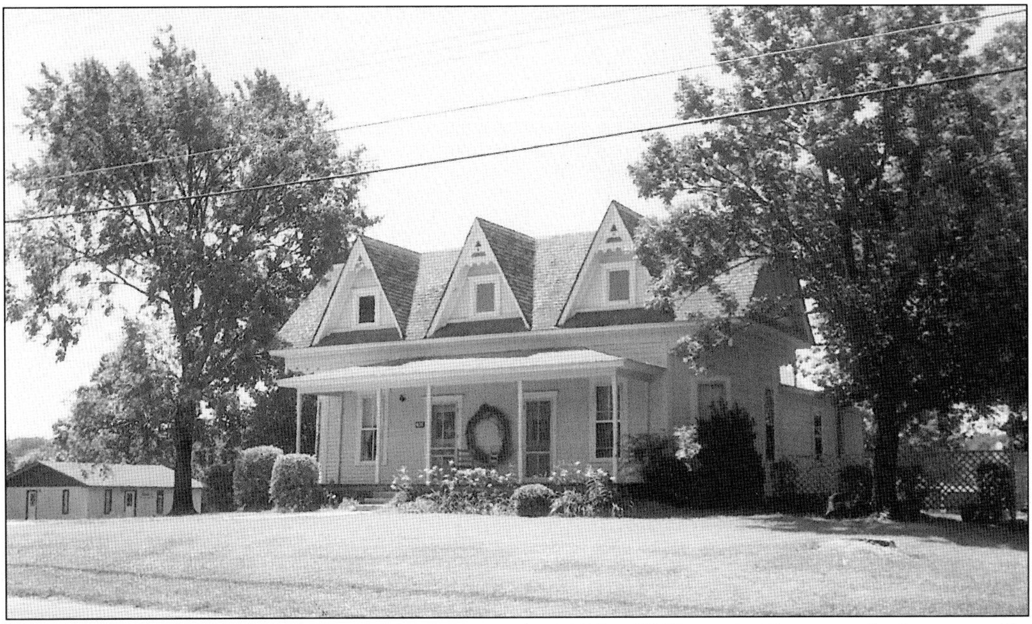

The historic Farnsworth House was built around 1907 by William G. Farnsworth. It originally had only the two large front rooms across the front and two small porches, but about mid-century, owner Herbert Castleberry added two rooms, a bath, and a back porch. It has a large dug well accessible on the back porch. This house was restored by Wanda M. Gray in 1980 and is currently owned by Mrs. Maurice Hunt. (Historian's Collection)

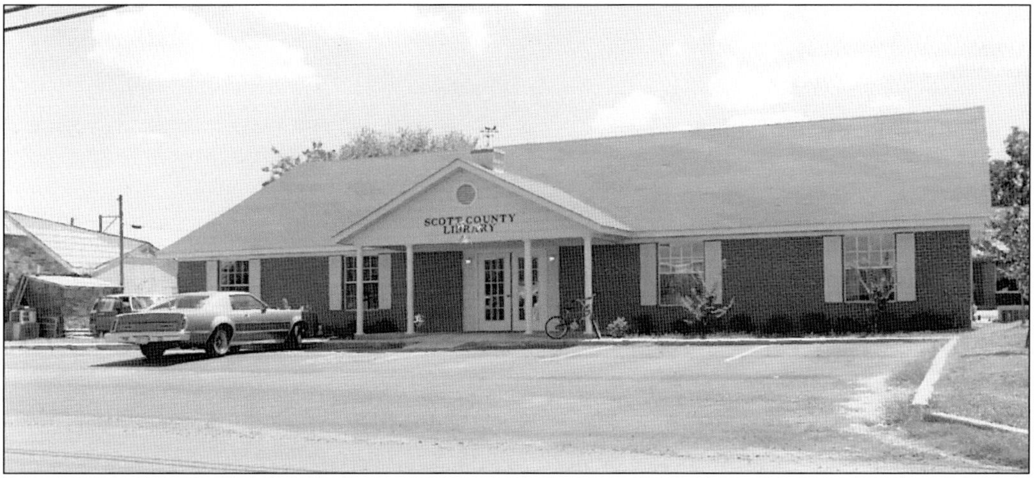

A great improvement to the landscape downtown and an outstanding contribution to the citizenry of the county was made when this 3,200-square-foot red-brick library was built on West Second Street, a block from the courthouse. This property joins the property of the old jail, housing the Historical Society. The driving forces behind the building of the library were the president of the library board, Wanda M. Gray, and County Judge Jim Hunt, who worked tirelessly to insure this educational institution became a reality. (Historian's Collection.)

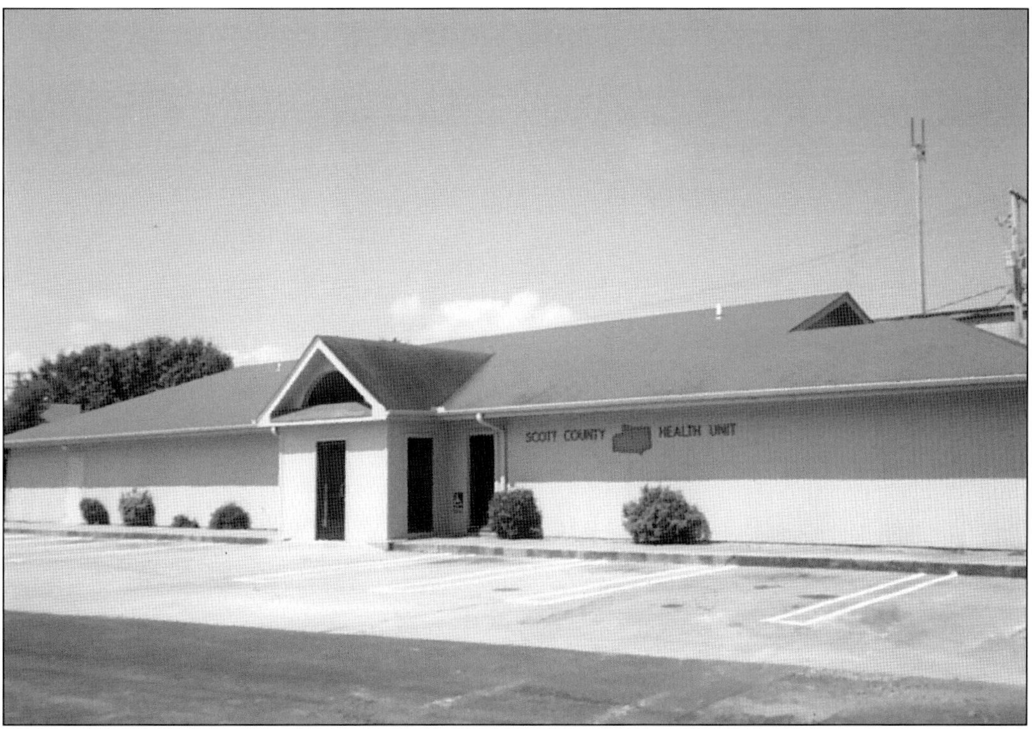

This building houses the Scott County Health Unit, which provides inexpensive medical service to local residents, especially the young and the elderly. This attractive building was first used by the Scott County Bank, but they soon outgrew it. It fronts Featherston Street, which runs parallel to Main Street and is directly across the street from the Italian family restaurant, Little Italy.(Historian's Collection.)

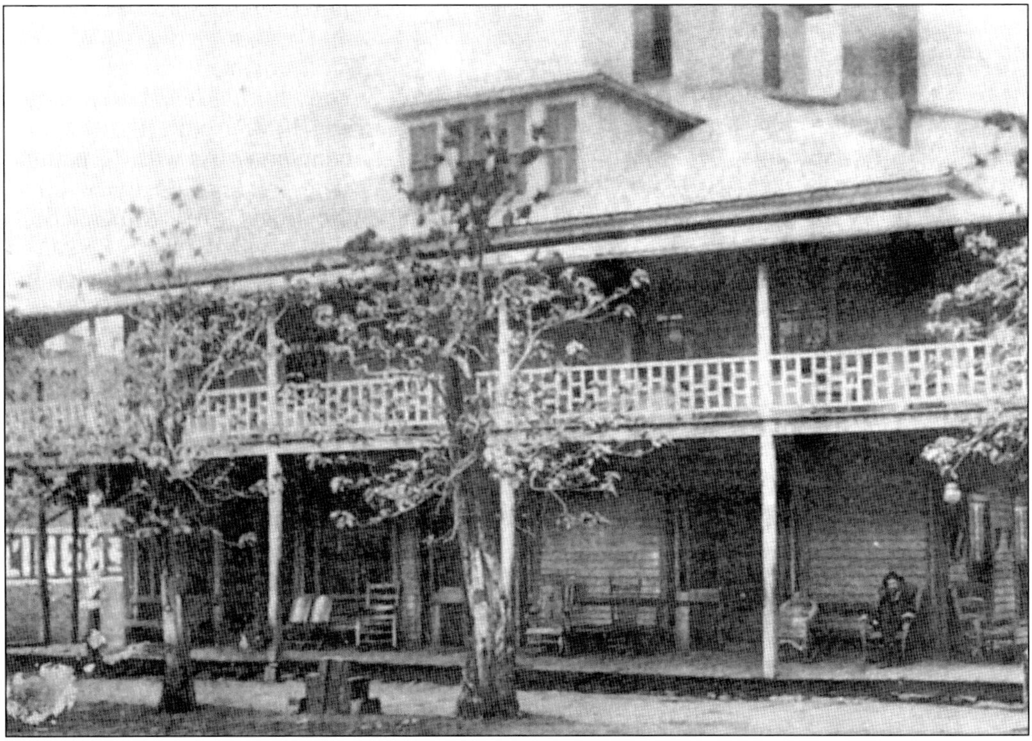

On the second story balcony of the Continental Hotel, patrons could enjoy a scene of the town up and down Main Street. One gentleman is enjoying a rocking chair on the porch, where he could greet passersby and spit tobacco juice onto the dust-covered Red River Road. This building was built by Free Malone in 1878 and has housed a bank and a post office. It was built near the site of the earliest business, the Featherston Tavern, if not on it. Today, it would be located directly east of and across Main Street from the Donut Shop, which is in the old First National Bank Building. (Historian's Collection.)

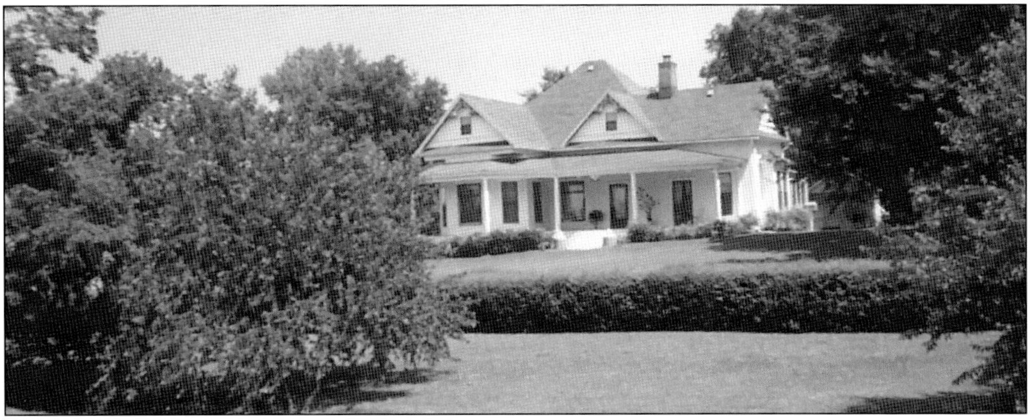

Edgar M. Fuller was a local businessman who owned and operated the first Chevrolet dealership. He also operated the Fuller-Judy Hardware Company for many years, which was located on Main Street next door to the Pines Theater (known today as the Scott County Theater). This building is located within two houses of where William G. Featherston built his home in the 1840s. In the 1880s, this home was restored by Mr. and Mrs. Dailey. (Historian's Collection.)

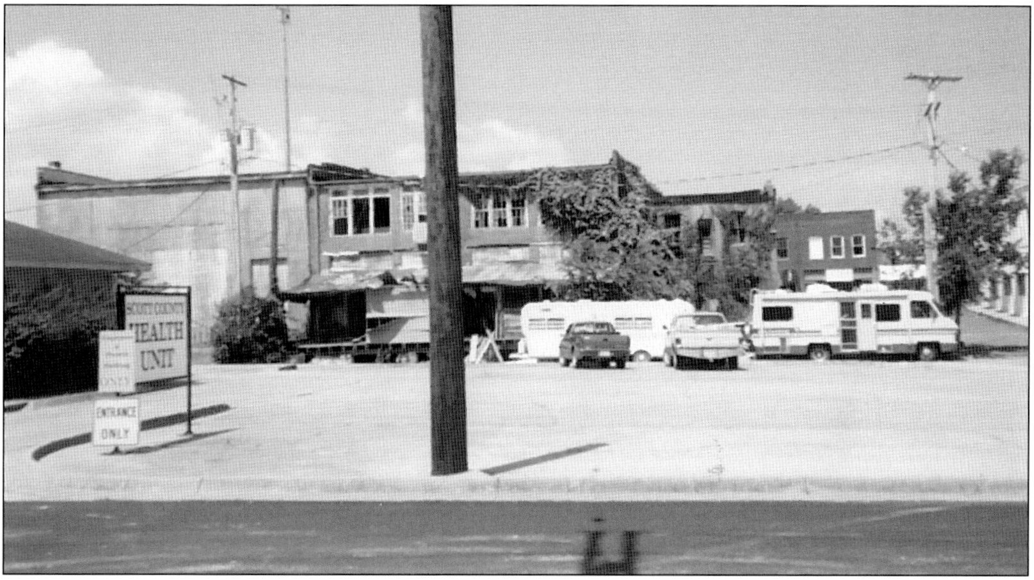

The rear view of the Fuller-Judy Mercantile Store on Main Street shows the ravages of time, but the building is now under new ownership and is being restored. In years past, this store carried an inventory of everything from coffins to harnesses for horses. The small building on the right is so badly deteriorated that it may have to be torn down. The motor home and the travel trailer in the alley between the Health Unit Parking Lot and the buildings are illustrative of the affluent leisurely lifestyle of the 1990s. (Historian's Collection.)

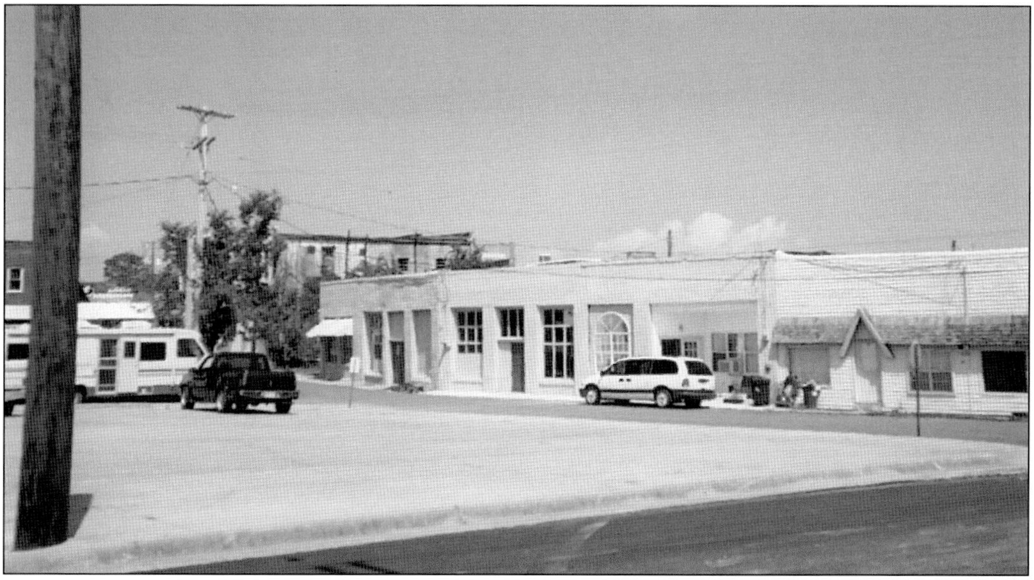

These white buildings, in the first block of Danville Street (formerly Winchester) off of Main Street, have been restored by a building contractor Paul Marrone in the last decade. The building on the right, in recent past, was the grocery store of Olgie Castleberry Crowley. The large building to the left of the white van was the Wayne Elliott Hardware Store. The building with the awning was the Hughes Insurance Office, more recently the Arkansas Headquarters for the Keetoowah Band of Cherokee Indians and, historically, in the 1890s, it was the Hansel Davis and T.J. Center Meat Market. (Historian's Collection.)

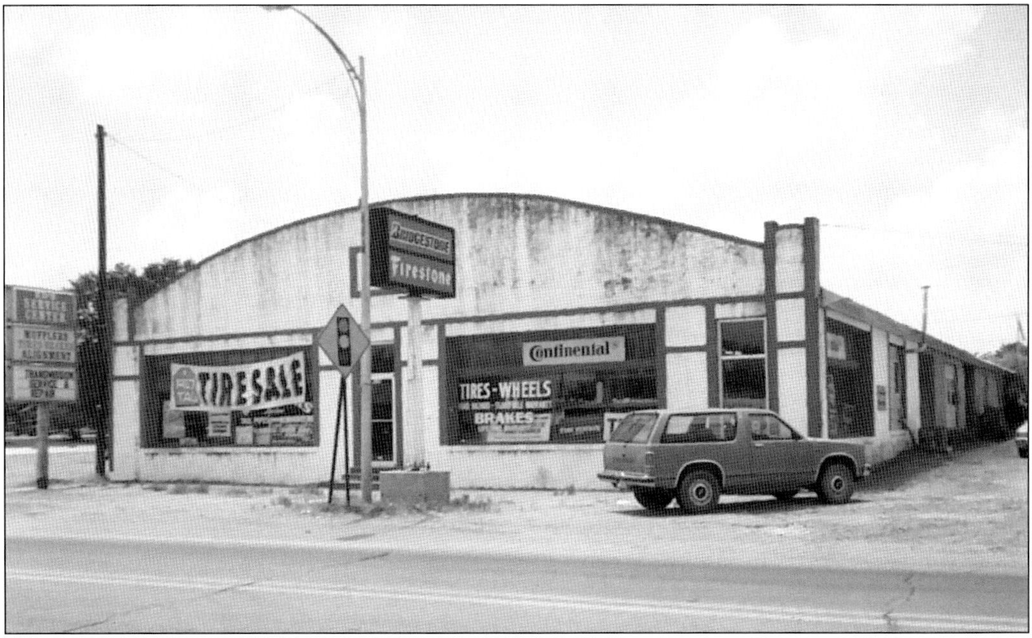

This post–World War II building fronting South Main Street in Waldron formerly belonged to the Harris Ford Company but now is the Firestone Tire business of Mr. Ed Hutchens. He has been in business for several years, and the people of the county are happy with the services he provides. It is directly across the street from the Rock Cafe and the Bulldog Car Wash. (Historian's Collection.)

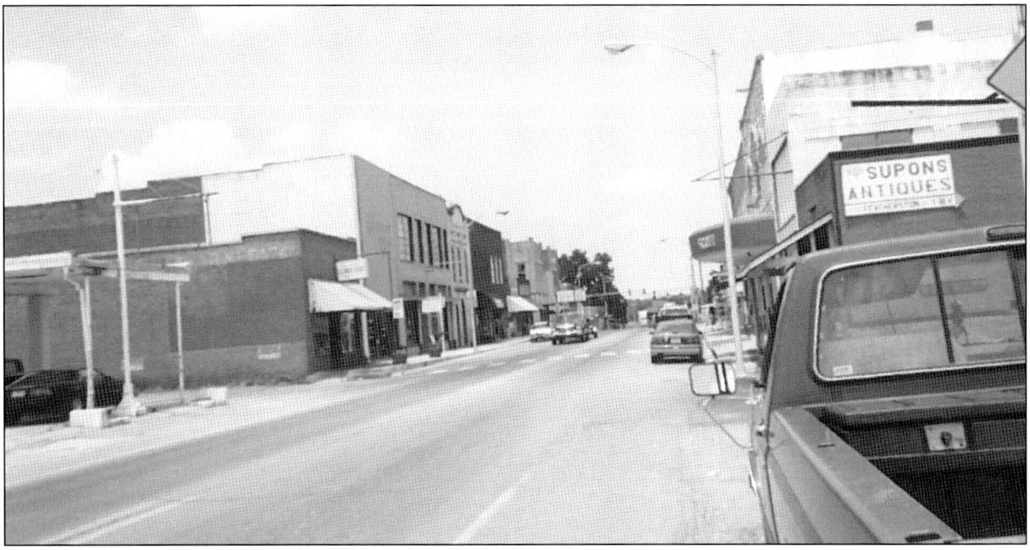

Over 160 years since historic Main Street in Waldron (looking north) on the Texas Road came into being, it slides into the 21st century looking a little faded and somewhat deserted. The Pine/Scott Theater has survived for almost a century thanks to Kenneth Hines, and many other buildings have as well; however, the occupancy of them change frequently due to lack of people shopping downtown. In the 1960s, businesses began moving towards the By-Pass Highway 71, west of town, and with the exception of a few, most of the large businesses have moved away from downtown. (Historian's Collection.)

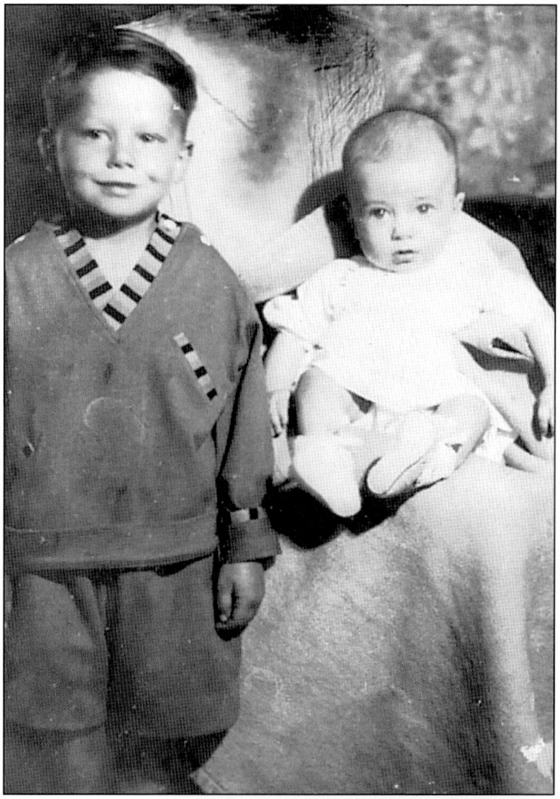

Ilustrative of the life and times of the first half of the 20th century are, from left to right, Wando Denton Newberry and Charles Donald Newberry. They are the sons of James Hilary Newberry and Florabell Doughty. Wando served in World War II as a tail gunner on an airplane and went to a watery grave in the English Channel, returning from an air raid over Germany. Charles returned safely from the war, married Marcine Taff, and enjoyed a useful and prosperous life. He died of lung cancer in the summer of 1999. (Historian's Collection)

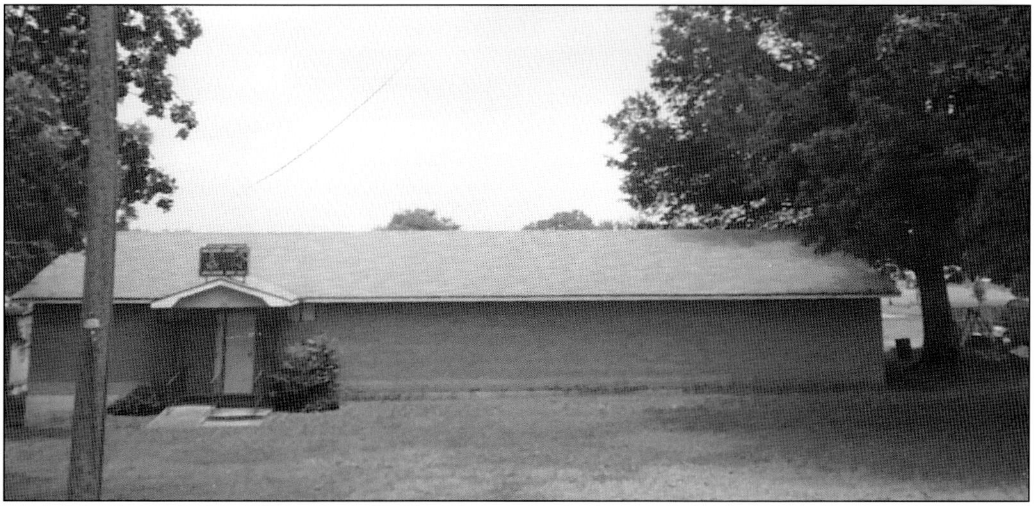

The brick 20-x-40-foot building, with light brown roof on Swinney Hill south of the high school, bears the noble insignia of Waldron Masonic Lodge No. 132. Since its beginning in 1858, with Dr. Elijah Leming serving as the first Worshipful Master, the group met in a log building, in a two-story structure near where the Continental Hotel stood, in the J.K. Bell building in 1882 which they rented for $75 a month, and in the upper story of the Donald Poe building on Second Street. The latter was reduced to a one story in 1997, thereby doing away with the last lodge prior to moving into this building. The land for this lodge was donated by Mrs. Charlye "Chard" Forester Davidson. (Historian's Collection.)

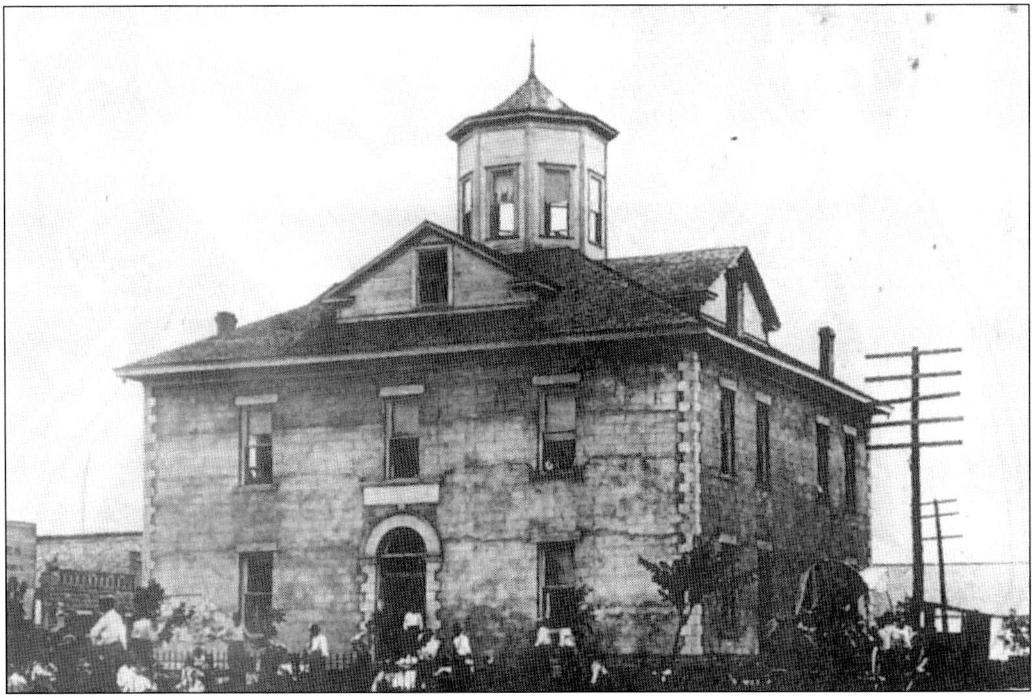

The arched doorway and rounded cupola lends a softness to the harsh square cut stone courthouse surrounded by a wrought iron fence. It is built on a site donated by William G. Featherston in the 1840s and was replaced by another courthouse in 1934, which still stands on the same site, though another courthouse was built a short distance away. Note the telephone and electric polls signifying more progressive times were coming. (Historian's Collection.)

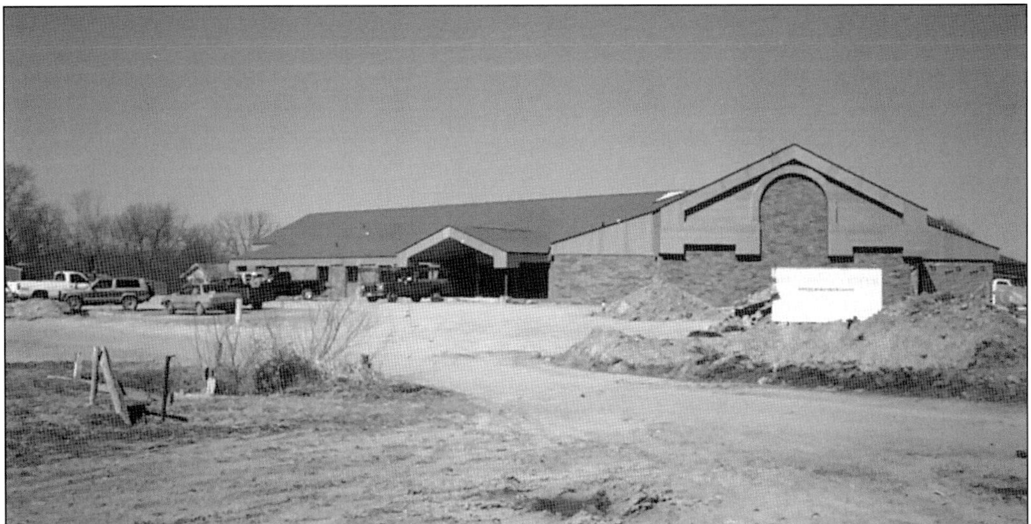

Under construction is the new million dollar courthouse paid for by a special 1¢ sales tax. It is a nice new building and has some advantages over the old one; however, it is too small to house the public records. Hundreds of older records were stored in a refrigerated truck trailer on the back of the courthouse lawn. Also, it is the first courthouse in history not to be built on the original Featherston Donation. (Historian's Collection.)

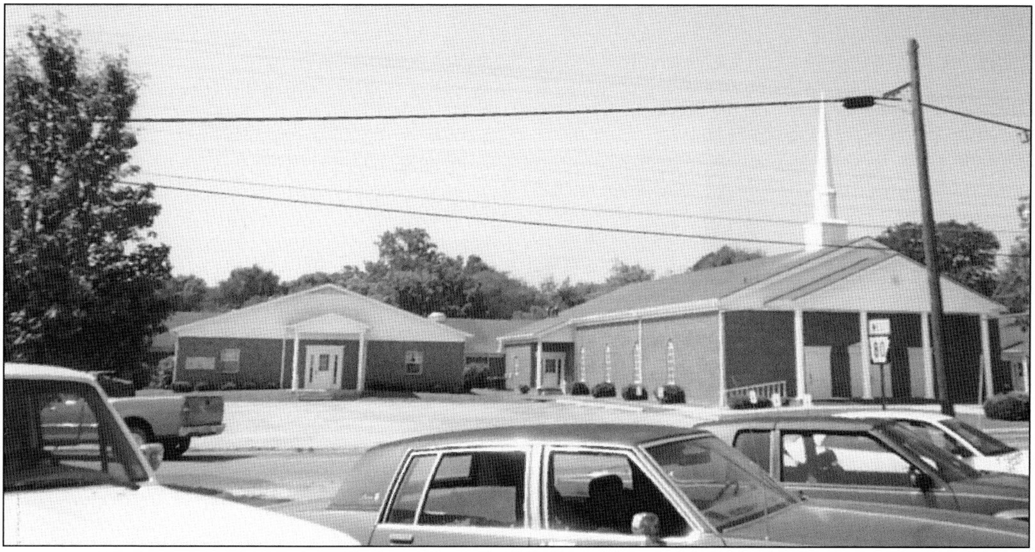

This modern First Baptist Church fronting Church Street at the corner of Main Street is located directly across the street from the Scott County Bank. To the regret of many, the old red-brick church, built in the same location in 1917, was torn down in the 1980s and replaced with this one, with a large parking area and more classrooms. This church was organized in 1884, under the direction of Rev. E.L. Compere. (Historian's Collection.)

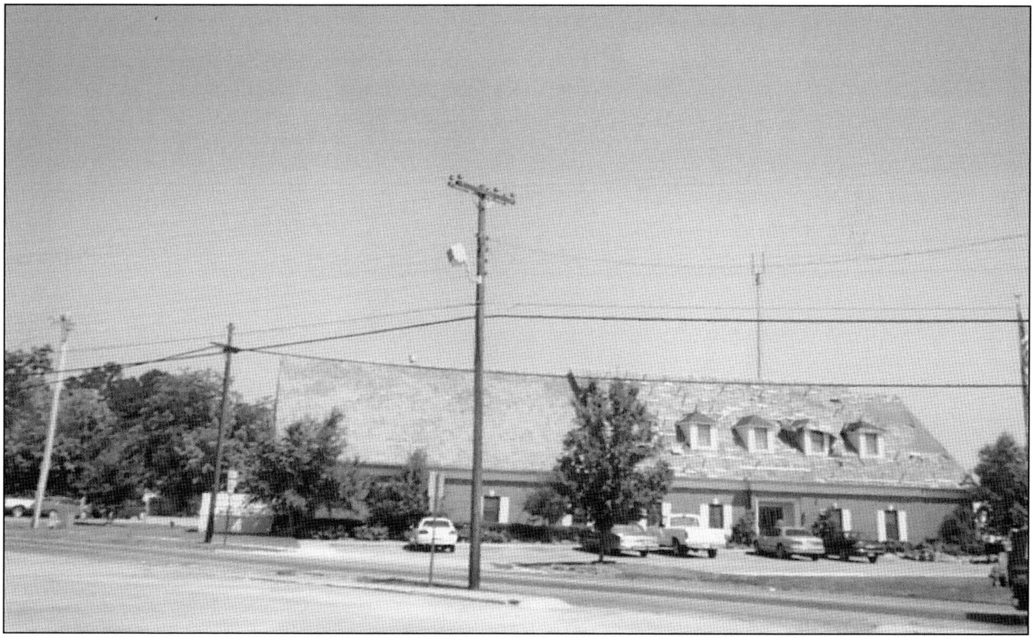

On the eve of the 21st century, the Scott County Bank is being adorned with a new split-wood shingle roof, reminiscent of the earliest style of roofs. This light brown brick structure was built in the 1970s, when the bank was moved from Featherston Street to the busy corner of Main and Church Streets and across the street north of the First Baptist Church. This site was also the location of the Magnolia Gas Station previously shown. It has been a fast growing bank and the first in Waldron to have a woman president, Mrs. Patsy Hawkins, who recently retired. (Historian's Collection.)

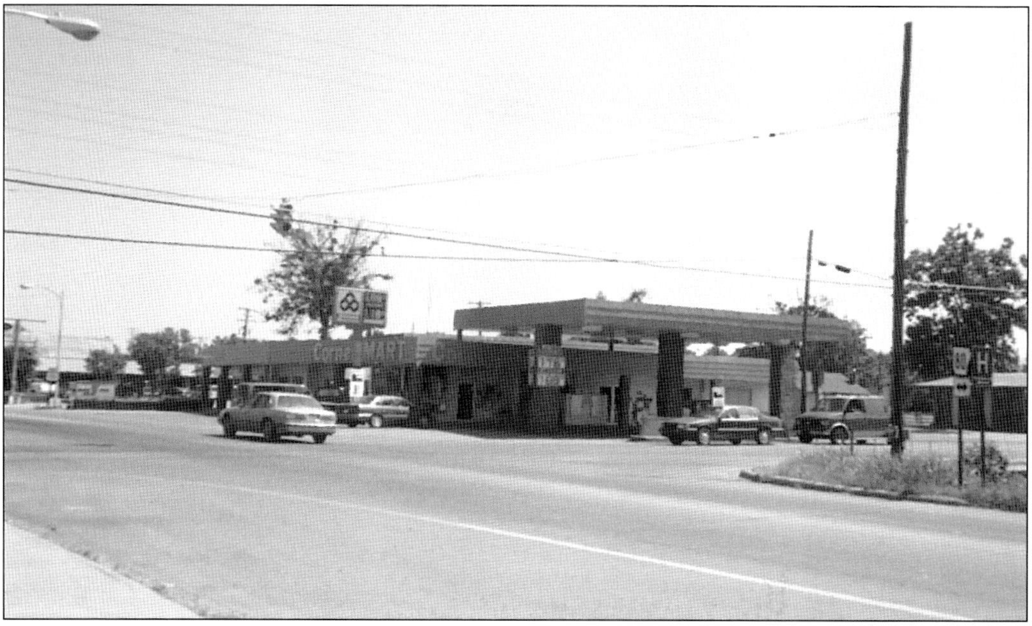

The corner of Main Street (Business Highway 71) and Church Street (Highway 80) is the busiest corner in Waldron. This building was enlarged by former owner Johnny Ward in the 1980s to include a late-20th-century business known as a convenience store (or mini mart) with soft drinks, milk, ice cream, ice, tobacco products, a limited supply of groceries, and gasoline. The surface area for the gasoline pumps is built over a drainage ditch that flows north to the South Fork of the Poteau River. (Historian's Collection.)

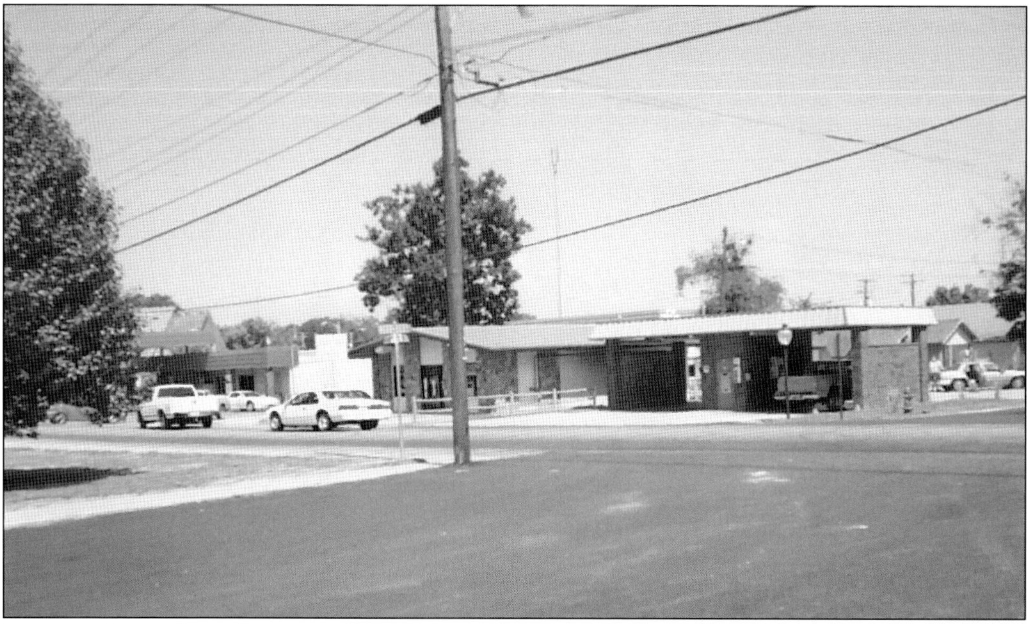

Looking forward to the year 2000 are two established businesses located at the corner of Featherston on East Church Streets in Waldron, the Idle Time Video Store (a natural rock building, with white car in front) and the much-used two bay car wash. The bartlett pear tree on the left of the image is on the Methodist church lawn. (Historian's Collection.)

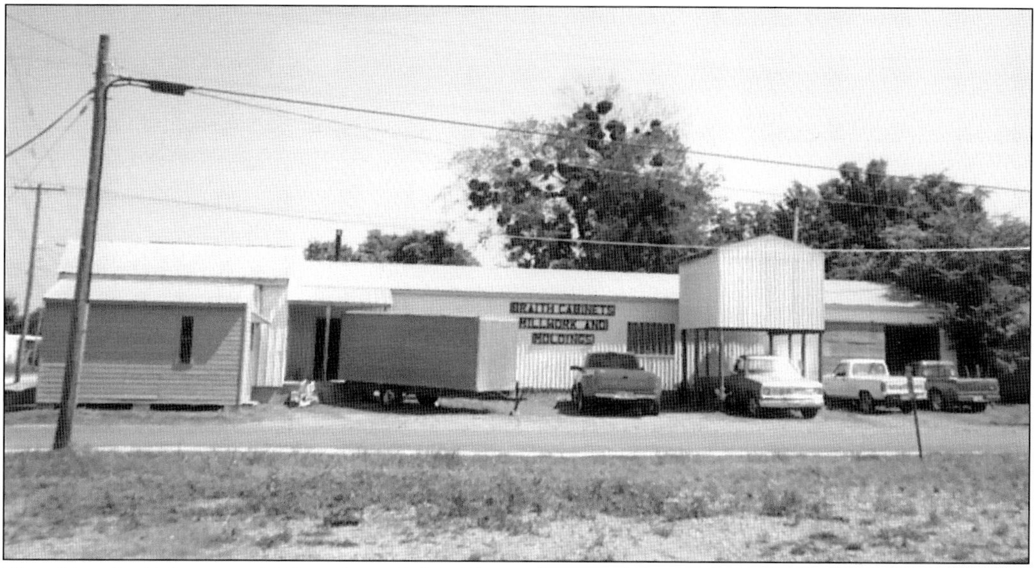

The Braith Cabinets, Millwork and Moldings factory has provided goods and services for county residents for almost a quarter of a century and is reaching for the year 2000 with eager anticipation. It is located at the corner of Featherston and Fifth Streets, east of City Hall. (Historian's Collection.)

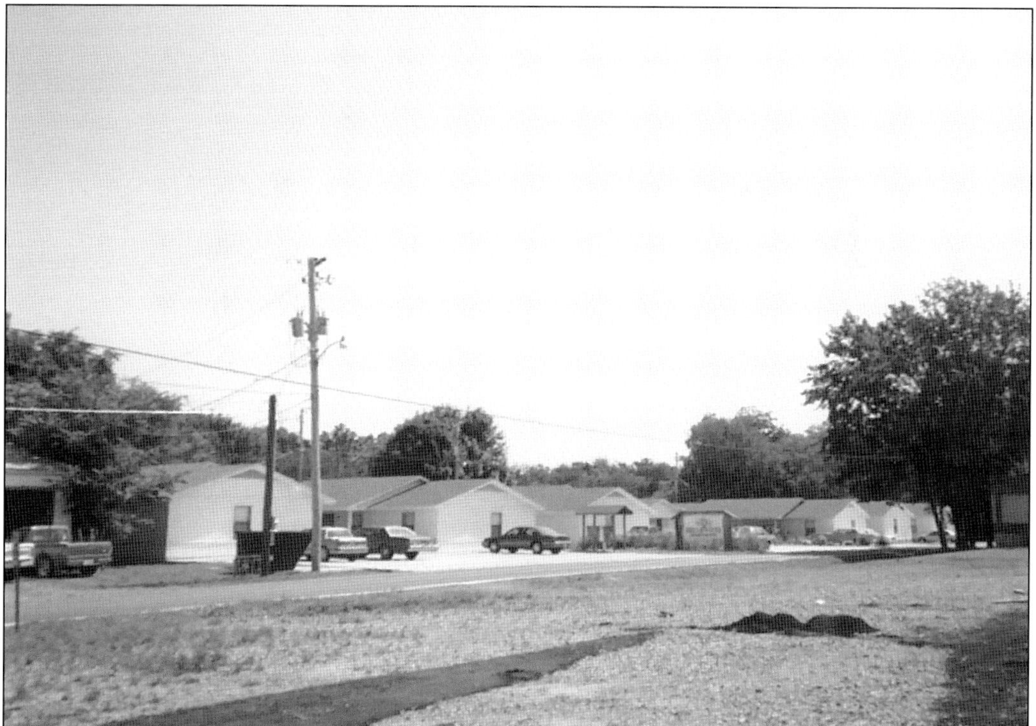

Pictured here are the light yellow, freshly painted Briarwood Apartments. The are next to the Braith Factory on Fifth Street in Waldron, just a stone's throw from City Hall. They are a welcome addition to the city as the need for apartment living has greatly increased with the coming of more industry. (Historian's Collection.)

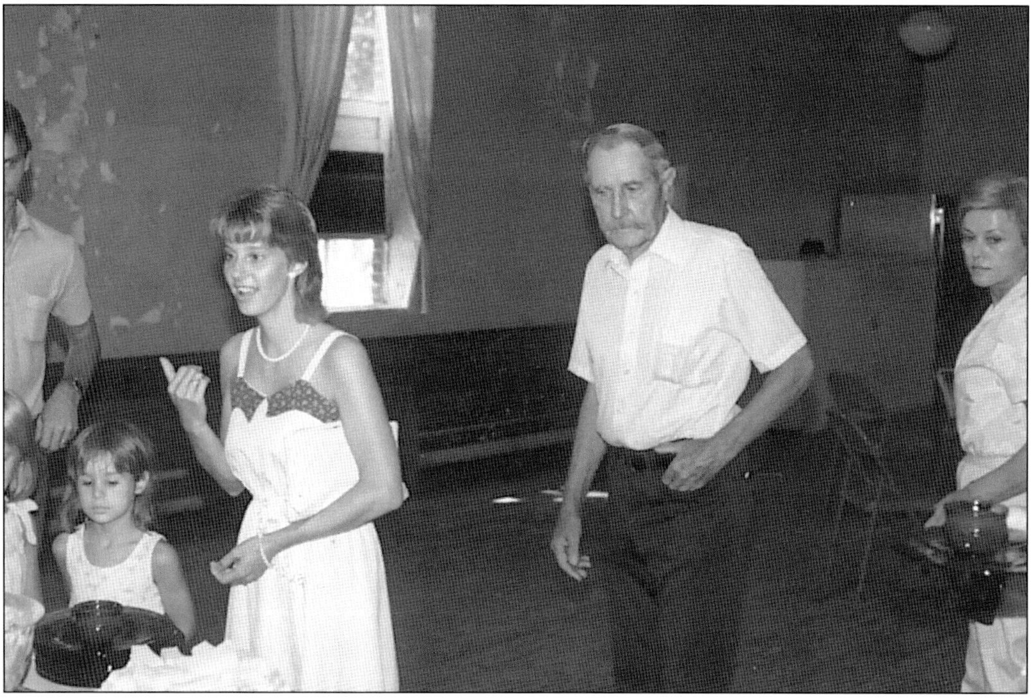

Little Jennifer Estes, with eyes glued to the refreshment table, is standing by Darleen K. Benton, who is followed by the legendary Bill Taff, at the reception for the founding day ceremony of the Historical Society. The handsome man with a moustache has not only a photographic memory but an avid interest in history and the ability to tell stories second to none. Bill was born in 1900 and is the son of Calvin C. Taff (1869–1899). In season, as a child, he picked blackberries in the morning, walked to town and sold them in the afternoon for ten¢ a gallon, and helped his mother and brothers raise corn, a garden, butcher hogs, and make ash-lye soap. He saw the first train to arrive in Waldron in 1903. (Historian's Collection.)

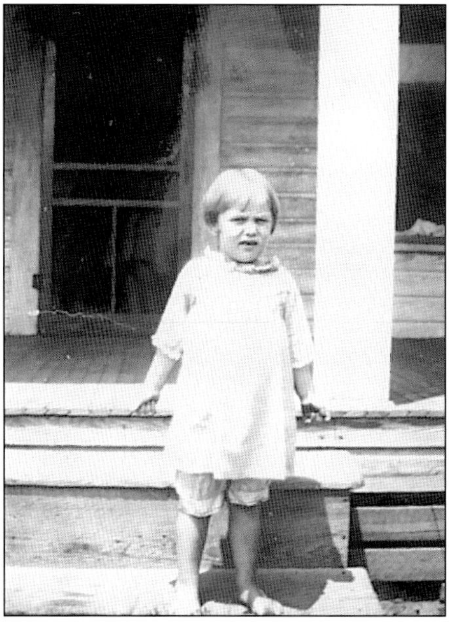

Posing on the steps of her grandfather's home, in her "every-day" clothes and barefeet, is Icy Beatrice Center when she was about two years old. In 1923, the little pantaloons extending below dresses for children were very common and were often called "bloomers." This same dress for young toddlers is also very fashionable today. When Beatrice grew to maturity, she married Mr. Ed Thompson and lived on a farm west of the Hon community. (Historian's Collection)

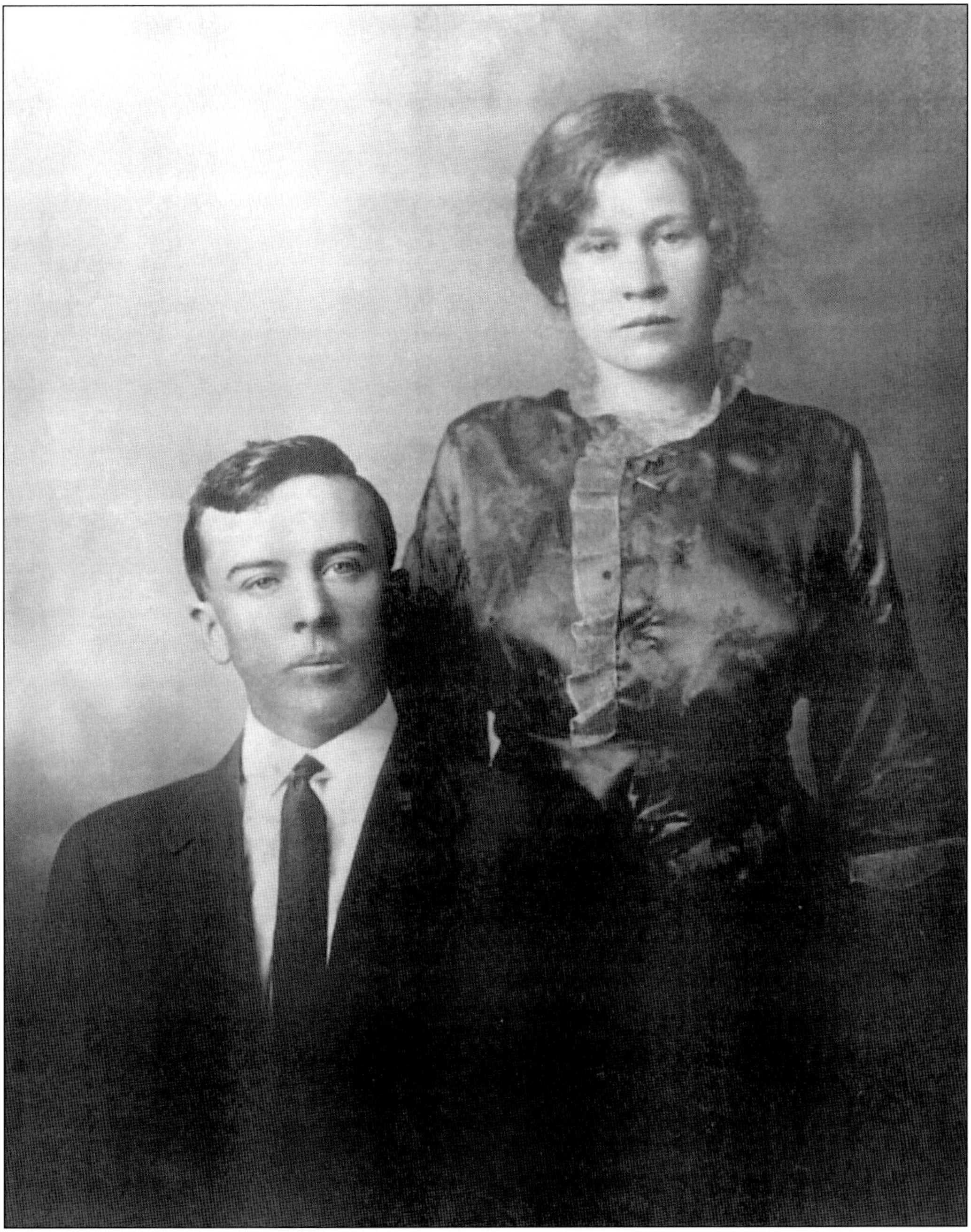

This image is the marriage portrait of a contemporary of Bill Taff, Arvil Almer Self (1891–1993) of Greenridge community. Arvil was born in Greenridge. His grandparents, Joseph L. Self (1824–1899) and Mary Jane Dyke (1830–1894), with his father, Alvin Walter Self (1858–1941), relocated from Walker County, Georgia, in 1870. Arvil Almer Self married Fern Ruth Houston, the daughter of James Harvey Houston. (Courtesy of Bryce W. Self, Redwood City, California.)

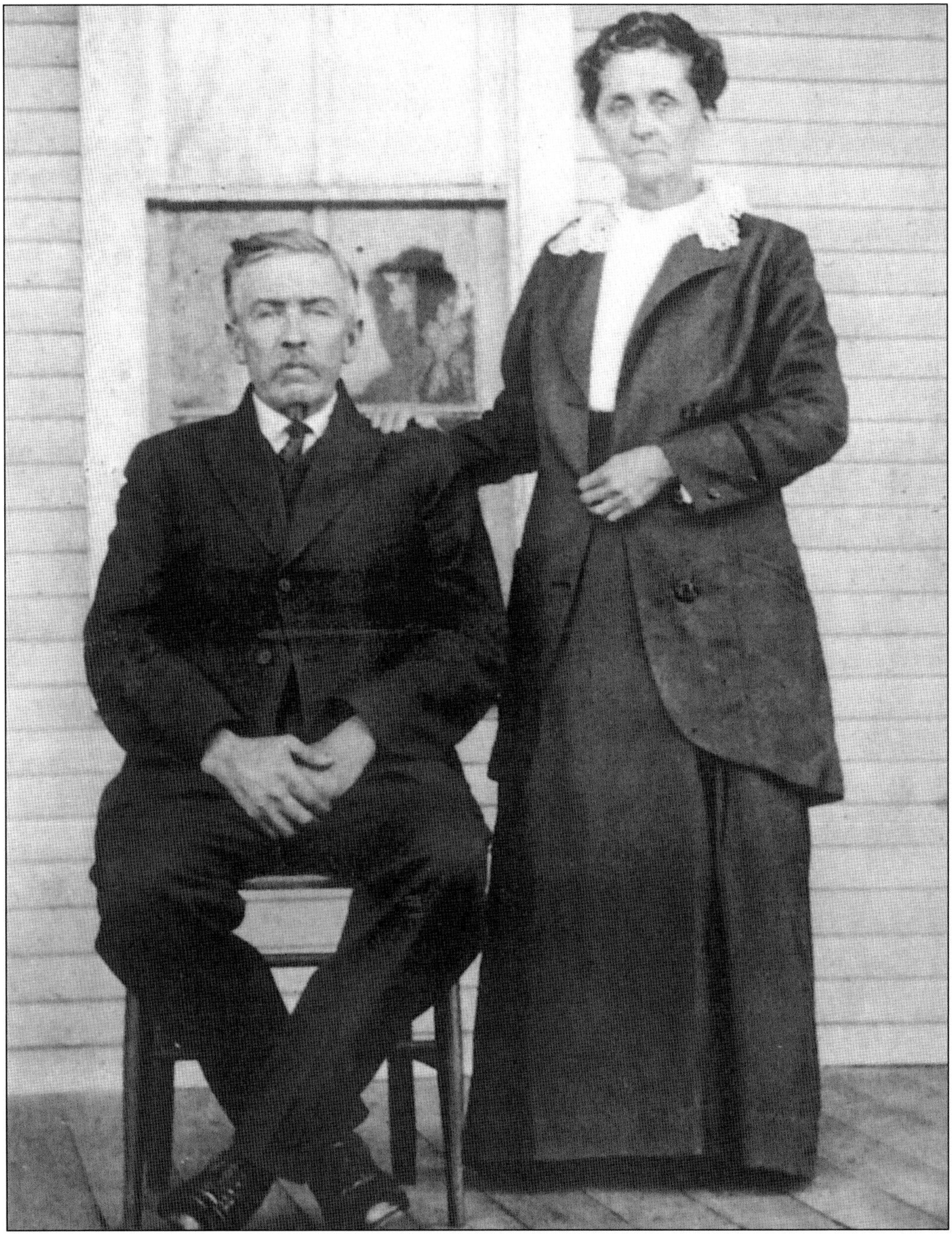

An image taken at the Self homestead shows the parents of Arvil Alvin Self, Alvin Walter Self (1858–1941) and wife, Rebecca Ann Highfill (1861–1959), from Blue Ball. He lived east of the Greenridge community and was in the merchandising and lumber business. He farmed as well, raising corn, wheat, oats, cattle, and horses. His home was built of logs, with a stick and dirt chimney. They used pine knots and candles formed at home for evening light. He lived in the era when clothes and shoes were made at home. He saw his first airplane flying over Waldron in 1915. (Courtesy of Bryce Self, Redwood City, California.)

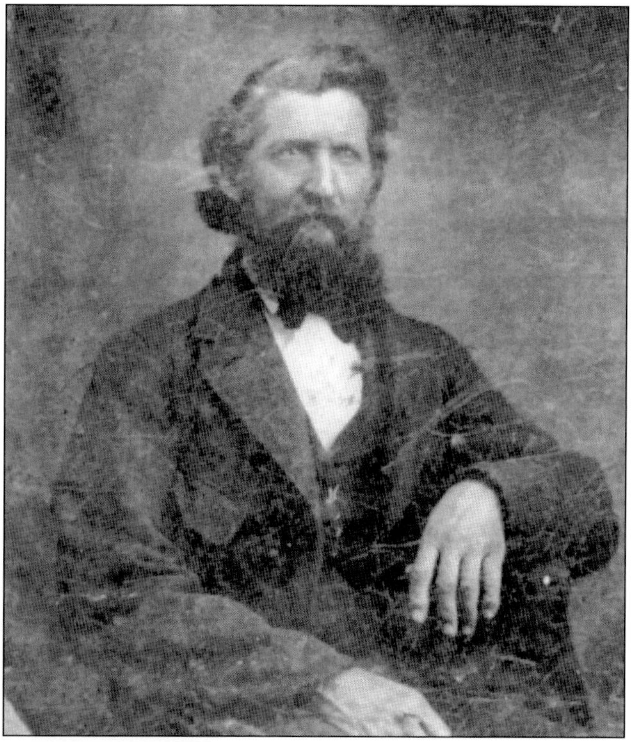

These formal portraits are of the first generation of the Self family to arrive in the county, Joseph L. Self (1824–1899) and his wife, Mary Jane Dyke (1830–1894). They traveled by train from Walker County, Georgia, to Chattanooga and then on to Memphis, Tennessee. From Memphis, they traveled by boat down the Mississippi and up the Arkansas River to the port at Ozark, then by wagon to Scott County, searching for a new home in the year 1870. Their diets were comprised of bread, hog meat, deer, turkey, squirrel, opossum, wild berries, poke sallet (cooked early leaves from the poke weed plant), and sassafras tea. (Courtesy of Bryce W. Self, Redwood City, California.)

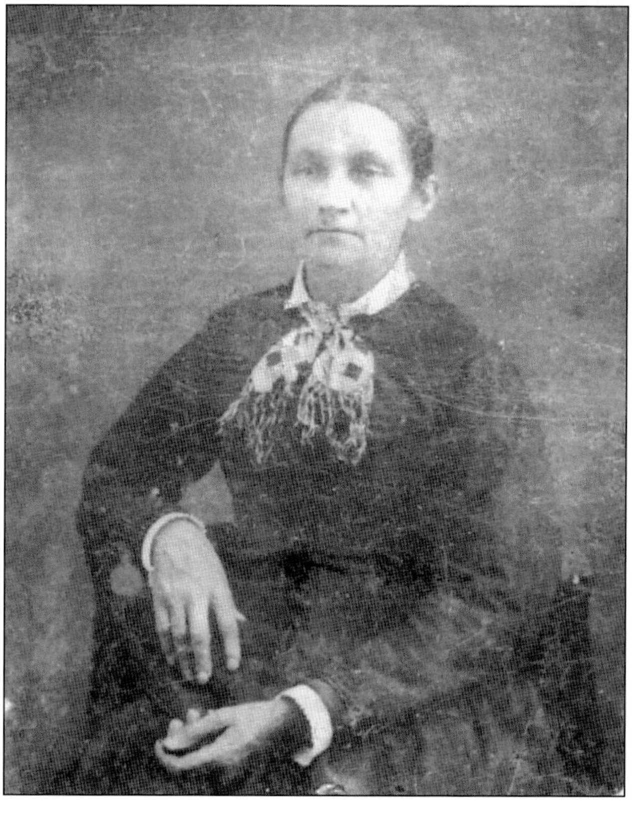

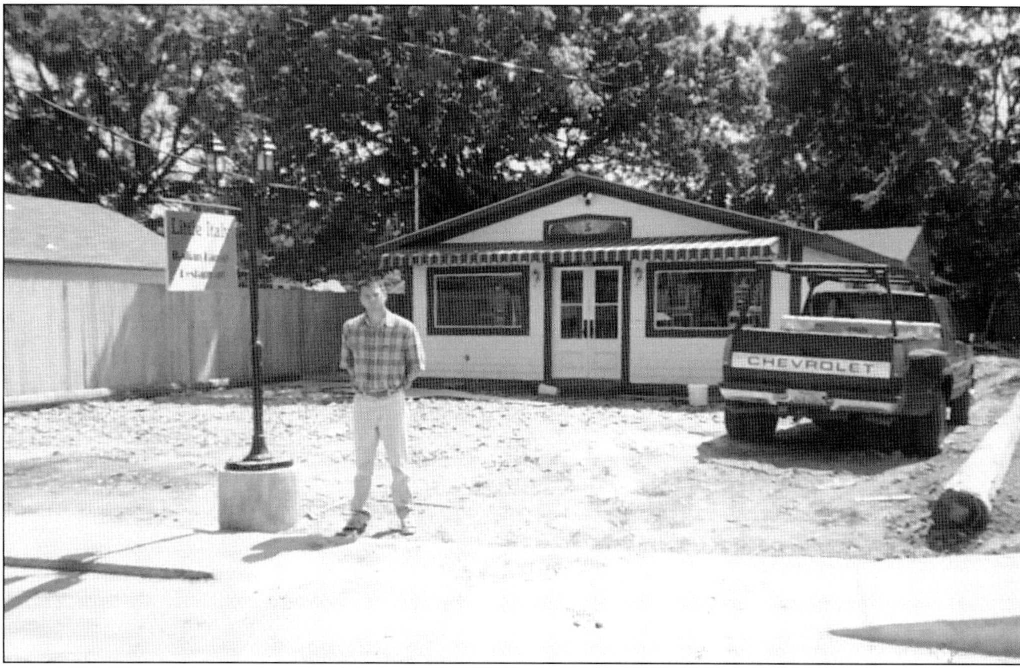

It is quite a dietary leap from "poke sallet" in 1870 to pizza at the Little Italy restaurant, where the proud owner, Joey Marrone, poses for the camera. The Little Italy restaurant is located on Featherston Street in Waldron, next door to where the historic Forester home stood on the corner of Danville Street. Proclaiming success in the 21st century, it opened it doors for business on June 14, 1999. It is owned by Mr. and Mrs. Joey Marrone and Joey's brother, Paul Marrone Jr. (Historian's Collection.)

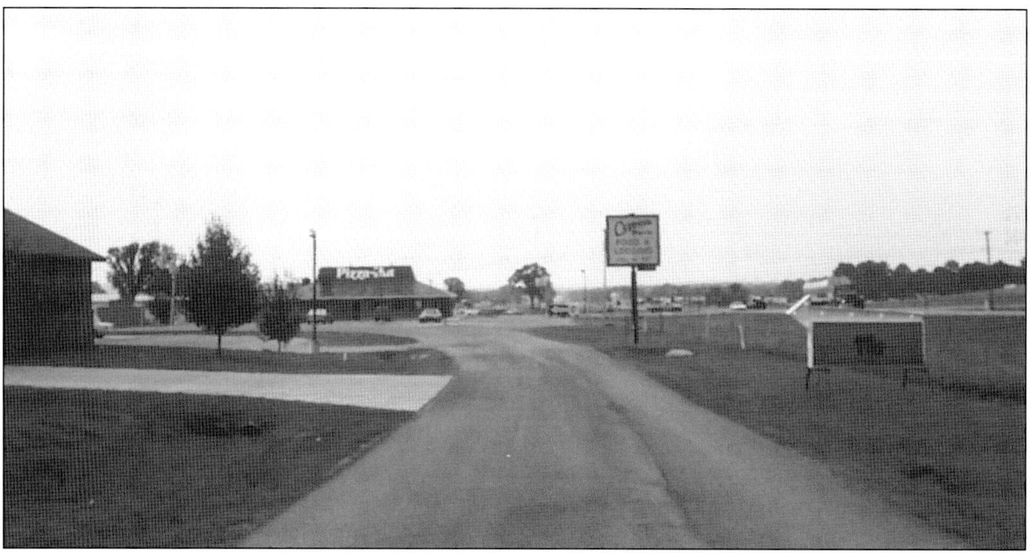

The Pizza Hut Restaurant is strategically situated on the by-pass at the corner of the Country Elite Addition along Highway 71 and Highway 80 West. It was built in the early 1980s and is next to Cypress Lodge and Cypress Barn Restaurant. For many years, this land belonged to Frank Hawkins and was good pasture land for his cattle to graze on until purchased by Frankie Newberry. (Historian's Collection.)

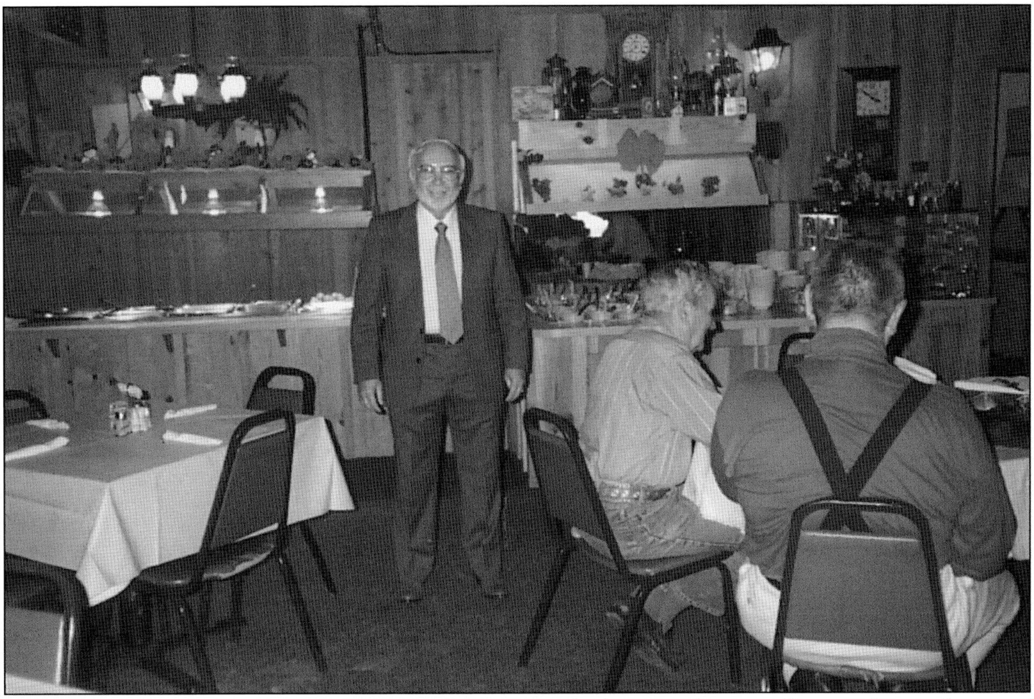

The smiling face of Frankie Newberry (1934–1999) glows as he proudly stands amid one of his business enterprises, the Cypress Barn Restaurant, the finest place to eat within a 50-mile radius. A self-made, ambitious man instilled with strong religious values, he aggressively pursued his life's work of building—first an auto parts business, next registered cattle, next land development in the North Gate and Country Elite Additions, and finally, the building of the Cypress Lodge. (Courtesy of Louise Newberry.)

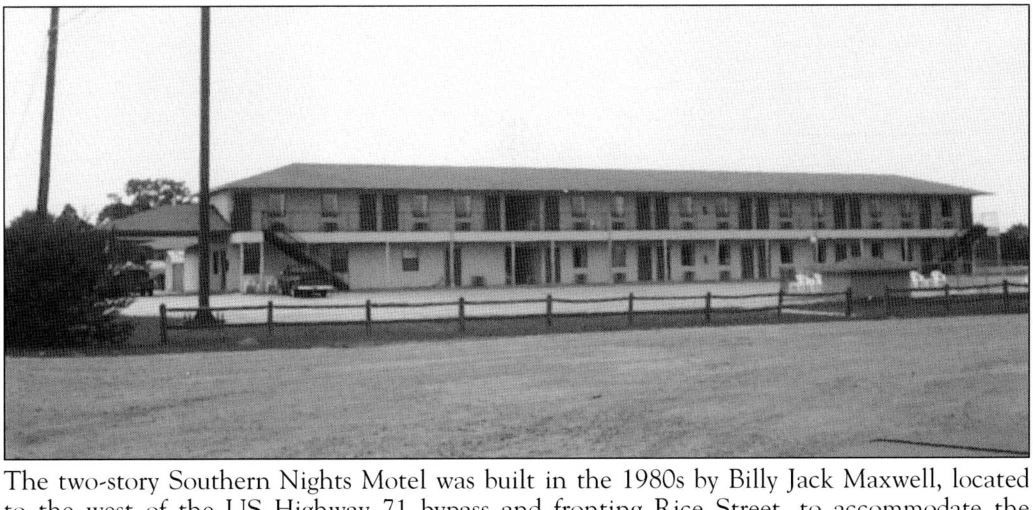

The two-story Southern Nights Motel was built in the 1980s by Billy Jack Maxwell, located to the west of the US Highway 71 bypass and fronting Rice Street, to accommodate the many travelers on this popular route. It was later sold to Lonnie Campbell; his son, Bruce, the congenial president of the Scott County Chamber of Commerce and Republican Party, operates the motel. It was constructed of concrete blocks, in lieu of timber, as are many commercial buildings of the late 1900s. One might expect to pay less than $35 a night for one room, which is lower than the cots of similar accommodations 50 miles away.

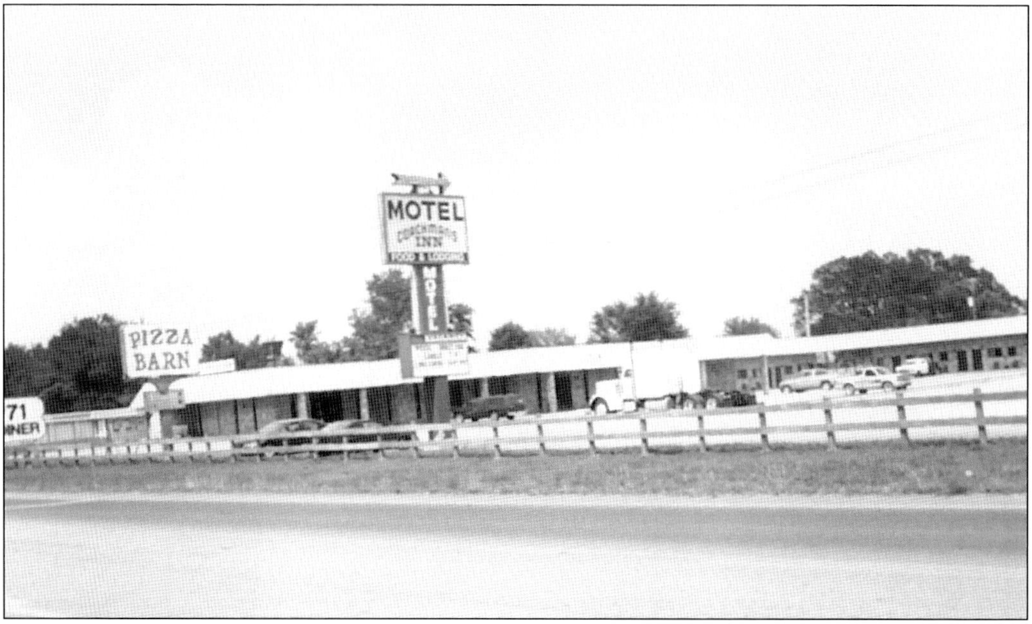

Pictured here is one of the first businesses built on the US Highway 71 bypass in the 1960s, to the west of Waldron: The Coachman Inn, Restaurant, and Pizza Barn. This complex was built by Jerry Parker and his wife, Jo, and has been enlarged to include a grocery store, an office building, and other stores, as well as gasoline pumps. The Parkers are supporters of the Democratic Party and friends of President Clinton and his wife, Hillary, who have visited this complex on numerous occasions. (Historian's Collection.)

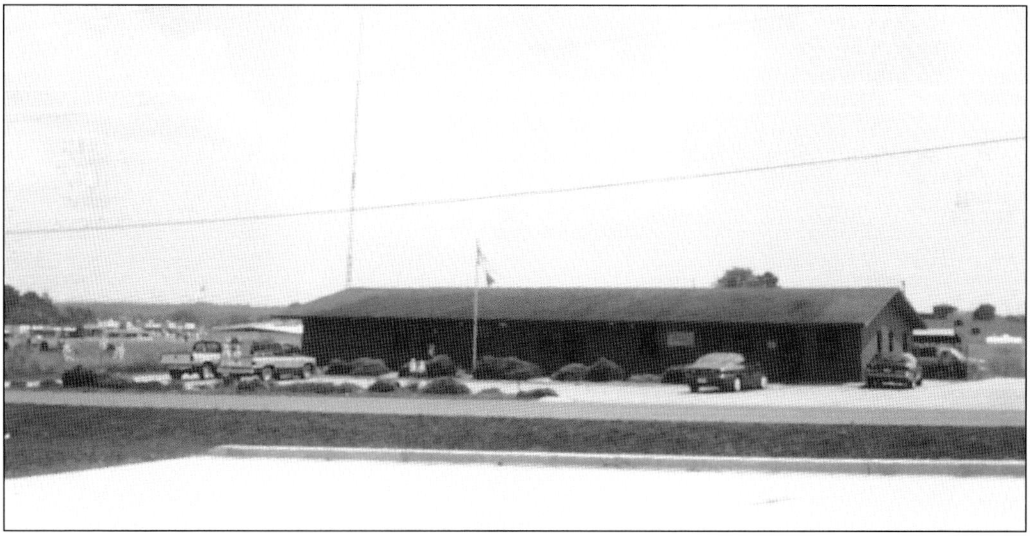

Built in the 1980s, this red-brick office building houses the fashionable ladies dress boutique of Ms. Helen Cain and the office of the U.S. Soil Conservation, where the very capable Joyce Parker, wife of Jerry, from the Winfield community, is employed. This building fronts Rice Street and is also west of the bypass. Both of these businesses moved from downtown to this area. In the background, the Parker Plaza can be seen (different family than Joyce Parker), where the Coachman Inn is located. There are three similar brick office buildings to the west of the building with the flagpole and the pick-up trucks in front. (Historian's Collection.)

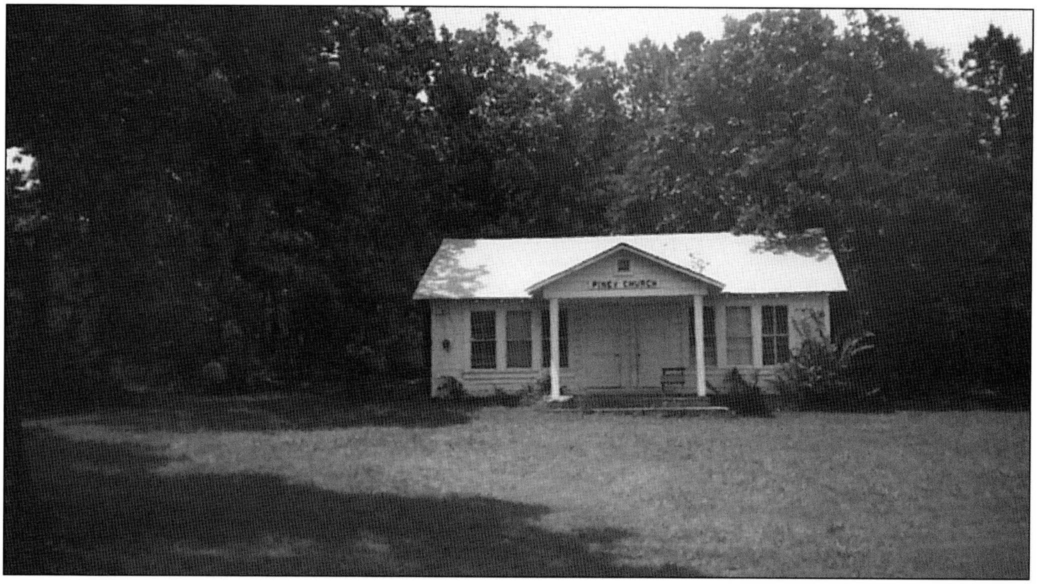

To reach the small, white wood-frame Piney Church nestled among the trees, one has to travel 20 miles over rough, mountainous roads to the southwest part of the county. Over the years, it has been the small, rural churches dotted across the landscape of the countryside that have held the small communities together. (Historian's Collection.)

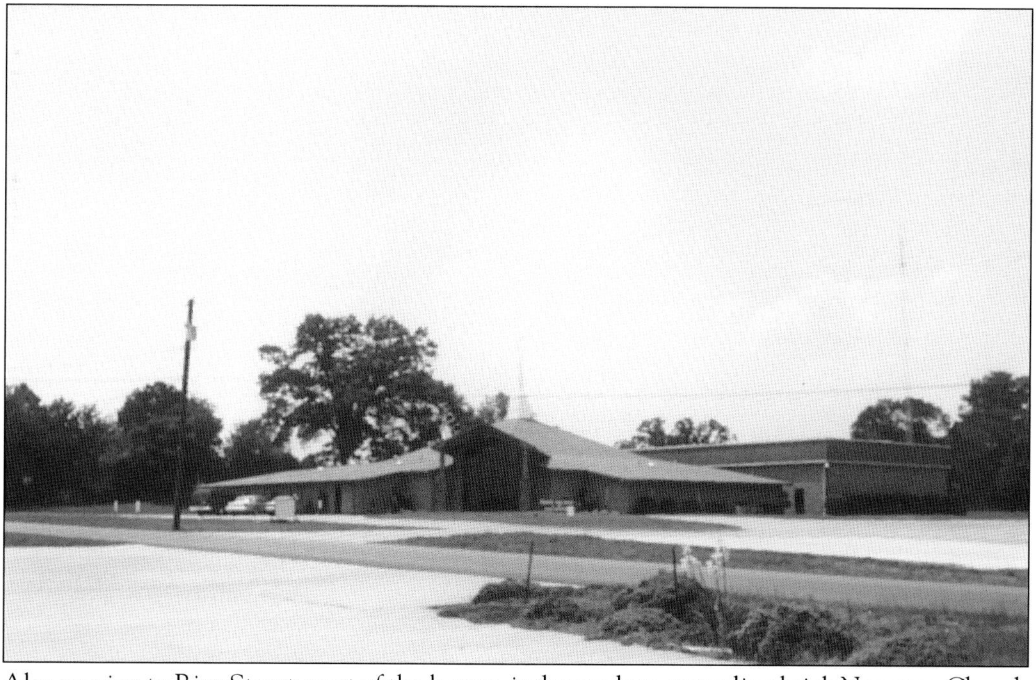

Also moving to Rice Street, west of the bypass, is the modern, sprawling brick Nazarene Church with its white steeple. It has a large, devout congregation, many of whom have been in the church since the early 1900s, when it was located across from the school building on West Church Street. It is especially noted for its youth programs and choir music, which is directed by Mrs. Johanna Newberry, wife of Bennie L. Newberry. This church is located across the street, north of the Soil Conservation offices complex. (Historian's Collection.)

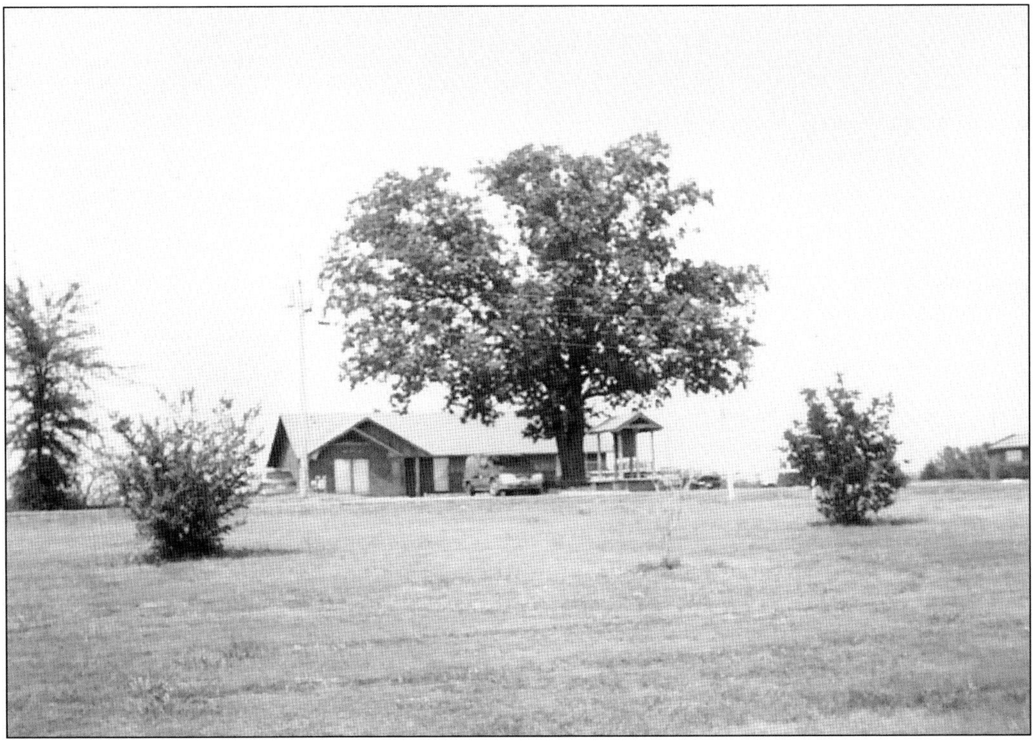

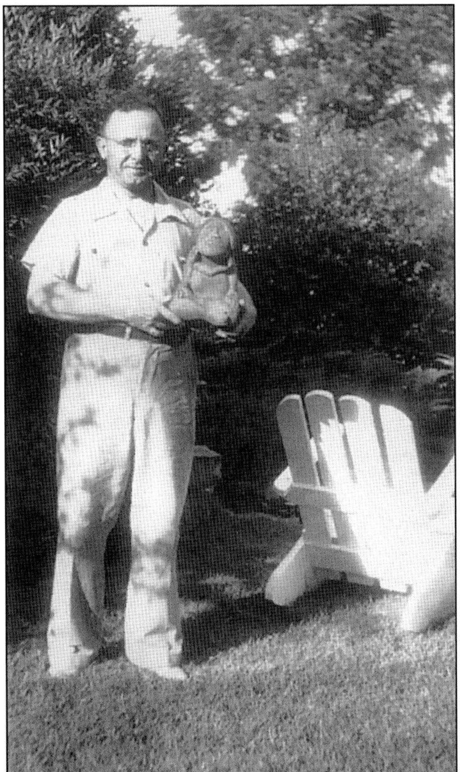

This office on the west end of Rice Street (west of Highway 71 bypass), on the top of a hill once covered in large oak trees, with a rear view overlooking the Poteau Valley to north, is the dental office of Dr. Mark Bailey. The two small shrubs in front are actually located on the front lawn of the Waldron Middle School. The rear corner of the building to the right is that of the medical clinic occupied by Dr. Young. (Historian's Collection.)

In his yard on West Second Street, Dr. Wilson, a dentist in Waldron, is holding one of his many American Indian artifacts. Though he did search for artifacts in the county, this object is from another area. He and his friend, John W. Black, enjoyed searching for American Indian relics in the county, as did earlier residents Samuel Sherrill, Dr. Cheves Bevill, and Bill Grandstaff. Dr. Wilson married a local lady, Miss Dorothy Crowley. (Courtesy of Lou Nell McCraw Davis, Lamar, AR.)

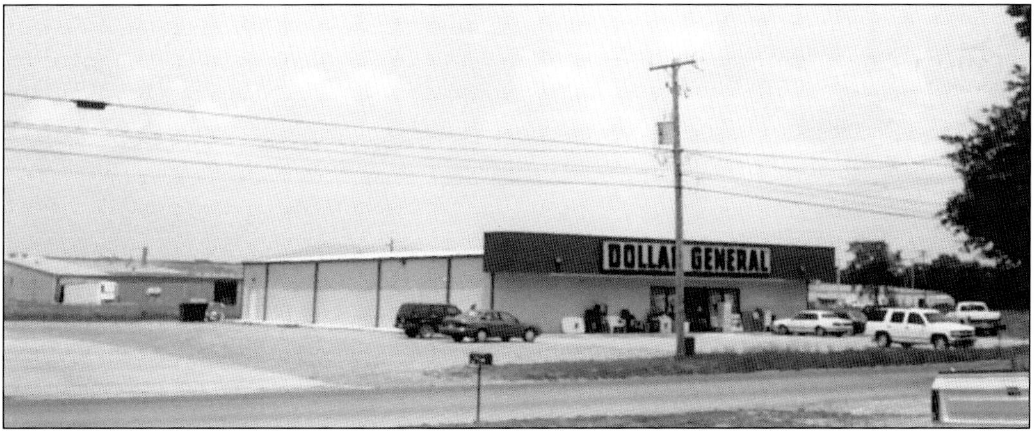

The Dollar General store on West Second Street follows the trend to establish businesses near the bypass and away from the downtown area. This business came into being in the latter part of the 1900s. This national franchise discount store provides less expensive shopping for many necessary items such as washing powder, clothing, sheets, toothpaste, garbage cans, and artificial flowers. (Historian's Collection.)

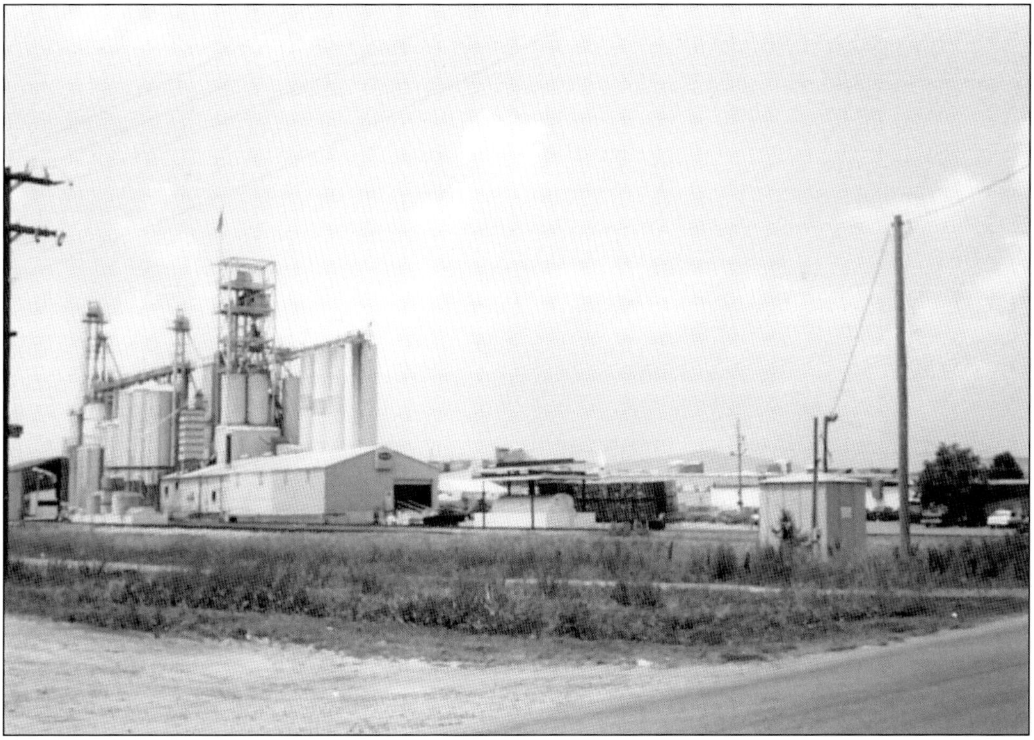

The 1902 railroad tracks in the foreground provide essential transportation for the large Tyson Foods, Inc. poultry processing plant almost a century later. The largest employer in the county supplies feed (silos on left) and baby chicks from their hatchery to poultry growers throughout the county, who have either broiler houses or laying houses where eggs are harvested. When broilers reach maturity, they are brought to this site for killing, cutting, freezing and shipping to the world market. When the farmers clean out their chicken houses, they apply the chicken litter to the land which greatly enriches the soil. (Historian's Collection.)

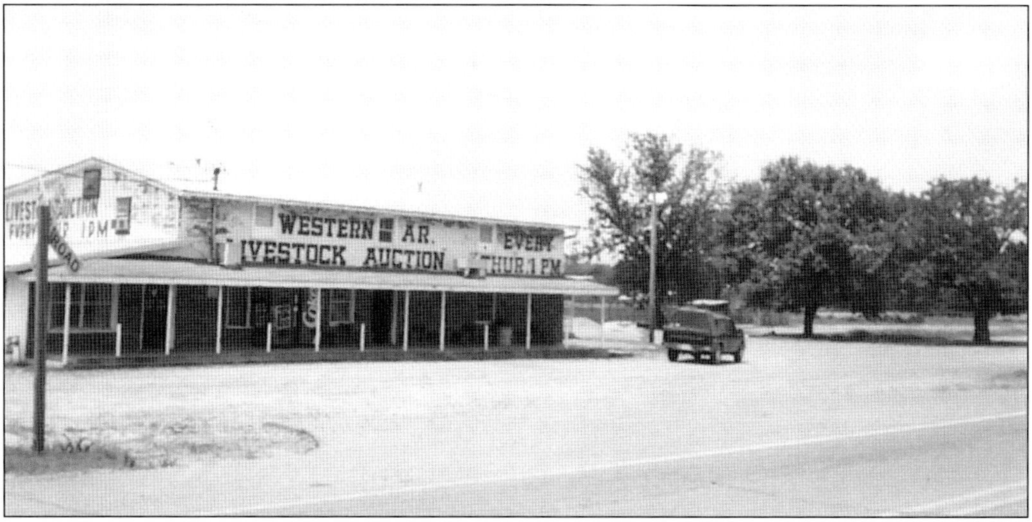

On the west side of North Main Street, just to the north of the railroad track and just south of the South Fork of the Poteau River, is the Western Arkansas Livestock Auction, where auctions are held each Thursday. Since the 1930s, when cropland was turned to pastureland for cattle to feed upon and from which hay was baled for winter feed, cattle, hogs, and horses have been raised and shipped to market from the county in large quantities from this "sale barn." In earlier years, a cotton gin was located on this site. (Historian's Collection.)

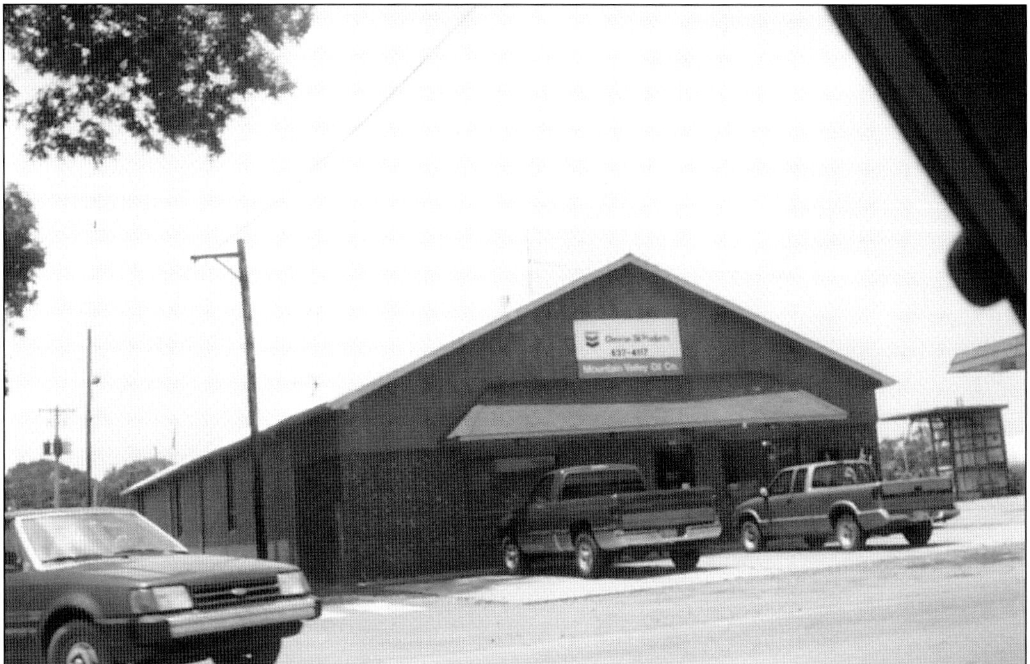

Two late-model pickup trucks are exemplary of the progress in the 20th century in the automobile industry, and the Chevron Oil Company, located on the corner of First and Main Streets, is an example of the other important industries created in response to the automobile. In years past, this building housed the Theo Money automobile agency and other oil product companies. (Historian's Collection.)

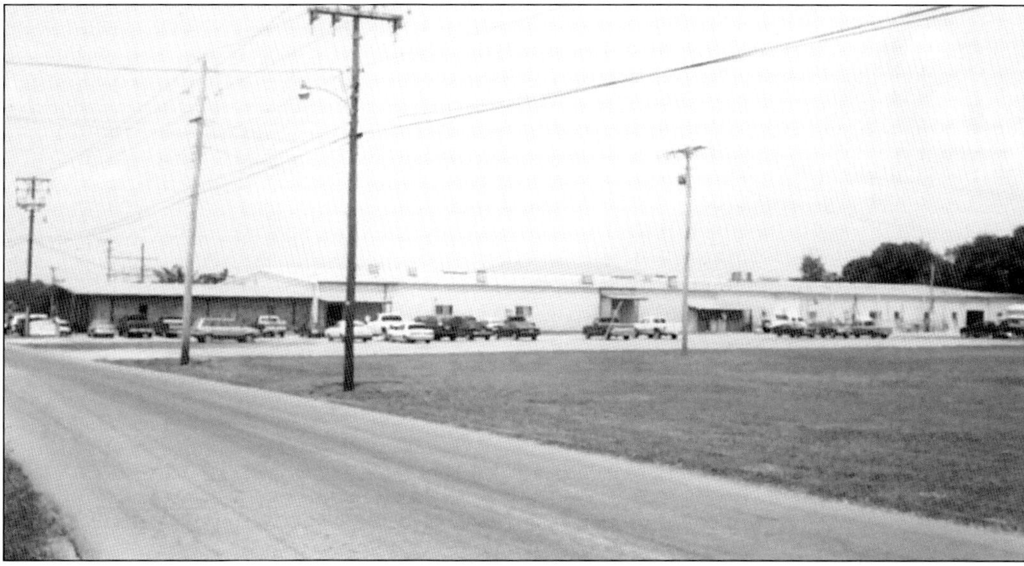

This image of the 5,200-square-foot factory that was founded by two local men, Dan and Carl Laird, as Sampling Technology Incorporated (STI) in the 1970s and later sold, is now known as Graeby S.T.I. and employs about 100 people. They manufacture the highly technical and regulatory controlled Continuous Emission Monitoring Equipment that measures the air quality in certain smokestacks of many industrial factories. Their employees install these computerized systems for their customers and provide technical training on its use. This company has entered the global market, but currently, about 90% of their business is in the United States. (Historian's Collection.)

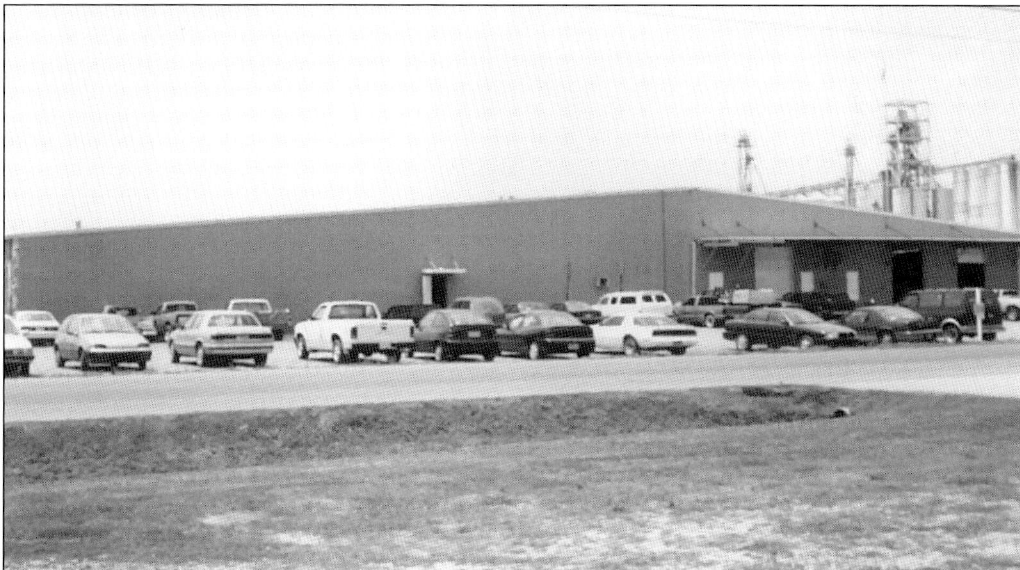

On the west side of Fur Street, a short distance north of Second Street and directly across from STI, you will find a dark blue building that manufacturers dog bones out of a by-product from the nearby Tyson poultry processing plant (the feed silos are in the background). They also manufacture children's furniture. This factory adds to the economic stability of the city and county by providing a steady income for many citizens. (Historian's Collection.)

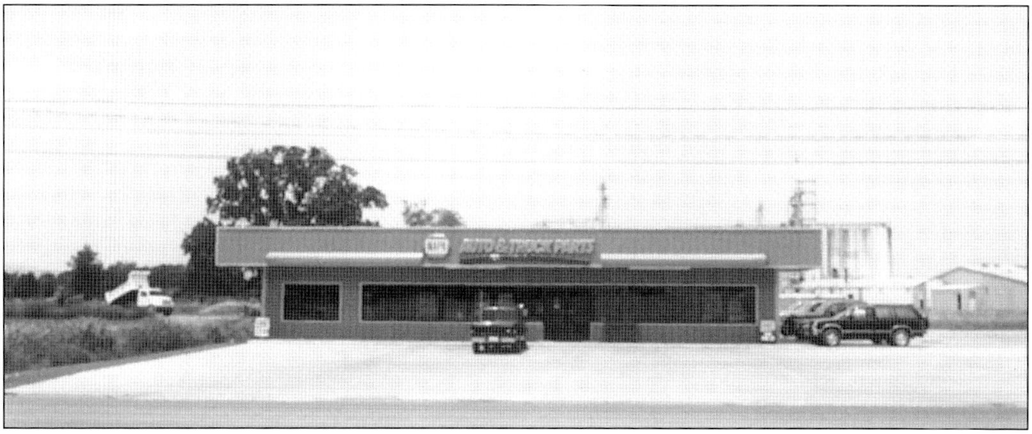

The automobile parts store selling Napa products owned by Neal Cherry built a new structure on West Second Street in Waldron and closed the one downtown. This building follows the trend of using metal buildings, as did the Dollar Store to the east. The Tyson Foods complex is to the north and can be seen in the background, as can the white dump truck with an uplifted bed. How the early farmers could have used a truck like this! Two of the most popular vehicles of the time are the small pickup truck in the front and the four-wheel-drive, carry-all vehicle on the right. (Historian's Collection.)

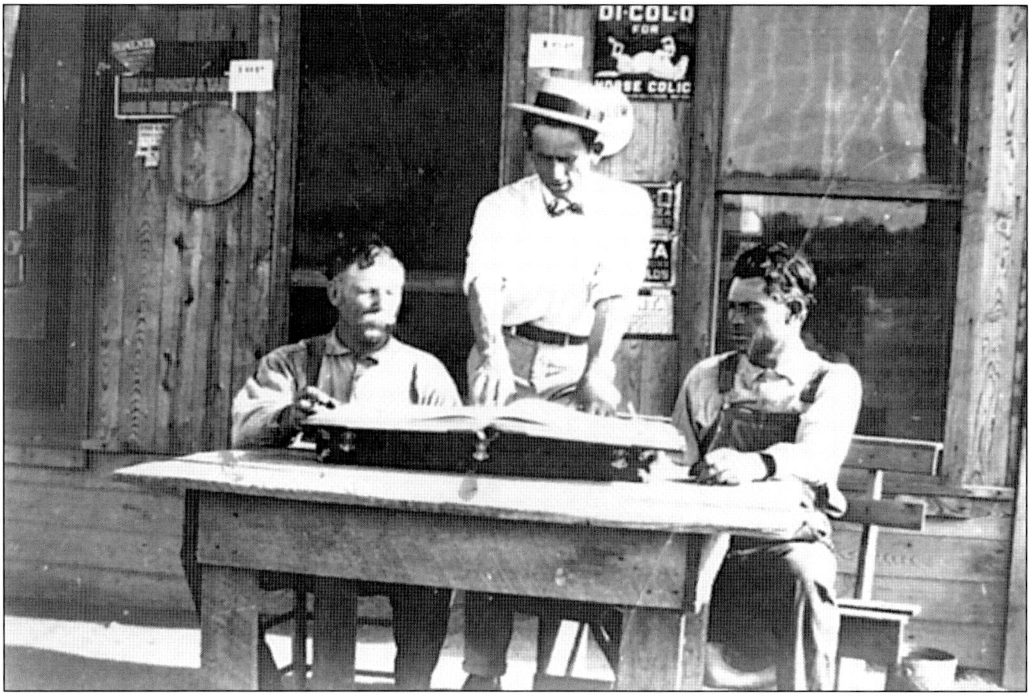

Seated in front of the small country store is an unidentified man (left) with Mr. Huddleston, the store owner. Standing in the straw hat with rolled up shirt sleeves, pointing to a line on the page of tax ledger, is assessor J.W. Black, who served from 1927 to 1930. This store building was only about 12 feet by 12 feet and had one glass topped gas pump in the front, which had a lever on the side to push back and forth to pump the gas. This large book was carried across the county by the assessor as he assessed property taxes. Today, it is much easier with the technological advances of the computer. (Courtesy of Lot Null McCraw Davis, Lamar, AR.)

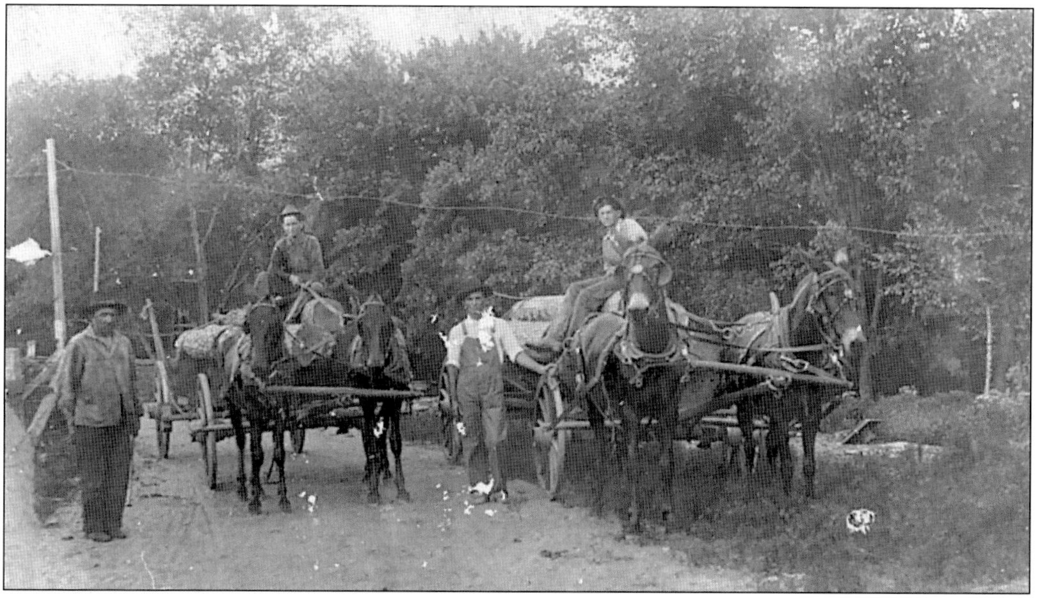

In the heavy forests surrounding the Blansett community in the southwest part of the county are two wagons heavily loaded with logs, on their way to the local sawmill. From the left, standing on the ground, is Dewey Whisenhunt; seated on the first wagon is Press Whisenhunt; standing between the wagons is Dick Dickens; and seated on the logs on the second wagon is Frank Lowrey. One of main topics of conversation among the men of this time period was about their team of horses and how they could pull their loads, and naturally, whose could do the best. Though trucks were destined to take over some of the log hauling, it was many years before many loggers could afford them. (Courtesy of Lou Nell McCraw Davis, Lamar, AR.)

The log truck replaced the wagon pulled by horses to transport logs to the sawmill and was a common sight in the county beginning as early as 1920. It continues today as many men, like Virgil Nichols (1900–1972), make a living transporting logs. Many men who made a living in the timber industry would cut down trees to make a road for the truck, then trim the limbs off, cut the tops off, load the huge logs onto a truck by use of a boom, then use long chains to secure their loads. (Courtesy of Ila Rhodes, Fresno, CA.)

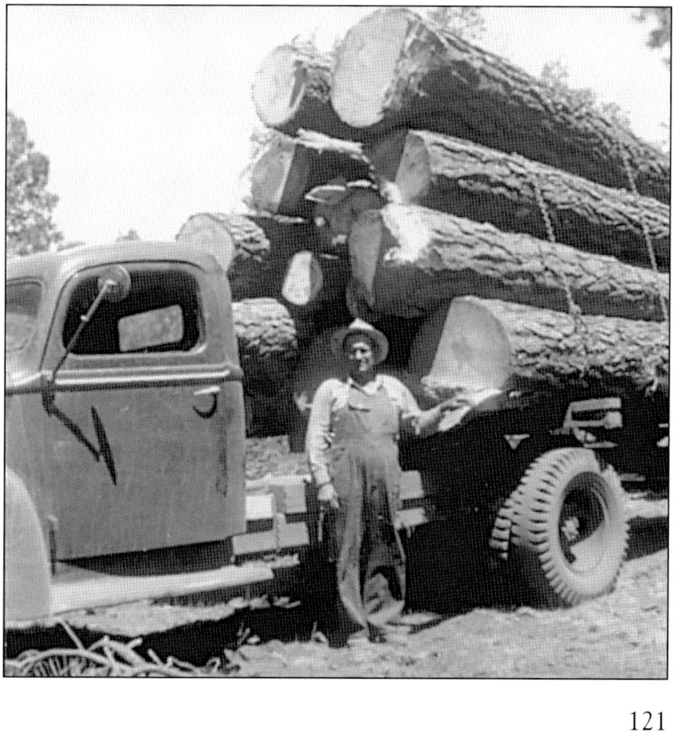

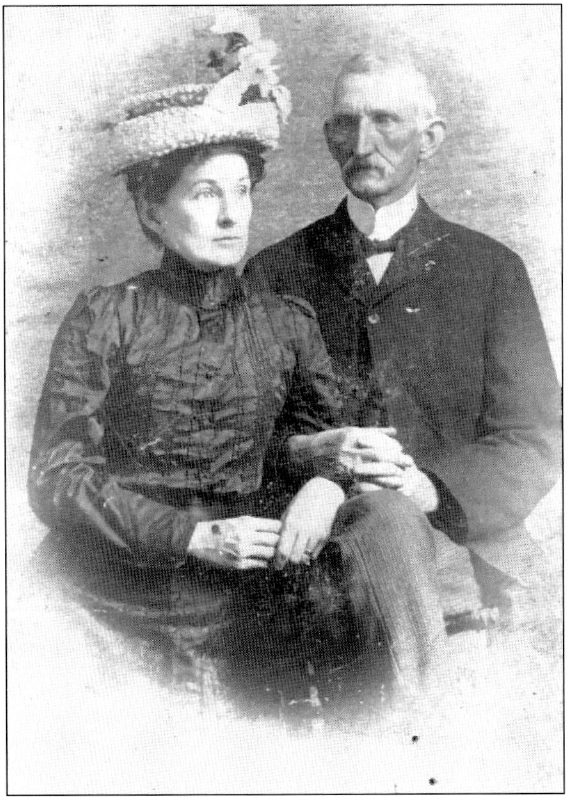

Dressed in dark formal attire, as was the custom of the times, South Carolinian Dr. Lucien Kaiser Robertson (1845–1936) and his beautiful wife, Virginia "Jenny" C. McCraw (1865–1959) pose for a formal portrait. Her flower-adorned hat attested to the millinery stores that did a big business at the turn of the 20th century, and her only jewelry was a wide gold wedding band. The standup collars on her dress and his shirt, with a simple circular black tie, are similar to fashions today. They made their home next door to her father, John Sanders McCraw, in the Parks community where Dr. Robertson practiced medicine. (Courtesy of Lou Nell McCraw Davis, Lamar, AR.)

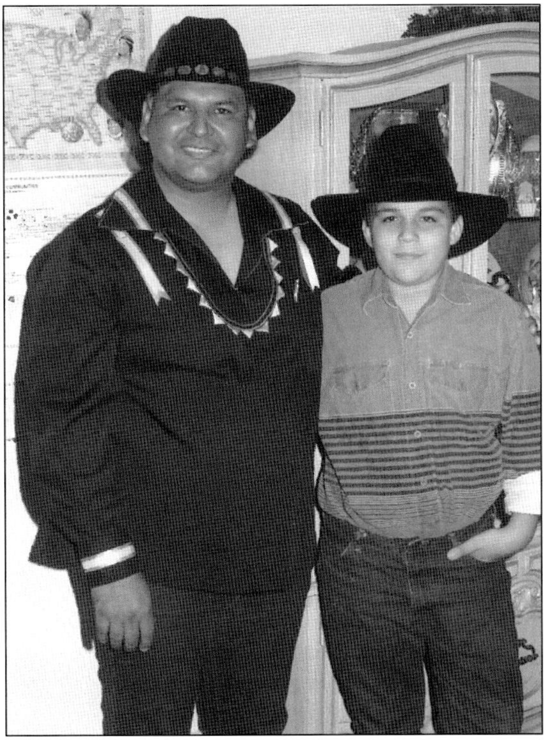

Attending a Heritage Day reception in his honor is Chief John Ross (left) from Oklahoma and local resident, Timothy Gilbert. They are pictured in the dining room of Waldron's historic Farnsworth house, in front of maps depicting the location of Native American tribes in the United States. Until 1998, Chief Ross was the Chief of the Keetoowah Band of Cherokee Indians, who had established a headquarters in Waldron. This historic tribe has many full-blooded Native Americans and strives to maintain their bloodline, language, customs, and heritage. You cannot be a member of this tribe unless you are at least one-quarter Native American; however, you can reside anywhere you choose. Members of Keetoowahs relocated to Arkansas as early as 1817 and were known as the "Old Settlers." They treatied out of the state in 1828, and they believe that to return to the east would enhance their chance of survival. (Courtesy of Jeff Gilbert, Waldron, AR.)

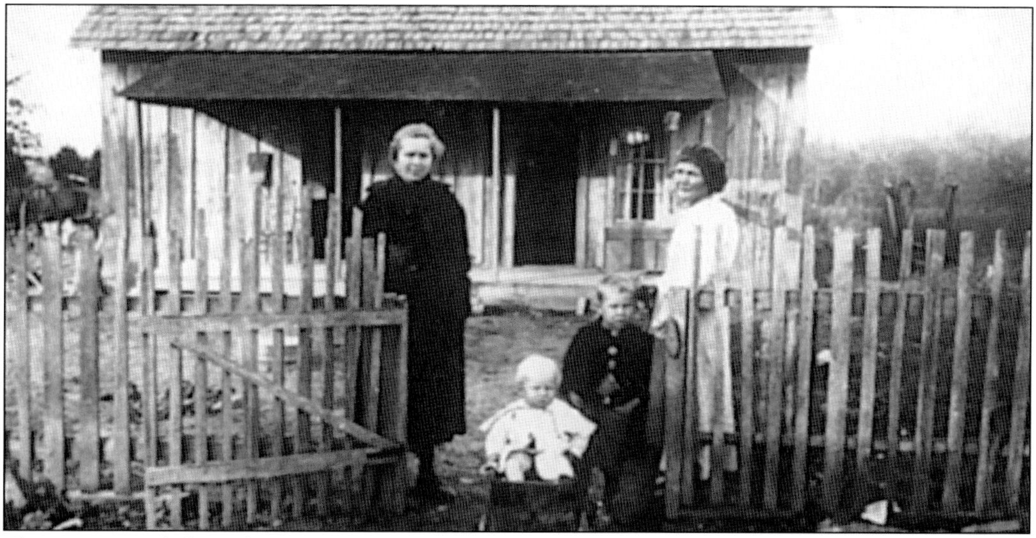

This unpainted "box" house, with board and batten siding, is typical of many found in the early years of the county and well into the 20th century. Some are found today but are used primarily for hunting cabins in the woods. Posing at the gate by the unpainted picket fence are, from left to right, as follows: Cara Roach Frizzell; sons, Lois (riding in the little red wagon) and Reno Frizzell; and mother-in-law, Mary Virginia Black Frizzell. Several descendants of the Roach and Frizzell families still reside in the county. (Courtesy of Lou Nell McCraw Davis, Lamar, AR.)

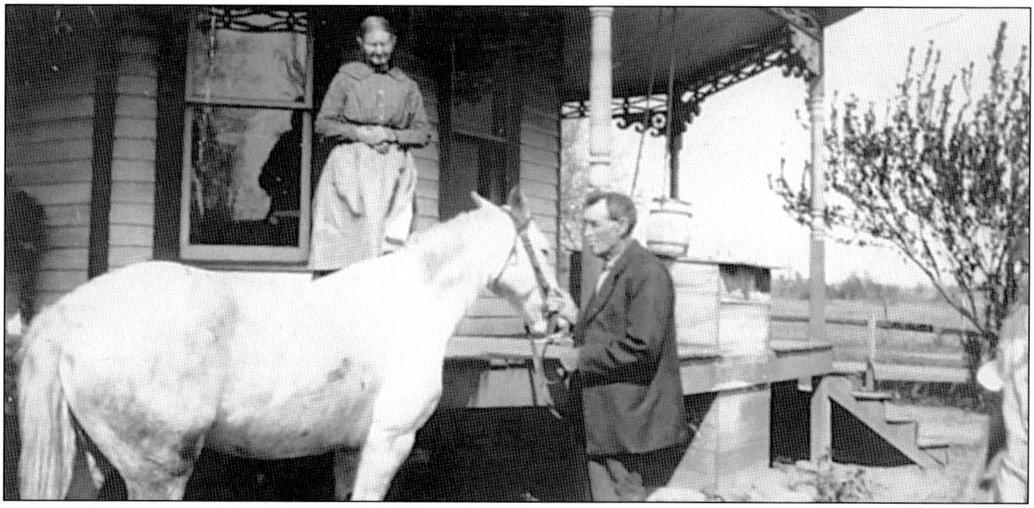

Today, many people at Hon continue to get their water from a well but not with a pulley and chain (sometimes used in lieu of rope) and a small barrel for a bucket (normally, an oak bucket was used). This hand-dug well is conveniently located on the porch and is framed up from the ground above the porch floor for ease in "drawing" the water while in a standing position. In the year 2000, and beyond, water will be extracted from the wells in the county by an electric pump and water pipelines made of plastic will be run to the house so that both the kitchen and indoor bathroom may have running water by the mere turning of a handle. Shown in this image is Uncle "Bess" Beam proudly showing his wife, Susie, a newly purchased grey mare. From her expression, she seems pleased. Members of the Beam family began arriving in the county from Alabama in the 1850s. As we near the year 2000, horses are used for pleasure riding in the county, not as work animals. (Courtesy of Lou Nell McCraw Davis, Lamar, AR.)

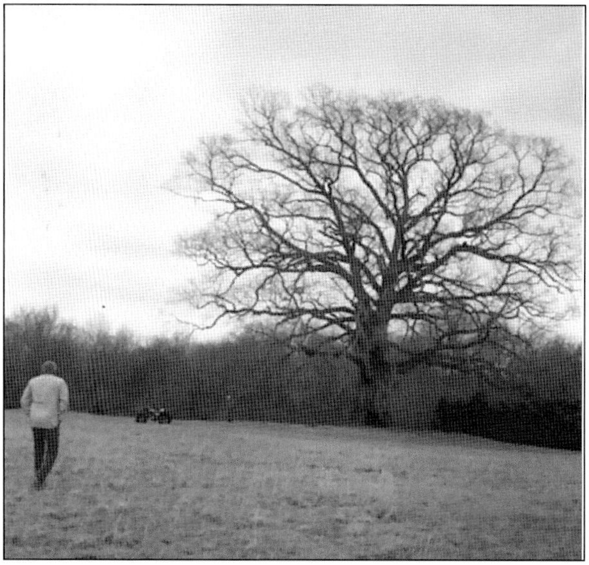

West of Waldron, in a large pasture on a 100-acre tract of land, stands the Arkansas Championship White Oak Tree. This sentinel of ages past is 86 feet and 6 inches high; has an east-west limb spread of 104 feet and 11 inches; and has a north-south limb spread of 102 feet and 3 inches. The circumference of the tree trunk is 20 feet and 2 inches. Years before, when row crops were planted in the pasture, many American Indian arrowheads were plowed up. (Historian's Collection.)

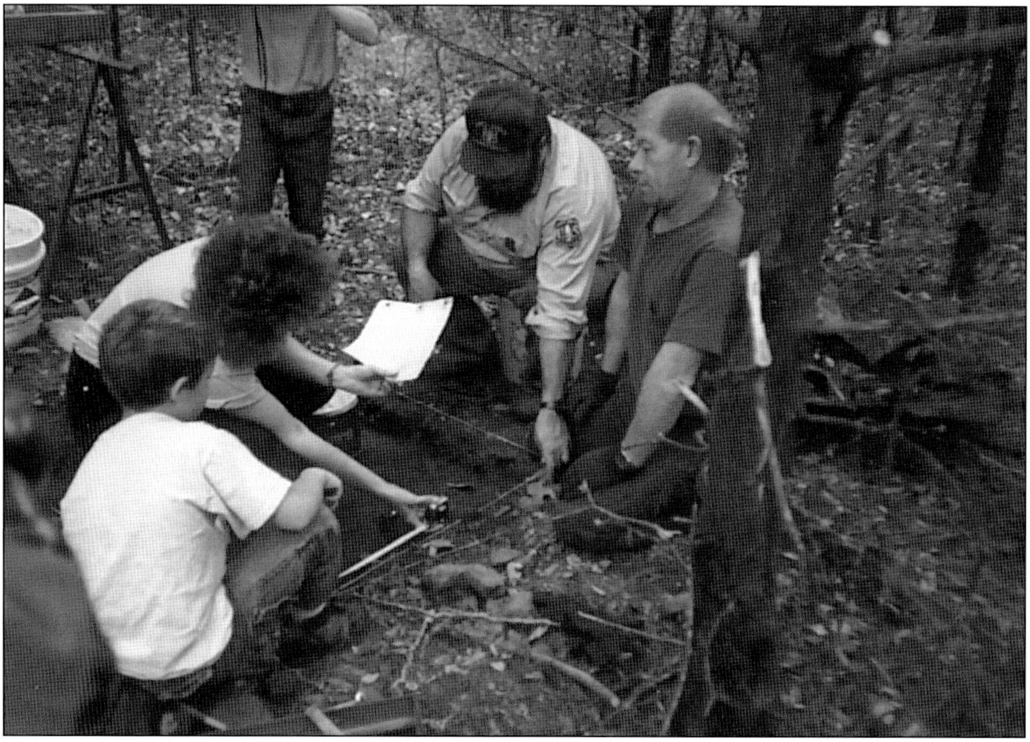

Looking back to Native American life in the county more than 5,000 years ago, an archeological team works at the Hicks Site near the Fourche LaFave River in the southeast part of the county. Holding the string taut is Freddie Woodral, archeological technician for the U.S. Forest Service for the Poteau District, while Melissa Bingham measures the dart point with the steel tape. Henry Hicks (right), the discoverer of the site, looks on, as does young Nathan Bingham. This archaic site was a stone, tool, and arrowhead factory. It is in knowing where we have been that we will be able to chart our paths into the 21st century. (Courtesy of Freddie Woodral.)

Index